Learning eBPF
Programming the Linux Kernel for Enhanced
Observability, Networking, and Security

Liz Rice

Beijing • Boston • Farnham • Sebastopol • Tokyo

Learning eBPF

by Liz Rice

Published by O'Reilly Media, Inc., 1005 Gravenstein Highway North, Sebastopol, CA 95472.

O'Reilly books may be purchased for educational, business, or sales promotional use. Online editions are also available for most titles (*http://oreilly.com*). For more information, contact our corporate/institutional sales department: 800-998-9938 or *corporate@oreilly.com*.

Acquisitions Editor: John Devins	**Indexer:** WordCo Indexing Services, Inc.
Development Editor: Rita Fernando	**Interior Designer:** David Futato
Production Editor: Chris Faucher	**Cover Designer:** Karen Montgomery
Copyeditor: Audrey Doyle	**Illustrator:** Kate Dullea
Proofreader: Kim Wimpsett	

March 2023:   First Edition

Revision History for the First Edition

2023-03-07:   First Release

See *http://oreilly.com/catalog/errata.csp?isbn=9781098135126* for release details.

978-1-098-13512-6

LSI

Table of Contents

Preface

In the cloud native community and beyond, eBPF has become one of the hottest technical topics of recent years. A new generation of powerful tools and projects (*https://ebpf.io/applications*) in networking, security, observability, and more have been built (and more continue to be created) using eBPF as a platform, offering better performance and accuracy compared to their predecessors. eBPF-related conferences such as the eBPF Summit (*https://ebpf.io/summit-2022*) and Cloud Native eBPF Day (*https://oreil.ly/q9-p3*) have attracted thousands of attendees and viewers, and at the time of this writing, the eBPF Slack (*http://ebpf.io/slack*) community has more than 14,000 members.

Why is eBPF being selected as the underlying technology for so many infrastructure tools? How does it deliver the promised improvements to performance? How is eBPF useful in such disparate technical fields, which range from performance tracing to network traffic encryption?

This book aims to answer these questions by giving the reader an understanding of how eBPF works, as well as providing an introduction to writing eBPF code.

Who This Book Is For

This book is for developers, system administrators, operators, and students who are curious about eBPF and want to know more about how it works. It will provide a foundation for those who want to explore writing eBPF programs themselves. Since eBPF provides a great platform for a whole new generation of instrumentation and tooling, there will likely be gainful employment for eBPF developers for some years to come.

But you don't necessarily need to be planning to write eBPF code yourself for this book to be useful to you. If you work in operations, security, or any other role that involves software infrastructure, you're likely to come across eBPF-based tooling, now or over the next few years. If you understand something about the internals of these tools, you'll be in a better position to use them effectively. For example, if you know how events can trigger eBPF programs, you'll have a better mental model for exactly what an eBPF-based tool is really measuring when it shows you performance metrics. If you're an application developer, you might also come into contact with some of these eBPF-based tools—for example, if you are performance tuning an application, you might use a tool like Parca (*https://www.parca.dev*) to generate flame graphs showing which functions are taking the most time. If you are evaluating security tools, this book will help you understand where eBPF shines and how to avoid using it in a naïve way that is less effective against attacks.

Even if you're not using eBPF tools today, I hope this book will give you interesting insights into areas of Linux that you might not have considered before. Most developers take the kernel for granted, as they use programming languages with convenient higher-level abstractions that allow them to focus on the work of application development—which is plenty hard enough! They use tools like debuggers and performance analyzers to help them do their job effectively. Knowing the internals of how a debugger or performance tool works might be interesting, but it's not essential. Yet, for many of us, it's fun and fulfilling to go down the rabbit hole to find out more.[1] In the same way, most people will use eBPF tools without having to worry about how they are built. Arthur C. Clarke wrote (*https://oreil.ly/gOV1D*) that "any sufficiently advanced technology is indistinguishable from magic," but personally, I like to dig in and find out how the magic trick works. You might be like me and feel compelled to explore eBPF programming to get a better feel for what is possible with this technology. If so, I think you'll enjoy this book.

What This Book Covers

eBPF continues to evolve at quite a rapid pace, which makes it rather difficult to write a comprehensive reference that doesn't constantly need updating. However, there are some fundamentals and basic principles that are unlikely to change significantly, and that's what this book discusses.

Chapter 1 sets the scene by describing why eBPF is so powerful as a technology and explaining how the ability to run custom programs in the operating system kernel enables so many exciting capabilities.

Things become more concrete in Chapter 2, where you'll see some "Hello World" examples that introduce you to the concepts of eBPF programs and maps.

---

1 At the dotGo Paris conference in 2017, I gave a talk that showed how a debugger works (*https://youtu.be/ TBrv17QyUE0*).

Chapter 3 dives into more detail about eBPF programs and how they run in the kernel, and Chapter 4 explores the interface between user space applications and eBPF programs.

One of the big challenges of eBPF in recent years has been the question of compatibility across kernel versions. Chapter 5 looks at the "compile once, run everywhere" (CO-RE) approach that solves this problem.

The verification process is perhaps the most important characteristic that distinguishes eBPF from kernel modules. I'll introduce you to the eBPF verifier in Chapter 6.

In Chapter 7 you'll get an introduction to the many different types of eBPF programs and their attachment points. Many of those attachment points are within the networking stack, and Chapter 8 explores the application of eBPF for networking features in more detail. Chapter 9 looks at how eBPF is being used to build security tools.

If you want to write a user space application that interacts with eBPF programs, there are many libraries and frameworks available to help. Chapter 10 gives an overview of the options for various programming languages.

Finally, in Chapter 11 I'll gaze into my crystal ball and tell you about some future developments that are likely to unfold in the eBPF world.

Prerequisite Knowledge

This book assumes you are comfortable with basic shell commands on Linux and with the idea of using a compiler to turn source code into an executable program. There are some simple example extracts from Makefiles, on the assumption that you have at least a minimal understanding of how make uses these files.

There are lots of code examples in Python, C, and Go. You won't need in-depth knowledge of those languages to get something out of these examples, but you'll get the most out of the book if you are generally happy to read some code. I'm also assuming you are familiar with the idea of *pointers*, which identify a memory location.

Example Code and Exercises

There are lots of code examples in this book. If you want to try them out for yourself, you'll find an accompanying GitHub repository and instructions for installing and running the code at *https://github.com/lizrice/learning-ebpf*.

I have also included exercises at the end of most of the chapters to help you explore eBPF programming by extending the examples or writing your own programs.

Because eBPF is continually evolving, the features available to you depend on the kernel version you're running. Many of the restrictions that apply to earlier versions have been lifted or relaxed in later versions. The Iovisor project has a useful overview of the kernel versions in which different BPF features were added (*https://oreil.ly/SsnEV*), and in this book I have attempted to note when the particular capabilities I'm describing were added. The examples were tested using version 5.15 of the kernel, and at the time of this writing some of the popular Linux distributions don't yet support such a recent kernel version. If you're reading this book shortly after it was published, you might find that some of the features won't work on the Linux kernel your organization uses in production.

Is eBPF Only for Linux?

eBPF was originally developed for Linux. There's no particular reason why the same approach couldn't be used in other operating systems too—indeed, Microsoft has been developing an eBPF implementation for Windows (*https://oreil.ly/k7AvA*). I discuss that briefly in Chapter 11, but throughout the rest of the book I focus on the Linux implementation, and all the examples will be from Linux.

Conventions Used in This Book

The following typographical conventions are used in this book:

Italic
Indicates new terms, URLs, email addresses, filenames, and file extensions.

`Constant width`
Used for program listings, as well as within paragraphs to refer to program elements such as variable or function names, databases, data types, environment variables, statements, and keywords.

`Constant width bold`
Shows commands or other text that should be typed literally by the user.

`Constant width italic`
Shows text that should be replaced with user-supplied values or by values determined by context.

This element signifies a tip or suggestion.

 This element signifies a general note.

This element indicates a warning or caution.

Using Code Examples

Supplemental material (code examples, exercises, etc.) is available for download at *https://github.com/lizrice/learning-ebpf*.

If you have a technical question or a problem using the code examples, please send email to *bookquestions@oreilly.com*.

This book is here to help you get your job done. In general, if example code is offered with this book, you may use it in your programs and documentation. You do not need to contact us for permission unless you're reproducing a significant portion of the code. For example, writing a program that uses several chunks of code from this book does not require permission. Selling or distributing examples from O'Reilly books does require permission. Answering a question by citing this book and quoting example code does not require permission. Incorporating a significant amount of example code from this book into your product's documentation does require permission.

We appreciate, but generally do not require, attribution. An attribution usually includes the title, author, publisher, and ISBN. For example: "*Learning eBPF* by Liz Rice (O'Reilly). Copyright 2023 Vertical Shift Ltd., 978-1-098-13512-6."

If you feel your use of code examples falls outside fair use or the permission given above, feel free to contact us at *permissions@oreilly.com*.

O'Reilly Online Learning

O'REILLY® For more than 40 years, *O'Reilly Media* has provided technology and business training, knowledge, and insight to help companies succeed.

Our unique network of experts and innovators share their knowledge and expertise through books, articles, and our online learning platform. O'Reilly's online learning platform gives you on-demand access to live training courses, in-depth learning paths, interactive coding environments, and a vast collection of text and video from O'Reilly and 200+ other publishers. For more information, visit *https://oreilly.com*.

How to Contact Us

Please address comments and questions concerning this book to the publisher:

O'Reilly Media, Inc.
1005 Gravenstein Highway North
Sebastopol, CA 95472
800-998-9938 (in the United States or Canada)
707-829-0515 (international or local)
707-829-0104 (fax)

We have a web page for this book, where we list errata, examples, and any additional information. You can access this page at *https://oreil.ly/learning-eBPF*.

Email *bookquestions@oreilly.com* to comment or ask technical questions about this book.

For news and information about our books and courses, visit *https://oreilly.com*.

Find us on LinkedIn: *https://linkedin.com/company/oreilly-media*.

Follow us on Twitter: *https://twitter.com/oreillymedia*.

Watch us on YouTube: *https://youtube.com/oreillymedia*.

Acknowledgments

I would like to thank the many people who have contributed enormously to the writing of this book:

- My technical reviewers—Timo Beckers, Jess Males, Quentin Monnet, Kevin Sheldrake, and Celeste Stinger—provided detailed, actionable feedback and great ideas for improving the examples, for which I'm very grateful.

- I'm standing on the shoulders of the giants who built, popularized, and continue to maintain eBPF, including Daniel Borkmann, Thomas Graf, Brendan Gregg, Andrii Nakryiko, Alexei Starovoitov, and countless others who have contributed not just code but also conference talks and blog posts to the community.

- Thank you to my talented and lovely colleagues at Isovalent, many of whom are eBPF and kernel specialists, from whom I continue to learn so much.

- Thanks also to the team at O'Reilly, especially my editor, Rita Fernando, who gave me endless support during the writing process, as well as the planning that helped keep the book on schedule; and John Devins, for encouraging me to write the book in the first place.

- Phil Pearl not only gave helpful feedback on the content, but he also made sure I ate and took breaks. I am forever grateful for his support and encouragement.

I also want to thank all the wonderful people who, over the years, have taken the time to make encouraging comments about my work, whether it's in person at an event or on social media. It's incredibly inspiring to know that something I have written or recorded has helped someone else get to grips with a technical concept or has given them the desire to build or write something themselves. Thank you!

CHAPTER 1

What Is eBPF, and Why Is It Important?

eBPF is a revolutionary kernel technology that allows developers to write custom code that can be loaded into the kernel dynamically, changing the way the kernel behaves. (Don't worry if you're not confident about what the kernel is—we'll come to that shortly in this chapter.)

This enables a new generation of highly performant networking, observability, and security tools. And as you'll see, if you want to instrument an app with these eBPF-based tools, you don't need to modify or reconfigure the app in any way, thanks to eBPF's vantage point within the kernel.

Just a few of the things you can do with eBPF include:

- Performance tracing of pretty much any aspect of a system
- High-performance networking, with built-in visibility
- Detecting and (optionally) preventing malicious activity

Let's take a brief journey through eBPF's history, starting with the Berkeley Packet Filter.

eBPF's Roots: The Berkeley Packet Filter

What we call "eBPF" today has its roots in the BSD Packet Filter, first described in 1993 in a paper[1] written by Lawrence Berkeley National Laboratory's Steven McCanne and Van Jacobson. This paper discusses a pseudomachine that can run

---

1 "The BSD Packet Filter: A New Architecture for User-level Packet Capture" (*https://oreil.ly/4GpgQ*) by Steven McCanne and Van Jacobson.

filters, which are programs written to determine whether to accept or reject a network packet. These programs were written in the BPF instruction set, a general-purpose set of 32-bit instructions that closely resembles assembly language. Here's an example taken directly from that paper:

```
ldh     [12]
jeq     #ETHERTYPE IP, L1, L2
L1:     ret     #TRUE
L2:     ret     #0
```

This tiny piece of code filters out packets that aren't Internet Protocol (IP) packets. The input to this filter is an Ethernet packet, and the first instruction (`ldh`) loads a 2-byte value starting at byte 12 in this packet. In the next instruction (`jeq`) that value is compared with the value that represents an IP packet. If it matches, execution jumps to the instruction labeled L1, and the packet is accepted by returning a nonzero value (identified here as #TRUE). If it doesn't match, the packet is not an IP packet and is rejected by returning 0.

You can imagine (or, indeed, refer to the paper to find examples of) more complex filter programs that make decisions based on other aspects of the packet. Importantly, the author of the filter can write their own custom programs to be executed within the kernel, and this is the heart of what eBPF enables.

BPF came to stand for "Berkeley Packet Filter," and it was first introduced to Linux in 1997, in kernel version 2.1.75,[2] where it was used in the tcpdump utility as an efficient way to capture the packets to be traced out.

Fast-forward to 2012, when seccomp-bpf was introduced in version 3.5 of the kernel. This enabled the use of BPF programs to make decisions about whether to allow or deny user space applications from making system calls. We'll explore this in more detail in Chapter 10. This was the first step in evolving BPF from the narrow scope of packet filtering to the general-purpose platform it is today. From this point on, the words *packet filter* in the name started to make less sense!

From BPF to eBPF

BPF evolved to what we call "extended BPF" or "eBPF" starting in kernel version 3.18 in 2014. This involved several significant changes:

- The BPF instruction set was completely overhauled to be more efficient on 64-bit machines, and the interpreter was entirely rewritten.

---

2 These and other details come from Alexei Starovoitov's 2015 NetDev presentation, "BPF – in-kernel virtual machine" (*https://oreil.ly/hISe1*).

- eBPF *maps* were introduced, which are data structures that can be accessed by BPF programs and by user space applications, allowing information to be shared between them. You'll learn about maps in Chapter 2.

- The bpf() system call was added so that user space programs can interact with eBPF programs in the kernel. You'll read about this system call in Chapter 4.

- Several BPF helper functions were added. You'll see a few examples in Chapter 2 and some more details in Chapter 6.

- The eBPF verifier was added to ensure that eBPF programs are safe to run. This is discussed in Chapter 6.

This put the basis for eBPF in place, but development did not slow down! Since then, eBPF has evolved significantly.

The Evolution of eBPF to Production Systems

A feature called *kprobes* (kernel probes) had existed in the Linux kernel since 2005, allowing for traps to be set on almost any instruction in the kernel code. Developers could write kernel modules that attached functions to kprobes for debugging or performance measurement purposes.[3]

The ability to attach eBPF programs to kprobes was added in 2015, and this was the starting point for a revolution in the way tracing is done across Linux systems. At the same time, hooks started to be added within the kernel's networking stack, allowing eBPF programs to take care of more aspects of networking functionality. We'll see more of this in Chapter 8.

By 2016, eBPF-based tools were being used in production systems. Brendan Gregg's (*https://www.brendangregg.com*) work on tracing at Netflix became widely known in infrastructure and operations circles, as did his statement (*https://oreil.ly/stV6v*) that eBPF "brings superpowers to Linux." In the same year, the Cilium project was announced, being the first networking project to use eBPF to replace the entire datapath in container environments.

The following year Facebook (now Meta) made Katran (*https://oreil.ly/X-WsL*) an open source project. Katran, a layer 4 load balancer, met Facebook's need for a highly scalable and fast solution (*https://oreil.ly/zl4yX*). Every single packet to Facebook.com since 2017 has passed through eBPF/XDP.[4] For me personally, this was the year that ignited my excitement about the possibilities enabled by this technology, after seeing

---

3 There is a good description of how kprobes work in the kernel documentation (*https://oreil.ly/Ue6Ii*).

4 This wonderful fact comes from Daniel Borkmann's KubeCon 2020 talk titled "eBPF and Kubernetes: Little Helper Minions for Scaling Microservices" (*https://oreil.ly/tIR9o*).

Thomas Graf's talk (*https://oreil.ly/g9ya0*) about eBPF and the Cilium project (*https://oreil.ly/doKbd*) at DockerCon in Austin, Texas.

In 2018, eBPF became a separate subsystem within the Linux kernel, with Daniel Borkmann (*http://borkmann.ch*) from Isovalent and Alexei Starovoitov (*https://oreil.ly/K8nXI*) from Meta as its maintainers (they were later joined by Andrii Nakryiko (*https://nakryiko.com*), also from Meta). The same year saw the introduction of BPF Type Format (BTF), which makes eBPF programs much more portable. We'll explore this in Chapter 5.

The year 2020 saw the introduction of LSM BPF, allowing eBPF programs to be attached to the Linux Security Module (LSM) kernel interface. This indicated that a third major use case for eBPF had been identified: it became clear that eBPF is a great platform for security tooling, in addition to networking and observability.

Over the years, eBPF's capabilities have grown substantially, thanks to the work of more than 300 kernel developers and many contributors to the associated user space tools (such as bpftool, which we'll meet in Chapter 3), compilers, and programming language libraries. Programs were once limited to 4,096 instructions, but that limit has grown to 1 million verified instructions[5] and has effectively been rendered irrelevant by support for tail calls and function calls (which you'll see in Chapters 2 and 3).

> For deeper insight into the history of eBPF, who better to refer to than the maintainers who have been working on it from the beginning?
>
> Alexei Starovoitov gave a fascinating presentation about the history of BPF (*https://youtu.be/DAvZH13725I*) from its roots in software-defined networking (SDN). In this talk, he discusses the strategies used to get the early eBPF patches accepted into the kernel and reveals that the official birthday of eBPF is September 26, 2014, which marked the acceptance of the first set of patches covering the verifier, BPF system call, and maps.
>
> Daniel Borkmann has also discussed the history of BPF and its evolution to support networking and tracing functionality. I highly recommend his talk "eBPF and Kubernetes: Little Helper Minions for Scaling Microservices" (*https://youtu.be/99jUcLt3rSk*), which is full of interesting nuggets of information.

---

5 For more details on the instruction limit and "complexity limit," see *https://oreil.ly/0iVer*.

Naming Is Hard

eBPF's applications range so far beyond packet filtering that the acronym is essentially meaningless now, and it has become a standalone term. And since the Linux kernels in widespread use these days all have support for the "extended" parts, the terms *eBPF* and *BPF* are largely used interchangeably. In the kernel source code and in eBPF programming, the common terminology is *BPF*. For example, as we'll see in Chapter 4, the system call for interacting with eBPF is `bpf()`, helper functions start with `bpf_`, and the different types of (e)BPF programs are identified with names that start with `BPF_PROG_TYPE`. Outside the kernel community, the name "eBPF" seems to have stuck, for example, in the community site ebpf.io (*https://ebpf.io*) and in the name of the eBPF Foundation (*http://ebpf.foundation*).

The Linux Kernel

To understand eBPF you'll need a solid grasp of the difference between the kernel and user space in Linux. I covered this in my report "What Is eBPF?"[6] and I've adapted some of that content for the next few paragraphs.

The Linux kernel is the software layer between your applications and the hardware they're running on. Applications run in an unprivileged layer called *user space*, which can't access hardware directly. Instead, an application makes requests using the system call (syscall) interface to request the kernel to act on its behalf. That hardware access can involve reading and writing to files, sending or receiving network traffic, or even just accessing memory. The kernel is also responsible for coordinating concurrent processes, enabling many applications to run at once. This is illustrated in Figure 1-1.

As application developers, we typically don't use the system call interface directly, because programming languages give us high-level abstractions and standard libraries that are easier interfaces to program. As a result, a lot of people are blissfully unaware of how much the kernel is doing while our programs run. If you want to get a sense of how often the kernel is invoked, you can use the `strace` utility to show all the system calls an application makes.

---

6 Extract from "What Is eBPF?" by Liz Rice. Copyright © 2022 O'Reilly Media. Used with permission.

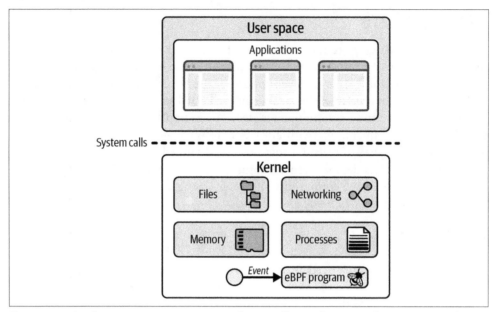

Figure 1-1. Applications in user space use the syscall interface to make requests to the kernel

Here's an example, where using `cat` to echo the word *hello* to the screen involves more than 100 system calls:

```
$ strace -c echo "hello"
hello
% time     seconds  usecs/call     calls    errors syscall
------ ----------- ----------- --------- --------- ----------------
 24.62    0.001693          56        30        12 openat
 17.49    0.001203          60        20           mmap
 15.92    0.001095          57        19           newfstatat
 15.66    0.001077          53        20           close
 10.35    0.000712         712         1           execve
  3.04    0.000209          52         4           mprotect
  2.52    0.000173          57         3           read
  2.33    0.000160          53         3           brk
  2.09    0.000144          48         3           munmap
  1.11    0.000076          76         1           write
  0.96    0.000066          66         1         1 faccessat
  0.76    0.000052          52         1           getrandom
  0.68    0.000047          47         1           rseq
  0.65    0.000045          45         1           set_robust_list
  0.63    0.000043          43         1           prlimit64
  0.61    0.000042          42         1           set_tid_address
  0.58    0.000040          40         1           futex
------ ----------- ----------- --------- --------- ----------------
100.00    0.006877          61       111        13 total
```

Because applications rely so heavily on the kernel, it means we can learn a lot about how an application behaves if we can observe its interactions with the kernel. With eBPF we can add instrumentation into the kernel to get these insights.

For example, if you are able to intercept the system call for opening files, you can see exactly which files any application accesses. But how could you do that interception? Let's consider what would be involved if we wanted to modify the kernel, adding new code to create some kind of output whenever that system call is invoked.

Adding New Functionality to the Kernel

The Linux kernel is complex, with around 30 million lines of code at the time of this writing.[7] Making a change to any codebase requires some familiarity with the existing code, so unless you're a kernel developer already, this is likely to present a challenge.

Additionally, if you want to contribute your change upstream, you'll be facing a challenge that isn't purely technical. Linux is a general-purpose operating system, used in all manner of environments and circumstances. This means that if you want your change to become part of an official Linux release, it's not simply a matter of writing code that works. The code has to be accepted by the community (and more specifically by Linus Torvalds, creator and main developer of Linux) as a change that will be for the greater good of all. This isn't a given—only one-third of submitted kernel patches are accepted.[8]

Let's suppose you've figured out a good technical approach for intercepting the system call for opening files. After some months of discussion and some hard development work on your part, let's imagine the change is accepted into the kernel. Great! But how long will it be until it arrives on everyone's machines?

There's a new release of the Linux kernel every two or three months, but even when a change has made it into one of these releases, it's still some time away from being available in most people's production environments. This is because most of us don't just use the Linux kernel directly—we use Linux distributions like Debian, Red Hat, Alpine, and Ubuntu that package up a version of the Linux kernel with various other components. You may well find that your favorite distribution is using a kernel release that's several years old.

For example, a lot of enterprise users employ Red Hat Enterprise Linux (RHEL). At the time of this writing, the current release is RHEL 8.5, dated November 2021, and it uses version 4.18 of the Linux kernel. This kernel was released in August 2018.

---

7 "Linux 5.12 Coming In At Around 28.8 Million Lines" (*https://oreil.ly/9zJP2*). Phoronix, March 2021.

8 Jiang Y, Adams B, German DM. 2013. "Will My Patch Make It? And How Fast?" (*https://oreil.ly/rj2P4*) (2013). According to this research paper, 33% of patches are accepted, and most take three to six months.

As illustrated in the cartoon in Figure 1-2, it takes literally years to get new functionality from the idea stage into a production environment Linux kernel.[9]

Figure 1-2. Adding features to the kernel (cartoon by Vadim Shchekoldin, Isovalent)

Kernel Modules

If you don't want to wait years for your change to make it into the kernel, there is another option. The Linux kernel was designed to accept kernel modules, which can be loaded and unloaded on demand. If you want to change or extend kernel behavior, writing a module is certainly one way to do it. A kernel module can be distributed for others to use independent of the official Linux kernel release, so it doesn't have to be accepted into the main upstream codebase.

The biggest challenge here is that this is still full-on kernel programming. Users have historically been very cautious about using kernel modules, for one simple reason: if kernel code crashes, it takes down the machine and everything running on it. How can a user be confident that a kernel module is safe to run?

---

9 Thankfully, security patches to existing functionality are made available more quickly.

Being "safe to run" doesn't just mean not crashing—the user wants to know that a kernel module is safe from a security perspective. Does it include vulnerabilities that an attacker could exploit? Do we trust the authors of the module not to put malicious code in it? Because the kernel is privileged code, it has access to everything on the machine, including all the data, so malicious code in the kernel would be a serious cause for concern. This applies to kernel modules too.

The safety of the kernel is one important reason why Linux distributions take so long to incorporate new releases. If other people have been running a kernel version in a variety of circumstances for months or years, this should have flushed out issues. The distribution maintainers can have some confidence that the kernel they ship to their users/customers is *hardened*—that is, it is safe to run.

eBPF offers a very different approach to safety: the *eBPF verifier*, which ensures that an eBPF program is loaded only if it's safe to run—it won't crash the machine or lock it up in a hard loop, and it won't allow data to be compromised. We'll discuss the verification process in more detail in Chapter 6.

Dynamic Loading of eBPF Programs

eBPF programs can be loaded into and removed from the kernel dynamically. Once they are attached to an event, they'll be triggered by that event regardless of what caused that event to occur. For example, if you attach a program to the syscall for opening files, it will be triggered whenever any process tries to open a file. It doesn't matter whether that process was already running when the program was loaded. This is a huge advantage compared to upgrading the kernel and then having to reboot the machine to use its new functionality.

This leads to one of the great strengths of observability or security tooling that uses eBPF—it instantly gets visibility over everything that's happening on the machine. In environments running containers, that includes visibility over all processes running inside those containers as well as on the host machine. I'll dig into the consequences of this for cloud native deployments later in this chapter.

Additionally, as illustrated in Figure 1-3, people can create new kernel functionality very quickly through eBPF without requiring every other Linux user to accept the same changes.

Figure 1-3. Adding kernel features with eBPF (cartoon by Vadim Shchekoldin, Isovalent)

High Performance of eBPF Programs

eBPF programs are a very efficient way to add instrumentation. Once loaded and JIT-compiled (which you'll see in Chapter 3), the program runs as native machine instructions on the CPU. Additionally, there's no need to incur the cost of transitioning between kernel and user space (which is an expensive operation) to handle each event.

The 2018 paper[10] that describes the eXpress Data Path (XDP) includes some illustrations of the kinds of performance improvements eBPF enables in networking. For example, implementing routing in XDP "improves performance with a factor of 2.5" compared to the regular Linux kernel implementation, and "XDP offers a performance gain of 4.3x over IPVS" for load balancing.

---

10 Høiland-Jørgensen T, Brouer JD, Borkmann D, et al. "The eXpress data path: fast programmable packet processing in the operating system kernel" (*https://oreil.ly/qyhLK*). *Proceedings of the 14th International Conference on emerging Networking EXperiments and Technologies* (CoNEXT '18). Association for Computing Machinery; 2018:54–66.

For performance tracing and security observability, another advantage of eBPF is that relevant events can be filtered within the kernel before incurring the costs of sending them to user space. Filtering only certain network packets was, after all, the point of the original BPF implementation. Today eBPF programs can collect information about all manner of events across a system, and they can use complex, customized programmatic filters to send only the relevant subset of information to user space.

eBPF in Cloud Native Environments

These days lots of organizations choose not to run applications by executing programs directly on servers. Instead, many use cloud native approaches: containers, orchestrators such as Kubernetes or ECS, or serverless approaches like Lambda, cloud functions, Fargate, and so on. These approaches all use automation to choose the server where each workload will run; in serverless, we're not even aware what server is running each workload.

Nevertheless, there are servers involved, and each of those servers (whether it's a virtual machine or bare-metal machine) runs a kernel. Where applications run in a container, if they're running on the same (virtual) machine, they share the same kernel. In a Kubernetes environment, this means all the containers in all the pods on a given node are using the same kernel. When we instrument that kernel with eBPF programs, all the containerized workloads on that node are visible to those eBPF programs, as illustrated in Figure 1-4.

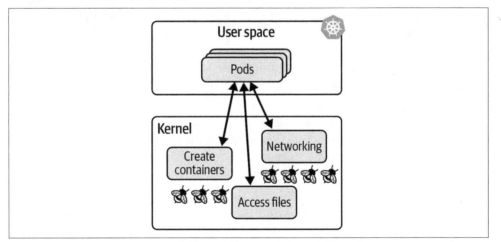

Figure 1-4. eBPF programs in the kernel have visibility of all applications running on a Kubernetes node

Visibility of all the processes on the node, combined with the ability to load eBPF programs dynamically, gives us the real superpowers of eBPF-based tooling in cloud native computing:

- We don't need to change our applications, or even the way they are configured, to instrument them with eBPF tooling.
- As soon as it's loaded into the kernel and attached to an event, an eBPF program can start observing preexisting application processes.

Contrast this with the *sidecar model*, which has been used to add functionality like logging, tracing, security, and service mesh functionality into Kubernetes apps. In the sidecar approach, the instrumentation runs as a container that is "injected" into each application pod. This process involves modifying the YAML that defines the application pods, adding in the definition of the sidecar container. This approach is certainly more convenient than adding the instrumentation into the source code of the application (which is what we had to do before the sidecar approach; for example, including a logging library in our application and making calls into that library at appropriate points in the code). Nevertheless, the sidecar approach has a few downsides:

- The application pod has to be restarted for the sidecar to be added.
- Something has to modify the application YAML. This is generally an automated process, but if something goes wrong, the sidecar won't be added, which means the pod doesn't get instrumented. For example, a deployment might be annotated to indicate that an admission controller should add the sidecar YAML to the pod spec for that deployment. But if the deployment isn't labeled correctly, the sidecar won't get added, and it's therefore not visible to the instrumentation.
- When there are multiple containers within a pod, they might reach readiness at different times, the ordering of which may not be predictable. Pod start-up time can be significantly slowed by the injection of sidecars, or worse, it can cause race conditions or other instabilities. For example, the Open Service Mesh documentation (*https://oreil.ly/z80Q5*) describes how application containers have to be resilient to all traffic being dropped until the Envoy proxy container is ready.
- Where networking functionality such as service mesh is implemented as a sidecar, it necessarily means that all traffic to and from the application container has to travel through the network stack in the kernel to reach a network proxy container, adding latency to that traffic; this is illustrated in Figure 1-5. We'll talk about improving network efficiency with eBPF in Chapter 9.

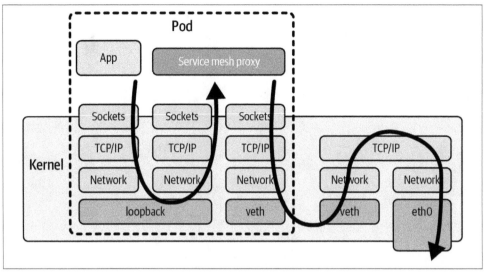

Figure 1-5. Path of a network packet using a service mesh proxy sidecar container

All these issues are inherent problems with the sidecar model. Fortunately, now that eBPF is available as a platform, we have a new model that can avoid these issues. Additionally, because eBPF-based tools can see everything that's happening on a (virtual) machine, they are harder for bad actors to sidestep. For example, if an attacker manages to deploy a cryptocurrency mining app on one of your hosts, they probably won't do you the courtesy of instrumenting it with the sidecars you're using on your application workloads. If you're relying on a sidecar-based security tool to prevent apps from making unexpected network connections, that tool isn't going to spot the mining app connecting to its mining pool if the sidecar isn't injected. In contrast, network security implemented in eBPF can police all traffic on the host machine, so this cryptocurrency mining operation could easily be stopped. The ability to drop network packets for security reasons is something we'll come back to in Chapter 8.

Summary

I hope this chapter has given you some insight into why eBPF as a platform is so powerful. It allows us to change the behavior of the kernel, providing us the flexibility to build bespoke tools or customized policies. eBPF-based tools can observe any event across the kernel, and hence across all applications running on a (virtual) machine, whether they are containerized or not. eBPF programs can also be deployed dynamically, allowing behavior to be changed on the fly.

So far we've discussed eBPF at a relatively conceptual level. In the next chapter we'll make it more concrete and explore the constituent parts of an eBPF-based application.

eBPF's "Hello World"

In the previous chapter I discussed why eBPF is so powerful, but it's OK if you don't yet feel you have a concrete grasp of what it really means to run eBPF programs. In this chapter I'll use a simple "Hello World" example to give you a better feel for it.

As you'll learn while you read through this book, there are several different libraries and frameworks for writing eBPF applications. As a warm-up, I'll show you what is probably the most accessible approach from a programming point of view: the BCC Python framework (*https://github.com/iovisor/bcc*). This offers a very easy way to write basic eBPF programs. For reasons that I'll cover in Chapter 5, it's not necessarily an approach I would recommend these days for production apps that you're intending to distribute to other users, but it's great for taking your first steps.

 If you want to try this code for yourself, it is available at *https://github.com/lizrice/learning-ebpf* in the *chapter2* directory.

You'll find the BCC project at *https://github.com/iovisor/bcc*, and the instructions for installing BCC are at *https://github.com/iovisor/bcc/blob/master/INSTALL.md*.

BCC's "Hello World"

The following is the full source code of *hello.py*, an eBPF "Hello World" application[1] written using BCC's Python library:

```
#!/usr/bin/python
from bcc import BPF
```

---

1 I originally wrote this for a talk titled "The Beginner's Guide to eBPF Programming." You can find the original code along with links to the slides and video at *https://github.com/lizrice/ebpf-beginners*.

```
program = r"""
int hello(void *ctx) {
    bpf_trace_printk("Hello World!");
    return 0;
}
"""

b = BPF(text=program)
syscall = b.get_syscall_fnname("execve")
b.attach_kprobe(event=syscall, fn_name="hello")

b.trace_print()
```

This code consists of two parts: the eBPF program itself that will run in the kernel, and some user space code that loads the eBPF program into the kernel and reads out the trace that it generates. As you can see in Figure 2-1, *hello.py* is the user space part of this application, and `hello()` is the eBPF program that runs in the kernel.

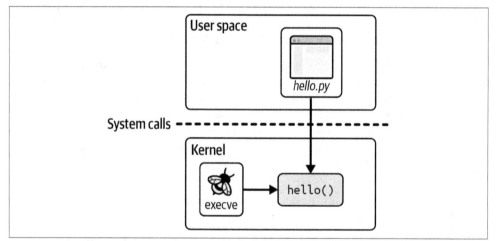

Figure 2-1. The user space and kernel components of "Hello World"

Let's dig into each line of the source code to understand it better.

The first line tells you this is Python code, and the program that can run it is the Python interpreter (*/usr/bin/python*).

The eBPF program itself is written in C code, and it's this part:

```
int hello(void *ctx) {
    bpf_trace_printk("Hello World!");
    return 0;
}
```

All the eBPF program does is use a helper function, `bpf_trace_printk()`, to write a message. Helper functions are another feature that distinguishes "extended" BPF from its "classic" predecessor. They are a set of functions that eBPF programs can call to interact with the system; I'll discuss them further in Chapter 5. For now you can just think of this as printing a line of text.

The entire eBPF program is defined as a string called `program` in the Python code. This C program needs to be compiled before it can be executed, but BCC takes care of that for you. (You'll see how to compile eBPF programs yourself in the next chapter.) All you need to do is pass this string as a parameter when creating a BPF object, as in the following line:

```
b = BPF(text=program)
```

eBPF programs need to be attached to an event, and for this example I've chosen to attach to the system call `execve`, which is the syscall used to execute a program. Whenever anything or anyone starts a new program executing on this machine, that will call `execve()`, which will trigger the eBPF program. Although the "execve()" name is a standard interface in Linux, the name of the function that implements it in the kernel depends on the chip architecture, but BCC gives us a convenient way to look up the function name for the machine we're running on:

```
syscall = b.get_syscall_fnname("execve")
```

Now, `syscall` represents the name of the kernel function I'm going to attach to, using a kprobe (you were introduced to the concept of kprobes in Chapter 1).[2] You can attach the `hello` function to that event, like this:

```
b.attach_kprobe(event=syscall, fn_name="hello")
```

At this point, the eBPF program is loaded into the kernel and attached to an event, so the program will be triggered whenever a new executable gets launched on the machine. All that's left to do in the Python code is to read the tracing that is output by the kernel and write it on the screen:

```
b.trace_print()
```

This `trace_print()` function will loop indefinitely (until you stop the program, perhaps with Ctrl+C), displaying any trace.

---

2 There is a more performant way to attach eBPF programs to functions, available from kernel version 5.5 onward, that uses fentry (and the corresponding fexit instead of kretprobe for the exit from a function). I'll discuss this later in the book, but for now I'm using kprobe to keep the example in this chapter as simple as possible.

Figure 2-2 illustrates this code. The Python program compiles the C code, loads it into the kernel, and attaches it to the execve syscall kprobe. Whenever any application on this (virtual) machine calls execve(), it triggers the eBPF hello() program, which writes a line of trace into a specific pseudofile. (I'll cover where that pseudofile is later in this chapter.) The Python program reads the trace message from the pseudofile and displays it to the user.

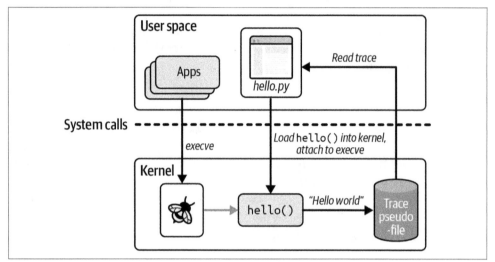

Figure 2-2. "Hello World" in operation

Running "Hello World"

Run this program, and depending on what is happening on the (virtual) machine you're using, you might see tracing being generated straightaway, because other processes could be executing programs[3] with the execve syscall. If you don't see anything, open a second terminal and execute any commands you like,[4] and you'll see the corresponding trace generated by "Hello World":

```
$ hello.py
b'      bash-5412    [001] .... 90432.904952: 0: bpf_trace_printk: Hello World'
```

---

3 I quite often use VScode remote to connect to a virtual machine in the cloud. This runs lots of node scripts on the virtual machine, which generates lots of tracing from this "Hello World" app.

4 Some commands (echo is a common example) might be shell built-ins that run as part of the shell process, rather than executing a new program. These won't trigger the execve() event, so no trace will be generated.

Since eBPF is so powerful, it requires special privileges to use it. Privileges are automatically assigned to the root user, so the easiest way to run eBPF programs is as root, perhaps by using `sudo`. For clarity I won't include `sudo` in the example commands in this book, but if you ever see an "Operation not permitted" error, the first thing to check is whether you're trying to run eBPF programs as an unprivileged user.

CAP_BPF was introduced in kernel version 5.8, and it gives sufficient privilege to perform some eBPF operations like creating certain types of map. However, you will probably need additional capabilities:

- CAP_PERFMON and CAP_BPF are both required to load tracing programs.
- CAP_NET_ADMIN and CAP_BPF are both required for loading networking programs.

There is a lot more detail on this in the blog post "Introduction to CAP_BPF" (*https://oreil.ly/G2zFO*) by Milan Landaverde.

As soon as the *hello* eBPF program is loaded and attached to an event, it gets triggered by events that are being generated from preexisting processes. This should reinforce a couple of points that you learned in Chapter 1:

- eBPF programs can be used to dynamically change the behavior of the system. There's no need to reboot the machine or restart existing processes. eBPF code starts taking effect as soon as it is attached to an event.
- There's no need to change anything about other applications for them to be visible to eBPF. Wherever you have terminal access on that machine, if you run an executable in it, that will use the `execve()` syscall, and if you have the *hello* program attached to that syscall, it will be triggered to generate tracing output. Likewise, if you have a script that runs executables, that will also trigger the *hello* eBPF program. You don't need to change anything about the terminal's shell, the script, or the executables you're running.

The trace output shows not only the `"Hello World"` string, but also some additional contextual information about the event that triggered the *hello* eBPF program to run. In the example output shown at the beginning of this section, the process that made the `execve` system call had a process ID of 5412, and it was running the command `bash`. For trace messages, this contextual information is added as part of the kernel tracing infrastructure (which isn't specific to eBPF), but as you'll see later in this chapter, it's also possible to retrieve contextual information like this within the eBPF program itself.

You might be wondering how the Python code knows where to read the tracing output from. The answer is not very sophisticated—the `bpf_trace_printk()` helper function in the kernel always sends output to the same predefined pseudofile location: */sys/kernel/debug/tracing/trace_pipe*. You can confirm this by using `cat` to view its contents; you'll need root privileges to access it.

A single trace pipe location is fine for a simple "Hello World" example or for basic debugging purposes, but it's very limited. There is very little flexibility in the format of the output, and it only supports the output of strings, so it's not terribly useful for passing structured information. Perhaps most importantly, there is just this one location on the (virtual) machine. If you had multiple eBPF programs running simultaneously, they would all write trace output to the same trace pipe, which could get very confusing for a human operator.

There's a much better way to get information out of an eBPF program: use an eBPF map.

BPF Maps

A *map* is a data structure that can be accessed from an eBPF program and from user space. Maps are one of the really significant features that distinguish extended BPF from its classic predecessor. (You might think this would mean they are commonly referred to as "eBPF maps," but you'll frequently see "BPF maps." As is generally the case, both terms are used interchangeably.)

Maps can be used to share data among multiple eBPF programs or to communicate between a user space application and eBPF code running in the kernel. Typical uses include the following:

- User space writing configuration information to be retrieved by an eBPF program
- An eBPF program storing state, for later retrieval by another eBPF program (or a future run of the same program)
- An eBPF program writing results or metrics into a map, for retrieval by the user space app that will present results

There are various types of BPF maps defined in Linux's *uapi/linux/bpf.h* file (*https://oreil.ly/1s1GM*), and there is some information about them in the kernel docs (*https://oreil.ly/5oUW7*). In general they are all key–value stores, and in this chapter you'll see examples of maps for hash tables, perf and ring buffers, and arrays of eBPF programs.

Some map types are defined as arrays, which always have a 4-byte index as the key type; other maps are hash tables that can use some arbitrary data type as the key.

There are map types that are optimized for particular types of operations, such as first-in-first-out queues (*https://oreil.ly/VSoEp*), first-in-last-out stacks (*https://oreil.ly/VSoEp*), least-recently-used data storage (*https://oreil.ly/vpsun*), longest-prefix matching (*https://oreil.ly/hZ5aM*), and Bloom filters (*https://oreil.ly/DzCTK*) (a probabilistic data structure designed to provide very fast results on whether an element exists).

Some eBPF map types hold information about specific types of objects. For example, sockmaps (*https://oreil.ly/UUTHO*) and devmaps (*https://oreil.ly/jzKYh*) hold information about sockets and network devices and are used by network-related eBPF programs to redirect traffic. A program array map stores a set of indexed eBPF programs, and (as you'll see later in this chapter) this is used to implement tail calls, where one program can call another. There's even a map-of-maps type (*https://oreil.ly/038tN*) to support storing information about maps.

Some map types have per-CPU variants, which is to say that the kernel uses a different block of memory for each CPU core's version of that map. This might have you wondering about concurrency concerns for maps that are *not* per-CPU, where multiple CPU cores could be accessing the same map simultaneously. Spin lock support for (some) maps was added in kernel version 5.1, and we'll return to this subject in Chapter 5.

The next example (*chapter2/hello-map.py* in the GitHub repository (*https://github.com/lizrice/learning-ebpf*)) shows some basic operations using a hash table map. It also demonstrates some of BCC's convenient abstractions that make it very easy to use maps.

Hash Table Map

Like the previous example in this chapter, this eBPF program will be attached to a kprobe at the entry to the execve system call. It's going to populate a hash table with key–value pairs, where the key is a user ID and the value is a counter for the number of times execve is called by a process running under that user ID. In practice, this example will show how many times each different user has run programs.

First, let's look at the C code for the eBPF program itself:

```
BPF_HASH(counter_table);                                    ❶

int hello(void *ctx) {
  u64 uid;
  u64 counter = 0;
  u64 *p;
```

```
uid = bpf_get_current_uid_gid() & 0xFFFFFFFF;          ❷
p = counter_table.lookup(&uid);                        ❸
if (p != 0) {                                          ❹
   counter = *p;
}
counter++;                                             ❺
counter_table.update(&uid, &counter);                  ❻
return 0;
}
```

❶ BPF_HASH() is a BCC macro that defines a hash table map.

❷ bpf_get_current_uid_gid() is a helper function used to obtain the user ID that is running the process that triggered this kprobe event. The user ID is held in the lowest 32 bits of the 64-bit value that gets returned. (The top 32 bits hold the group ID, but that part is masked out.)

❸ Look for an entry in the hash table with a key matching the user ID. It returns a pointer to the corresponding value in the hash table.

❹ If there is an entry for this user ID, set the counter variable to the current value in the hash table (pointed to by p). If there is no entry for this user ID in the hash table, the pointer will be 0, and the counter value will be left at 0.

❺ Whatever the current counter value is, it gets incremented by one.

❻ Update the hash table with the new counter value for this user ID.

Take a closer look at the lines of code that access the hash table:

```
p = counter_table.lookup(&uid);
```

And later:

```
counter_table.update(&uid, &counter);
```

If you're thinking "that's not proper C code!" you're absolutely right. C doesn't support defining methods on structures like that.[5] This is a great example where BCC's version of C is very loosely a C-like language that BCC rewrites before it sends the code to the compiler. BCC offers some convenient shortcuts and macros that it converts into "proper" C.

Just like in the previous example, the C code is defined as a string called program. The program is compiled, loaded into the kernel, and attached to the execve kprobe, in exactly the same way as the previous "Hello World" example:

---

5 C++ does, but not C.

```
b = BPF(text=program)
syscall = b.get_syscall_fnname("execve")
b.attach_kprobe(event=syscall, fn_name="hello")
```

This time a little more work is required on the Python side to read the information out of the hash table:

```
while True:                                   ❶
    sleep(2)
    s = ""
    for k,v in b["counter_table"].items():    ❷
        s += f"ID {k.value}: {v.value}\t"
    print(s)
```

❶ This part of the code loops indefinitely, looking for output to display every two seconds.

❷ BCC automatically creates a Python object to represent the hash table. This code loops through any values and prints them to the screen.

When you run this example, you'll want a second terminal window where you can run some commands. Here's some example output I obtained, annotated on the right side with the commands I ran in another terminal:

```
Terminal 1                          Terminal 2
$ ./hello-map.py
                                    [blank line(s) until I run something]
ID 501: 1                           ls
ID 501: 1
ID 501: 2                           ls
ID 501: 3      ID 0: 1             sudo ls
ID 501: 4      ID 0: 1             ls
ID 501: 4      ID 0: 1
ID 501: 5      ID 0: 2             sudo ls
```

This example generates a line of output every two seconds, whether anything has happened or not. At the end of this output, the hash table contains two entries:

- key=501, value=5

- key=0, value=2

In the second terminal, I have the user ID of 501. Running the ls command with this user ID increments the execve counter. When I run sudo ls, this results in two calls to execve: one is the execution of sudo, under user ID 501; the other is the execution of ls, under root's user ID of 0.

In this example, I used a hash table to convey data from the eBPF program to user space. (I could also have used an array type of map here, since the key was an integer; hash tables let you use an arbitrary type as the key.) Hash tables are very convenient when the data is naturally in key–value pairs, but the user space code has to keep polling the table on a regular basis. The Linux kernel already supported the perf subsystem (*https://oreil.ly/nTvvH*) for sending data from the kernel to user space, and eBPF includes support for using perf buffers and their successor, BPF ring buffers. Let's take a look.

Perf and Ring Buffer Maps

In this section I'm going to describe a slightly more sophisticated version of "Hello World" that uses BCC's `BPF_PERF_OUTPUT` capabilities, which let you write data in a structure of your choosing into a perf ring buffer map.

 There is a newer construct called "BPF ring buffers" that are now generally preferred over BPF perf buffers, if you have a kernel of version 5.8 or above. Andrii Nakryiko discusses the difference in his BPF ring buffer (*https://oreil.ly/ARRyV*) blog post. You'll see an example of BCC's `BPF_RINGBUF_OUTPUT` in Chapter 4.

Ring Buffers

Ring buffers are by no means unique to eBPF, but I'll explain them just in case you haven't come across them before. You can think of a ring buffer as a piece of memory logically organized in a ring, with separate "write" and "read" pointers. Data of some arbitrary length gets written to wherever the write pointer is, with the length information included in a header for that data. The write pointer moves to after the end of that data, ready for the next write operation.

Similarly, for a read operation, data gets read from wherever the read pointer is, using the header to determine how much data to read. The read pointer moves along in the same direction as the write pointer so that it points to the next available piece of data. This is illustrated in Figure 2-3, showing a ring buffer with three items of different length available for reading.

If the read pointer catches up with the write pointer, it simply means there's no data to read. If a write operation would make the write pointer overtake the read pointer, the data doesn't get written and a *drop counter* gets incremented. Read operations include the drop counter to indicate whether data has been lost since the last successful read.

If read and write operations happened at precisely the same rate with no variability, and they always contained the same amount of data, you could at least in theory get away with a ring buffer just big enough to accommodate that data size. In most applications there will be some variation in the time between reads, writes, or both, so the buffer size needs to be tuned to account for this.

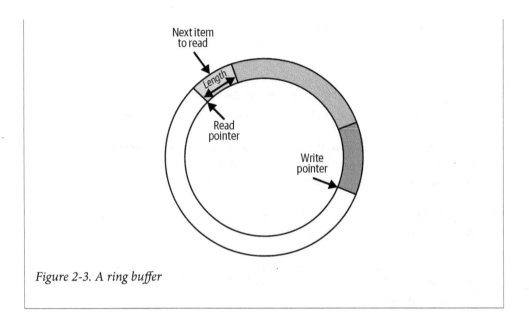

Figure 2-3. A ring buffer

You'll find the source code for this example in *chapter2/hello-buffer.py* in the *Learning eBPF* GitHub repository (*http://github.com/lizrice/learning-ebpf*). As in the first "Hello World" example you saw early in this chapter, this version will write the string "Hello World" to the screen every time the execve() syscall is used. It will also look up the process ID and the name of the command that makes each execve() call so that you'll get similar output to the first example. This gives me the opportunity to show you a couple more examples of BPF helper functions.

Here's the eBPF program that will be loaded into the kernel:

```
BPF_PERF_OUTPUT(output);                                          ❶

struct data_t {                                                   ❷
    int pid;
    int uid;
    char command[16];
    char message[12];
};

int hello(void *ctx) {
    struct data_t data = {};                                      ❸
    char message[12] = "Hello World";

    data.pid = bpf_get_current_pid_tgid() >> 32;                  ❹
    data.uid = bpf_get_current_uid_gid() & 0xFFFFFFFF;            ❺

    bpf_get_current_comm(&data.command, sizeof(data.command));    ❻
    bpf_probe_read_kernel(&data.message, sizeof(data.message), message); ❼
```

```
    output.perf_submit(ctx, &data, sizeof(data));                    ❽

    return 0;
}
```

❶ BCC defines the macro `BPF_PERF_OUTPUT` for creating a map that will be used to pass messages from the kernel to user space. I've called this map `output`.

❷ Every time `hello()` is run, the code will write a structure's worth of data. This is the definition of that structure, which has fields for the process ID, the name of the currently running command, and a text message.

❸ `data` is a local variable that holds the data structure to be submitted, and `message` holds the `"Hello World"` string.

❹ `bpf_get_current_pid_tgid()` is a helper function that gets the ID of the process that triggered this eBPF program to run. It returns a 64-bit value with the process ID in the top 32 bits.[6]

❺ `bpf_get_current_uid_gid()` is the helper function you saw in the previous example for obtaining the user ID.

❻ Similarly, `bpf_get_current_comm()` is a helper function for getting the name of the executable (or "command") that's running in the process that made the exe cve syscall. This is a string, not a numeric value like the process and user IDs, and in C you can't simply assign a string using =. You have to pass the address of the field where the string should be written, `&data.command`, as an argument to the helper function.

❼ For this example, the message is `"Hello World"` every time. `bpf_probe_read_kernel()` copies it into the right place in the data structure.

❽ At this point the data structure is populated with the process ID, command name, and message. This call to `output.perf_submit()` puts that data into the map.

---

6 The lower 32 bits are the *thread group ID*. For a single-threaded process, this is the same as the process ID, but additional threads for the process would be given different IDs. The docs for the GNU C library have a good description of the difference between process and thread group IDs (*https://oreil.ly/Wo9k3*).

Just as in the first "Hello World" example, this C program is assigned to a string called program in the Python code. What follows is the rest of the Python code:

```
b = BPF(text=program)                            ❶
syscall = b.get_syscall_fnname("execve")
b.attach_kprobe(event=syscall, fn_name="hello")

def print_event(cpu, data, size):                ❷
    data = b["output"].event(data)
    print(f"{data.pid} {data.uid} {data.command.decode()} " + \
          f"{data.message.decode()}")

b["output"].open_perf_buffer(print_event)        ❸
while True:                                       ❹
    b.perf_buffer_poll()
```

❶ The lines that compile the C code, load it into the kernel, and attach it to the syscall event are unchanged from the version of "Hello World" you saw earlier.

❷ print_event is a callback function that will output a line of data to the screen. BCC does some heavy lifting so that I can refer to the map simply as b["output"] and grab data from it using b["output"].event().

❸ b["output"].open_perf_buffer() opens the perf ring buffer. The function takes print_event as an argument to define that this is the callback function to be used whenever there is data to read from the buffer.

❹ The program will now loop indefinitely,[7] polling the perf ring buffer. If there is any data available, print_event will get called.

Running this code gives us output that's fairly similar to the original "Hello World":

```
$ sudo ./hello-buffer.py
11654 node Hello World
11655 sh Hello World
...
```

As before, you might need to open a second terminal to the same (virtual) machine and run some commands to trigger some output.

The big difference between this and the original "Hello World" example is that instead of using a single, central trace pipe, the data is now being passed via a ring buffer map called output that was created by this program for its own use, as shown in Figure 2-4.

---

7 This is just example code, so I'm not worrying about cleaning up on keyboard interrupt or any other niceties!

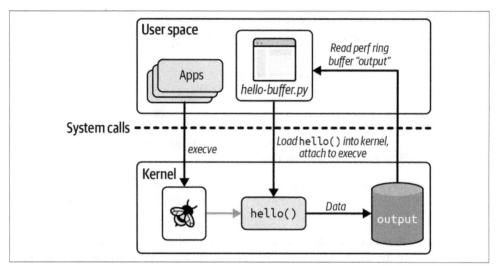

Figure 2-4. Using a perf ring buffer for passing data from the kernel to user space

You can verify that the information isn't going to the trace pipe by using `cat /sys/kernel/debug/tracing/trace_pipe`.

As well as demonstrating the use of a ring buffer map, this example shows some eBPF helper functions for retrieving contextual information about the event that triggered the eBPF program to run. Here you've seen helper functions getting the user ID, the process ID, and the name of the current command. As you'll see in Chapter 7, the set of contextual information that's available and the set of valid helper functions that can be used to retrieve it depend on what type of program it is and what event triggered it.

The fact that contextual information like this is available to the eBPF code is what makes it so valuable for observability. Whenever an event occurs, an eBPF program can report not only the fact that the event happened but also relevant information about what happened to trigger the event. It's also highly performant, since all this information can be gathered within the kernel, without the need for any synchronous context switching to user space.

You'll see further examples in this book where eBPF helper functions are used to gather other contextual data, as well as examples where eBPF programs change the contextual data or even block events from happening altogether.

Function Calls

You've seen that eBPF programs can call helper functions provided by the kernel, but what if you want to split the code you're writing into functions? Generally, in software development it's considered good practice[8] to pull common code into a function that you can call from multiple places, rather than duplicating the same lines over and over again. But in the early days, eBPF programs were not permitted to call functions other than helper functions. To work around this, programmers have directed the compiler to "always inline" their functions, like this:

```
static __always_inline void my_function(void *ctx, int val)
```

Generally, a function in source code results in the compiler emitting a jump instruction, which causes execution to jump to the set of instructions that make up the called function (and then to jump back again when that function has completed). You can see this illustrated on the left side of Figure 2-5. The right side shows what happens when a function is inlined: there is no jump instruction; instead, a copy of the function's instructions is emitted directly within the calling function.

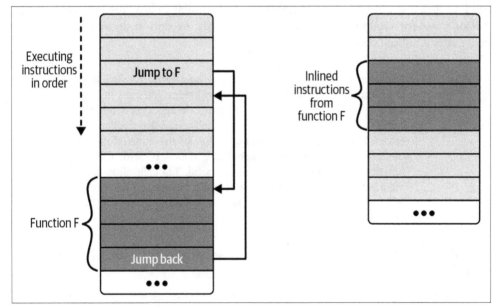

Figure 2-5. Layout of noninlined and inlined function instructions

---

8 This principle is often called "DRY" ("Don't Repeat Yourself"), as popularized by The Pragmatic Programmer (*https://oreil.ly/QFich*).

If the function is called from multiple places, that results in multiple copies of that function's instructions in the compiled executable. (Sometimes the compiler might choose to inline a function for optimization purposes, and that is one reason why you might not be able to attach a kprobe to certain kernel functions. I'll come back to this in Chapter 7.)

Starting from Linux kernel 4.16 and LLVM 6.0, the restriction requiring functions to be inlined was lifted so that eBPF programmers could write function calls more naturally. However, this feature, called "BPF to BPF function calls" or "BPF subprograms," isn't currently supported by the BCC framework, so let's come back to it in the next chapter. (You can, of course, continue to use functions with BCC if they are inlined.)

There is another mechanism for decomposing complex functionality into smaller parts in eBPF: tail calls.

Tail Calls

As described at ebpf.io (*https://oreil.ly/Loyuz*), "tail calls can call and execute another eBPF program and replace the execution context, similar to how the execve() system call operates for regular processes." In other words, execution doesn't return to the caller after a tail call completes.

> Tail calls (*https://oreil.ly/cOA1r*) are by no means exclusive to eBPF programming. The general motivation behind tail calls is to avoid adding frames to the stack over and over again as a function is called recursively, which can eventually lead to stack overflow errors. If you can arrange your code to call a recursive function as the last thing it does, the stack frame associated with the calling function isn't really doing anything useful. Tail calls allow for calling a series of functions without growing the stack. This is particularly useful in eBPF where the stack is limited to 512 bytes (*https://oreil.ly/SZmkd*).

Tail calls are made using the bpf_tail_call() helper function, which has the following signature:

```
long bpf_tail_call(void *ctx, struct bpf_map *prog_array_map, u32 index)
```

The three arguments to this function have the following meanings:

- ctx allows passing the context from the calling eBPF program to the callee.
- prog_array_map is an eBPF map of type BPF_MAP_TYPE_PROG_ARRAY, which holds a set of file descriptors that identify eBPF programs.
- index indicates which of that set of eBPF programs should be invoked.

This helper is somewhat unusual in that if it succeeds, it never returns. The currently running eBPF program is replaced on the stack by the program being called. The helper could fail, for example, if the indicated program doesn't exist in the map, in which case the calling program carries on executing.

User space code has to load all the eBPF programs into the kernel (as usual), and it also sets up the program array map.

Let's look at a simple example written in Python using BCC; you'll find the code in the GitHub repo (*http://github.com/lizrice/learning-ebpf*) as *chapter2/hello-tail.py*. The main eBPF program is attached to a tracepoint at the common entry point for all syscalls. This program uses tail calls to trace out specific messages for certain syscall opcodes. If there isn't a tail call for a given opcode, the program traces out a generic message.

If you're using the BCC framework, to make a tail call (*https://oreil.ly/rT9e1*) you can use a line of the slightly simpler form:

```
prog_array_map.call(ctx, index)
```

Before passing the code to the compilation step, BCC will rewrite the preceding line to this:

```
bpf_tail_call(ctx, prog_array_map, index)
```

Here is the source code for the eBPF program and its tail calls:

```
BPF_PROG_ARRAY(syscall, 300);                              ❶

int hello(struct bpf_raw_tracepoint_args *ctx) {          ❷
    int opcode = ctx->args[1];                            ❸
    syscall.call(ctx, opcode);                            ❹
    bpf_trace_printk("Another syscall: %d", opcode);      ❺
    return 0;
}

int hello_execve(void *ctx) {                             ❻
    bpf_trace_printk("Executing a program");
    return 0;
}

int hello_timer(struct bpf_raw_tracepoint_args *ctx) {    ❼
    if (ctx->args[1] == 222) {
        bpf_trace_printk("Creating a timer");
    } else if (ctx->args[1] == 226) {
        bpf_trace_printk("Deleting a timer");
    } else {
        bpf_trace_printk("Some other timer operation");
    }
    return 0;
}
```

```
int ignore_opcode(void *ctx) {                              ❽
    return 0;
}
```

❶ BCC provides a `BPF_PROG_ARRAY` macro for easily defining maps of type `BPF_MAP_TYPE_PROG_ARRAY`. I have called the map `syscall` and allowed for 300 entries,[9] which is going to be sufficient for this example.

❷ In the user space code that you'll see shortly, I'm going to attach this eBPF program to the `sys_enter` raw tracepoint, which gets hit whenever any syscall is made. The context passed to an eBPF program attached to a raw tracepoint takes the form of this `bpf_raw_tracepoint_args` structure.

❸ In the case of `sys_enter`, the raw tracepoint arguments include the opcode identifying which syscall is being made.

❹ Here we make a tail call to the entry in the program array whose key matches the opcode. This line of code will be rewritten by BCC to a call to the `bpf_tail_call()` helper function before it passes the source code to the compiler.

❺ If the tail call succeeds, this line tracing out the opcode value will never be hit. I've used this to provide a default line of trace for opcodes for which there isn't a program entry in the map.

❻ `hello_exec()` is a program that will be loaded into the syscall program array map, to be executed as a tail call when the opcode indicates it's an `execve()` syscall. It's just going to generate a line of trace to tell the user a new program is being executed.

❼ `hello_timer()` is another program that will be loaded into the syscall program array. In this case it's going to be referred to by more than one entry in the program array.

❽ `ignore_opcode()` is a tail call program that does nothing. I'll use this for syscalls where I don't want any trace to be generated at all.

---

9 There are some 300 syscalls in Linux, and since I'm not using any recently added syscalls for this example, this is good enough.

Now let's look at the user space code that loads and manages this set of eBPF programs:

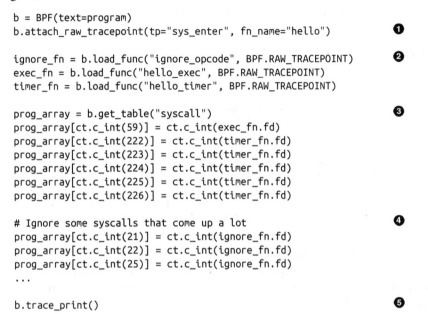

```
b = BPF(text=program)
b.attach_raw_tracepoint(tp="sys_enter", fn_name="hello")        ❶

ignore_fn = b.load_func("ignore_opcode", BPF.RAW_TRACEPOINT)    ❷
exec_fn = b.load_func("hello_exec", BPF.RAW_TRACEPOINT)
timer_fn = b.load_func("hello_timer", BPF.RAW_TRACEPOINT)

prog_array = b.get_table("syscall")                             ❸
prog_array[ct.c_int(59)] = ct.c_int(exec_fn.fd)
prog_array[ct.c_int(222)] = ct.c_int(timer_fn.fd)
prog_array[ct.c_int(223)] = ct.c_int(timer_fn.fd)
prog_array[ct.c_int(224)] = ct.c_int(timer_fn.fd)
prog_array[ct.c_int(225)] = ct.c_int(timer_fn.fd)
prog_array[ct.c_int(226)] = ct.c_int(timer_fn.fd)

# Ignore some syscalls that come up a lot                       ❹
prog_array[ct.c_int(21)] = ct.c_int(ignore_fn.fd)
prog_array[ct.c_int(22)] = ct.c_int(ignore_fn.fd)
prog_array[ct.c_int(25)] = ct.c_int(ignore_fn.fd)
...

b.trace_print()                                                 ❺
```

❶   Instead of attaching to a kprobe, as you saw earlier, this time the user space code attaches the main eBPF program to the sys_enter tracepoint.

❷   These calls to b.load_func() return a file descriptor for each tail call program. Notice that tail calls need to have the same program type as their parent— BPF.RAW_TRACEPOINT in this case. Also, it bears pointing out that each tail call program is an eBPF program in its own right.

❸   The user space code creates entries in the syscall map. The map doesn't have to be fully populated for every possible opcode; if there is no entry for a particular opcode, it simply means no tail call will be executed. Also, it's perfectly fine to have multiple entries that point to the same eBPF program. In this case, I want the hello_timer() tail call to be executed for any of a set of timer-related syscalls.

❹   Some syscalls get run so frequently by the system that a line of trace for each of them clutters up the trace output to the point of unreadability. I've used the ignore_opcode() tail call for several syscalls.

❺   Print the trace output to the screen, until the user terminates the program.

Running this program generates trace output for every syscall that runs on the (virtual) machine, unless the opcode has an entry that links it to the `ignore_opcode()` tail call. Here's some example output from running `ls` in another terminal (some details have been omitted for readability):

```
./hello-tail.py
b'    hello-tail.py-2767      ... Another syscall: 62'
b'    hello-tail.py-2767      ... Another syscall: 62'
...
b'            bash-2626      ... Executing a program'
b'            bash-2626      ... Another syscall: 220'
...
b'            <...>-2774      ... Creating a timer'
b'            <...>-2774      ... Another syscall: 48'
b'            <...>-2774      ... Deleting a timer'
...
b'              ls-2774      ... Another syscall: 61'
b'              ls-2774      ... Another syscall: 61'
...
```

The particular syscalls being executed are beside the point, but you can see that the different tail calls are getting called and are generating trace messages. You can also see the default message `Another syscall` for opcodes that don't have an entry in the tail call program map.

 Check out Paul Chaignon's blog post about the cost of BPF tail calls (*https://oreil.ly/jTxcb*) on various different kernel versions.

Tail calls have been supported in eBPF since kernel version 4.2, but for a long time they were incompatible with making BPF to BPF function calls. This restriction was lifted in kernel 5.10.[10]

The fact that you can chain up to 33 tail calls together, combined with the instruction complexity limit per eBPF program of 1 million instructions, means that today's eBPF programmers have a lot of leeway to write very complex code to run entirely in the kernel.

---

10 Making tail calls from a BPF subprogram requires support from the JIT compiler, which you'll meet in the next chapter. In the kernel version I used to write the examples in this book, only the JIT compiler on x86 has this support, although support has been added to ARM in kernel 6.0 (*https://oreil.ly/KYUYS*).

Summary

I hope that by showing some concrete examples of an eBPF program, this chapter helped you consolidate your mental model of eBPF code running in the kernel, triggered by events. You've also seen examples of data being passed from the kernel to user space using BPF maps.

Using the BCC framework hides many of the details of how the program is built, loaded into the kernel, and attached to events. In the next chapter I'll show you a different approach to writing "Hello World," and we'll dive deeper into those hidden details.

Exercises

Here are some optional activities you might like to try (or think about) if you want to explore "Hello World" a bit further:

1. Adapt the *hello-buffer.py* eBPF program to output different trace messages for odd and even process IDs.

2. Modify *hello-map.py* so that the eBPF code gets triggered by more than one syscall. For example, openat() is commonly called to open files, and write() is called to write data to a file. You can start by attaching the *hello* eBPF program to multiple syscall kprobes. Then try having modified versions of the *hello* eBPF program for different syscalls, demonstrating that you can access the same map from multiple different programs.

3. The *hello-tail.py* eBPF program is an example of a program that attaches to the sys_enter raw tracepoint that is hit whenever *any* syscall is called. Change *hello-map.py* to show the total number of syscalls made by each user ID, by attaching it to that same sys_enter raw tracepoint.

   Here's some example output I got after making that change:

```
$ ./hello-map.py
ID 104: 6      ID 0: 225
ID 104: 6      ID 101: 34    ID 100: 45    ID 0: 332    ID 501: 19
ID 104: 6      ID 101: 34    ID 100: 45    ID 0: 368    ID 501: 38
ID 104: 6      ID 101: 34    ID 100: 45    ID 0: 533    ID 501: 57
```

4. The `RAW_TRACEPOINT_PROBE` macro provided by BCC (*https://oreil.ly/kh-j4*) simplifies attaching to raw tracepoints, telling the user space BCC code to automatically attach it to a specified tracepoint. Try it in *hello-tail.py*, like this:

   - Replace the definition of the `hello()` function with `RAW_TRACEPOINT_PROBE(sys_enter)`.

   - Remove the explicit attachment call `b.attach_raw_tracepoint()` from the Python code.

   You should see that BCC automatically creates the attachment and the program works exactly the same. This is an example of the many convenient macros that BCC provides.

5. You could further adapt *hello_map.py* so that the key in the hash table identifies a particular syscall (rather than a particular user). The output will show how many times that syscall has been called across the whole system.

Anatomy of an eBPF Program

In the previous chapter you saw a simple eBPF "Hello World" program written using the BCC framework. In this chapter there's an example version of a "Hello World" program written entirely in C so that you can see some of the details BCC took care of behind the scenes.

This chapter also shows you the stages an eBPF program goes through on its journey from source code to execution, as illustrated in Figure 3-1.

Figure 3-1. C (or Rust) source code is compiled into eBPF bytecode, which is either JIT-compiled or interpreted into native machine code instructions

An eBPF program is a set of eBPF bytecode instructions. It's possible to write eBPF code directly in this bytecode, much as it's possible to program in assembly language. Humans typically find a higher-level programming language easier to deal with, and at least at the time of this writing, I'd say the vast majority of eBPF code is written in C[1] and then compiled to eBPF bytecode.

Conceptually, this bytecode runs in an eBPF virtual machine within the kernel.

---

1 Increasingly, eBPF programs are also being written in Rust, since the Rust compiler supports eBPF bytecode as a target.

The eBPF Virtual Machine

The eBPF virtual machine, like any virtual machine, is a software implementation of a computer. It takes in a program in the form of eBPF bytecode instructions, and these have to be converted to native machine instructions that run on the CPU.

In early implementations of eBPF, the bytecode instructions were interpreted within the kernel—that is, every time an eBPF program runs, the kernel examines the instructions and converts them into machine code, which it then executes. Interpreting has since been largely replaced by JIT (just-in-time) compilation for performance reasons and to avoid the possibility of some Spectre-related vulnerabilities in the eBPF interpreter. *Compilation* means the conversion to native machine instructions happens just once, when the program is loaded into the kernel.

eBPF bytecode consists of a set of instructions, and those instructions act on (virtual) eBPF registers. The eBPF instruction set and register model were designed to map neatly to common CPU architectures so that the step of compiling or interpreting from bytecode to machine code is reasonably straightforward.

eBPF Registers

The eBPF virtual machine uses 10 general-purpose registers, numbered 0 to 9. Additionally, Register 10 is used as a stack frame pointer (and can only be read, but not written). As a BPF program is executed, values get stored in these registers to keep track of state.

It's important to understand that these eBPF registers in the eBPF virtual machine are implemented in software. You can see them enumerated from BPF_REG_0 to BPF_REG_10 in the *include/uapi/linux/bpf.h* header file (*https://oreil.ly/_ZhU2*) of the Linux kernel's source code.

The context argument to an eBPF program is loaded into Register 1 before its execution begins. The return value from the function is stored in Register 0.

Before calling a function from eBPF code, the arguments to that function are placed in Register 1 through Register 5 (not all the registers are used if there are fewer than five arguments).

eBPF Instructions

The same *linux/bpf.h* header file (*https://oreil.ly/_ZhU2*) defines a structure called bpf_insn, which represents a BPF instruction:

```
struct bpf_insn {
    __u8 code;          /* opcode */                        ❶
    __u8 dst_reg:4;     /* dest register */                 ❷
    __u8 src_reg:4;     /* source register */
    __s16 off;        /* signed offset */                   ❸
    __s32 imm;        /* signed immediate constant */
};
```

❶ Each instruction has an opcode, which defines what operation the instruction is to perform: for example, adding a value to the contents of a register, or jumping to a different instruction in the program.[2] The Iovisor project's "Unofficial eBPF spec" (*https://oreil.ly/FXcPu*) has a list of the valid instructions.

❷ Different operations might involve up to two registers.

❸ Depending on the operation, there might be an offset value and/or an "immediate" integer value.

This bpf_insn structure is 64 bits (or 8 bytes) long. However, sometimes an instruction might need to span more than 8 bytes. If you want to set a register to a 64-bit value, you can't somehow squeeze all 64 bits of that value into the structure, along with the opcode and register information. In these cases, the instruction uses *wide instruction encoding* that is 16 bytes long in total. You'll see an example of this in this chapter.

When loaded into the kernel, the bytecode of an eBPF program is represented by a series of these bpf_insn structures. The verifier performs several checks on this information to ensure that the code is safe to run. You'll learn more about the verification process in Chapter 6.

Most of the different opcodes fall into the following categories:

- Loading a value into a register (either an immediate value or a value read from memory or from another register)
- Storing a value from a register into memory
- Performing arithmetic operations such as adding a value to the contents of a register
- Jumping to a different instruction if a particular condition is satisfied

---

2 There are a few instructions where the operation is "modified" by the value of other fields in the instruction. For example, there are a set of atomic instructions (*https://oreil.ly/oyTI7*) introduced in kernel 5.12 that include an arithmetic operation (ADD, AND, OR, XOR) that is specified in the imm field.

For an overview of eBPF architecture, I recommend the BPF and XDP Reference Guide (*https://oreil.ly/rvm1i*) that's included as part of the Cilium project's documentation. If you'd like more details, the kernel documentation (*https://oreil.ly/_2XDT*) describes the eBPF instructions and encoding quite clearly.

Let's use another simple example of an eBPF program and follow its journey from C source code, through eBPF bytecode, to machine code instructions.

If you want to build and run this code yourself, you'll find the code along with instructions for setting up an environment to do so at *github.com/lizrice/learning-ebpf*. The code for this chapter is in the *chapter3* directory.

The examples in this chapter are written in C using a library called *libbpf*. You'll learn more about this library in Chapter 5.

eBPF "Hello World" for a Network Interface

The examples in the previous chapter emitted the trace "Hello World" triggered by a system call kprobe; this time I'm going to show an eBPF program that writes a line of trace when triggered by the arrival of a network packet.

Packet processing is a very common application of eBPF. I'll cover this in a lot more detail in Chapter 8, but for now it might be helpful to be aware of the basic idea of an eBPF program that is triggered for every packet of data that arrives on a network interface. The program can inspect and even modify the contents of that packet, and it makes a decision (or *verdict*) on what the kernel should do with that packet. The verdict could tell the kernel to carry on processing it as usual, drop it, or redirect it elsewhere.

In the simple example I'm showing here, the program doesn't do anything with the network packet; it simply writes out the words *Hello World* and a counter to the trace pipe every time a network packet is received.

The example program is in *chapter3/hello.bpf.c*. It's a fairly common convention to put eBPF programs into filenames ending with *bpf.c* to distinguish them from user space C code that might live in the same source code directory. Here's the entire program:

```
#include <linux/bpf.h>                          ❶
#include <bpf/bpf_helpers.h>

int counter = 0;                                ❷

SEC("xdp")                                      ❸
int hello(void *ctx) {                          ❹
    bpf_printk("Hello World %d", counter);
```

```
    counter++;
    return XDP_PASS;
}

char LICENSE[] SEC("license") = "Dual BSD/GPL";  ❺
```

❶ This example starts by including some header files. Just in case you're not familiar with C coding, every program has to include the header files that define any
structures or functions the program is going to use. You can guess from the
names that these header files are related to BPF.

❷ This example shows how eBPF programs can use global variables. This counter
will get incremented every time the program runs.

❸ The macro SEC() defines a section called xdp that you'll be able to see in the
compiled object file. I'll come back to how the section name is used in Chapter 5,
but for now you can simply think of it as defining that it's an eXpress Data Path
(XDP) type of eBPF program.

❹ Here you can see the actual eBPF program. In eBPF, the program name is the
function name, so this program is called hello. It uses a helper function,
bpf_printk, to write a string of text, increments the global variable counter, and
then returns the value XDP_PASS. This is the verdict indicating to the kernel that it
should process this network packet as normal.

❺ Finally there is another SEC() macro that defines a license string, and this is a
crucial requirement for eBPF programs. Some of the BPF helper functions in the
kernel are defined as "GPL only." If you want to use any of these functions, your
BPF code has to be declared as having a GPL-compatible license. The verifier
(which we will discuss in Chapter 6) will object if the declared license is not compatible with the functions a program uses. Certain eBPF program types, including those that use BPF LSM (which you'll learn about in Chapter 9), are also
required to be GPL compatible (*https://oreil.ly/ItahV*).

> You might be wondering why the previous chapter used
> bpf_trace_printk() and this version uses bpf_printk(). The
> short answer is that BCC's version is called bpf_trace_printk()
> and *libbpf*'s version is bpf_printk(), but both of those are wrap-
> pers around the kernel function bpf_trace_printk(). Andrii Nak-
> ryiko wrote a good post (*https://oreil.ly/9mNSY*) on this on his
> blog.

This is an example of an eBPF program that attaches to the XDP hook point on a network interface. You can think of the XDP event being triggered the moment a network packet arrives inbound on a (physical or virtual) network interface.

 Some network cards support offloading XDP programs so that they can be executed on the network card itself. This means each network packet that arrives can be processed on the card, before it gets anywhere near the machine's CPU. XDP programs can inspect and even modify each network packet, so this is very useful for doing things like DDoS protection, firewalling, or load balancing in a highly performant way. You'll learn more about this in Chapter 8.

You have seen the C source code, so the next step is to compile it into an object the kernel can understand.

Compiling an eBPF Object File

Our eBPF source code needs to be compiled into the machine instructions that the eBPF virtual machine can understand: eBPF bytecode. The Clang compiler from the LLVM project (*https://llvm.org*) will do this if you specify `-target bpf`. The following is an extract from a Makefile that will do the compilation:

```
hello.bpf.o: %.o: %.c
    clang \
        -target bpf \
        -I/usr/include/$(shell uname -m)-linux-gnu \
        -g \
        -O2 -c $< -o $@
```

This generates an object file called *hello.bpf.o* from the source code in *hello.bpf.c*. The -g flag is optional here,[3] but it generates debug information so that you can see the source code alongside the bytecode when you inspect the object file. Let's inspect this object file to better understand the eBPF code it contains.

Inspecting an eBPF Object File

The file utility is commonly used to determine the contents of a file:

```
$ file hello.bpf.o
hello.bpf.o: ELF 64-bit LSB relocatable, eBPF, version 1 (SYSV), with debug_info,
not stripped
```

---

3 The -g flag is required to generate BTF information that you'll need for CO-RE eBPF programs, which I'll cover in Chapter 5.

This shows it's an ELF (Executable and Linkable Format) file, containing eBPF code, for a 64-bit platform with LSB (least significant bit) architecture. It includes debug information if you used the -g flag at the compilation step.

You can inspect this object further with llvm-objdump to see the eBPF instructions:

```
$ llvm-objdump -S hello.bpf.o
```

Even if you're not familiar with disassembly, the output from this command isn't too hard to understand:

```
hello.bpf.o:    file format elf64-bpf                          ❶

Disassembly of section xdp:                                     ❷

0000000000000000 <hello>:                                       ❸
; bpf_printk("Hello World %d", counter");                       ❹
       0:    18 06 00 00 00 00 00 00 00 00 00 00 00 00 00 00 r6 = 0 ll
       2:    61 63 00 00 00 00 00 00 r3 = *(u32 *)(r6 + 0)
       3:    18 01 00 00 00 00 00 00 00 00 00 00 00 00 00 00 r1 = 0 ll
       5:    b7 02 00 00 0f 00 00 00 r2 = 15
       6:    85 00 00 00 06 00 00 00 call 6
; counter++;                                                    ❺
       7:    61 61 00 00 00 00 00 00 r1 = *(u32 *)(r6 + 0)
       8:    07 01 00 00 01 00 00 00 r1 += 1
       9:    63 16 00 00 00 00 00 00 *(u32 *)(r6 + 0) = r1
; return XDP_PASS;                                              ❻
      10:    b7 00 00 00 02 00 00 00 r0 = 2
      11:    95 00 00 00 00 00 00 00 exit
```

❶ The first line gives further confirmation that *hello.bpf.o* is a 64-bit ELF file with eBPF code (there's no particular rhyme or reason why some tools use the term *BPF* and others *eBPF*; as I said earlier, these terms are now practically interchangeable).

❷ Next comes the disassembly of the section labeled xdp, which matches the SEC() definition in the C source code.

❸ This section is a function called hello.

❹ There are five lines of eBPF bytecode instructions that correspond to the source line bpf_printk("Hello World %d", counter");.

❺ Three lines of eBPF bytecode instructions increment the counter variable.

❻ And another two lines of bytecode are generated from the source code return XDP_PASS;.

Unless you're particularly keen to do so, there's no real need to understand exactly how each line of bytecode relates to the source. The compiler takes care of generating the bytecode so that you don't have to think about it! But let's examine the output in a little more detail so you can get a feel for how this output relates to the eBPF instructions and registers you learned about earlier in this chapter.

To the left of each line of bytecode you can see the offset of that instruction from wherever hello is located in memory. As described earlier in this chapter, eBPF instructions are generally 8 bytes long, and since on a 64-bit platform each memory location can hold 8 bytes, the offset is usually incremented by one for each instruction. However, the first instruction in this program happens to be a wide instruction encoding that requires 16 bytes in order to set Register 6 to a 64-bit value of 0. That places the instruction in the second line of output at offset 2. After that there is another 16-byte instruction, setting Register 1 to a 64-bit value of 0. And after that, the remaining instructions each fit in 8 bytes, so the offset increments by one in each line.

The first byte of each line is the opcode that tells the kernel what operation to perform, and on the right side of each instruction line is the human-readable interpretation of the instruction. At the time of this writing, the Iovisor project has the most complete documentation (*https://oreil.ly/nLbLp*) of the eBPF opcodes, but the official Linux kernel documentation (*https://oreil.ly/yp-jW*) is catching up, and the eBPF Foundation is working on standard documentation (*https://oreil.ly/7ZWzj*) that is not tied to a specific operating system.

For example, let's take the instruction at offset 5, which looks like this:

```
5:    b7 02 00 00 0f 00 00 00 r2 = 15
```

The opcode is 0xb7, and the documentation tells us the pseudocode corresponding to this is dst = imm, which can be read as "Set the destination to the immediate value." The destination is defined by the second byte, 0x02, which means "Register 2." The "immediate" (or literal) value here is 0x0f, which is 15 in decimal. So we can understand that this instruction tells the kernel to "set Register 2 to value 15." This corresponds to the output we see on the right side of the instruction: r2 = 15.

The instruction at offset 10 is similar:

```
10:    b7 00 00 00 02 00 00 00 r0 = 2
```

This line also has opcode 0xb7, and this time it's setting the value of Register 0 to 2. When an eBPF program finishes running, Register 0 holds the return code, and XDP_PASS has the value 2. This matches the source code, which always returns XDP_PASS.

You now know that *hello.bpf.o* contains an eBPF program in bytecode. The next step is to load it into the kernel.

Loading the Program into the Kernel

For this example we'll use a utility called `bpftool`. You can also load programs programmatically, and you'll see examples of that later in the book.

 Some Linux distributions provide a package that includes `bpftool`, or you can compile it from source code (*https://github.com/libbpf/bpftool*). You can find more details about installing or building this tool on Quentin Monnet's blog (*https://oreil.ly/Yqepv*), as well as additional documentation and usage on the Cilium site (*https://oreil.ly/rnTIg*).

The following is an example of using `bpftool` to load a program into the kernel. Note that you'll likely need to be root (or use `sudo`) to get the BPF privileges that `bpftool` requires.

```
$ bpftool prog load hello.bpf.o /sys/fs/bpf/hello
```

This loads the eBPF program from our compiled object file and "pins" it to the location */sys/fs/bpf/hello*.[4] No output response to this command indicates success, but you can confirm that the program is in place using `ls`:

```
$ ls /sys/fs/bpf
hello
```

The eBPF program has been successfully loaded. Let's use the `bpftool` utility to find out more about the program and its status within the kernel.

Inspecting the Loaded Program

The `bpftool` utility can list all the programs that are loaded into the kernel. If you try this yourself you'll probably see several preexisting eBPF programs in this output, but for clarity I will just show the lines that relate to our "Hello World" example:

```
$ bpftool prog list
...
540: xdp  name hello  tag d35b94b4c0c10efb  gpl
        loaded_at 2022-08-02T17:39:47+0000  uid 0
        xlated 96B  jited 148B  memlock 4096B  map_ids 165,166
        btf_id 254
```

---

4 In general, this is optional—eBPF programs can be loaded into the kernel without being pinned to a file location—but it's not optional for `bpftool`, which always has to pin the programs it loads. The reason for this is covered further in "BPF Program and Map References" on page 67.

The program has been assigned the ID 540. This identity is a number assigned to each program as it's loaded. Knowing the ID, you can ask `bpftool` to show more information about this program. This time, let's get the output in prettified JSON format so that the field names are visible, as well as the values:

```
$ bpftool prog show id 540 --pretty
{
    "id": 540,
    "type": "xdp",
    "name": "hello",
    "tag": "d35b94b4c0c10efb",
    "gpl_compatible": true,
    "loaded_at": 1659461987,
    "uid": 0,
    "bytes_xlated": 96,
    "jited": true,
    "bytes_jited": 148,
    "bytes_memlock": 4096,
    "map_ids": [165,166
    ],
    "btf_id": 254
}
```

Given the field names, a lot of this is straightforward to understand:

- The program's ID is 540.

- The `type` field tells us this program can be attached to a network interface using the XDP event. Several other types of BPF programs can be attached to different sorts of events, and we'll discuss this more in Chapter 7.

- The name of the program is `hello`, which is the function name from the source code.

- The `tag` is another identifier for this program, which I'll describe in more detail shortly.

- The program is defined with a GPL-compatible license.

- There's a timestamp showing when the program was loaded.

- User ID 0 (which is root) loaded the program.

- There are 96 bytes of translated eBPF bytecode in this program, which I'll show you shortly.

- This program has been JIT-compiled, and the compilation resulted in 148 bytes of machine code. I'll cover this shortly too.

- The `bytes _memlock` field tells us this program reserves 4,096 bytes of memory that won't be paged out.

- This program refers to BPF maps with IDs 165 and 166. This might seem surprising, since there is no obvious reference to maps in the source code. You'll see later in this chapter how map semantics are used to handle global data in eBPF programs.

- You'll learn about BTF in Chapter 5, but for now just know that btf_id indicates there is a block of BTF information for this program. This information is included in the object file only if you compile with the -g flag.

The BPF Program Tag

The tag is a SHA (Secure Hashing Algorithm) sum of the program's instructions, which can be used as another identifier for the program. The ID can vary every time you load or unload the program, but the tag will remain the same. The bpftool utility accepts references to a BPF program by ID, name, tag, or pinned path, so in the example here, all of the following would give the same output:

- bpftool prog show id 540
- bpftool prog show name hello
- bpftool prog show tag d35b94b4c0c10efb
- bpftool prog show pinned /sys/fs/bpf/hello

You could have multiple programs with the same name, and even multiple instances of programs with the same tag, but the ID and pinned path will always be unique.

The Translated Bytecode

The bytes_xlated field tells us how many bytes of "translated" eBPF code there are. This is the eBPF bytecode after it has passed through the verifier (and possibly been modified by the kernel for reasons I'll discuss later in this book).

Let's use bpftool to show this translated version of our "Hello World" code:

```
$ bpftool prog dump xlated name hello
int hello(struct xdp_md * ctx):
; bpf_printk("Hello World %d", counter);
   0: (18) r6 = map[id:165][0]+0
   2: (61) r3 = *(u32 *)(r6 +0)
   3: (18) r1 = map[id:166][0]+0
   5: (b7) r2 = 15
   6: (85) call bpf_trace_printk#-78032
; counter++;
   7: (61) r1 = *(u32 *)(r6 +0)
   8: (07) r1 += 1
   9: (63) *(u32 *)(r6 +0) = r1
```

```
; return XDP_PASS;
  10: (b7) r0 = 2
  11: (95) exit
```

This looks very similar to the disassembled code you saw earlier in the output from llvm-objdump. The offset addresses are the same, and the instructions look similar—for example, we can see the instruction at offset 5 is r2=15.

The JIT-Compiled Machine Code

The translated bytecode is pretty low level, but it's not quite machine code yet. eBPF uses a JIT compiler to convert eBPF bytecode to machine code that runs natively on the target CPU. The bytes_jited field shows that after this conversation the program is 108 bytes long.

 For higher performance, eBPF programs are generally JIT-compiled. The alternative is to interpret the eBPF bytecode at runtime. The eBPF instruction set and registers were designed to map fairly closely to native machine instructions to make this interpretation straightforward and therefore relatively fast, but compiled programs will be faster, and most architectures now support JIT.[5]

The bpftool utility can generate a dump of this JITed code in assembly language. Don't worry if you're not familiar with assembly language and this looks entirely incomprehensible! I have included it only to illustrate all the transformations the eBPF code goes through from source code to the executable machine instructions. Here is the command and its output:

```
$ bpftool prog dump jited name hello
int hello(struct xdp_md * ctx):
bpf_prog_d35b94b4c0c10efb_hello:
; bpf_printk("Hello World %d", counter);
   0:   hint    #34
   4:   stp     x29, x30, [sp, #-16]!
   8:   mov     x29, sp
   c:   stp     x19, x20, [sp, #-16]!
  10:   stp     x21, x22, [sp, #-16]!
  14:   stp     x25, x26, [sp, #-16]!
  18:   mov     x25, sp
  1c:   mov     x26, #0
  20:   hint    #36
  24:   sub     sp, sp, #0
```

---

5 The kernel setting CONFIG_BPF_JIT needs to be enabled to take advantage of JIT compilation, and it can be enabled or disabled at runtime with the net.core.bpf_jit_enable sysctl setting. See the docs (*https://oreil.ly/4-xi6*) for more information on JIT support on different chip architectures.

```
28:    mov     x19, #-140733193388033
2c:    movk    x19, #2190, lsl #16
30:    movk    x19, #49152
34:    mov     x10, #0
38:    ldr     w2, [x19, x10]
3c:    mov     x0, #-205419695833089
40:    movk    x0, #709, lsl #16
44:    movk    x0, #5904
48:    mov     x1, #15
4c:    mov     x10, #-6992
50:    movk    x10, #29844, lsl #16
54:    movk    x10, #56832, lsl #32
58:    blr     x10
5c:    add     x7, x0, #0
; counter++;
60:    mov     x10, #0
64:    ldr     w0, [x19, x10]
68:    add     x0, x0, #1
6c:    mov     x10, #0
70:    str     w0, [x19, x10]
; return XDP_PASS;
74:    mov     x7, #2
78:    mov     sp, sp
7c:    ldp     x25, x26, [sp], #16
80:    ldp     x21, x22, [sp], #16
84:    ldp     x19, x20, [sp], #16
88:    ldp     x29, x30, [sp], #16
8c:    add     x0, x7, #0
90:    ret
```

 Some packaged distributions of bpftool don't yet include support for dumping the JITed output, and if that's the case, you'll see "Error: No libbfd support." You can build bpftool for yourself by following the instructions at *https://github.com/libbpf/bpftool*.

You've seen that the "Hello World" program has been loaded into the kernel, but at this point it's not yet associated with an event, so nothing will trigger it to run. It needs to be attached to an event.

Attaching to an Event

The program type has to match the type of event it's being attached to; you'll learn more about this in Chapter 7. In this case it's an XDP program, and you can use bpftool to attach the example eBPF program to the XDP event on a network interface, like this:

```
$ bpftool net attach xdp id 540 dev eth0
```

At the time of this writing, the `bpftool` utility doesn't support the ability to attach all program types, but it has recently been extended (*https://oreil.ly/Tt99p*) to auto-attach k(ret)probes, u(ret)probes, and tracepoints.

Here I have used the program's ID of 540, but you can also use the name (provided it is unique) or tag to identify the program being attached. In this example, I have attached the program to the network interface `eth0`.

You can view all the network-attached eBPF programs using `bpftool`:

```
$ bpftool net list
xdp:
eth0(2) driver id 540

tc:

flow_dissector:
```

The program with ID 540 is attached to the XDP event on the `eth0` interface. This output also gives some clues about some other potential events in the network stack that you can attach eBPF programs to: `tc` and `flow_dissector`. More on this in Chapter 7.

You can also inspect the network interfaces using `ip link`, and you'll see output that looks something like this (some details have been removed for clarity):

```
1: lo: <LOOPBACK,UP,LOWER_UP> mtu 65536 qdisc noqueue state UNKNOWN mode DEFAULT
group default qlen 1000
    ...
2: eth0: <BROADCAST,MULTICAST,UP,LOWER_UP> mtu 1500 xdp qdisc fq_codel state UP
mode DEFAULT group default qlen 1000
    ...
    prog/xdp id 540 tag 9d0e949f89f1a82c jited
    ...
```

In this example there are two interfaces: the loopback interface `lo`, which is used to send traffic to processes on this machine; and the `eth0` interface, which connects this machine to the outside world. This output also shows that `eth0` has a JIT-compiled eBPF program, with identity 540 and tag `9d0e949f89f1a82c`, attached to its XDP hook.

You can also use `ip link` to attach and detach XDP programs to a network interface. I have included this as an exercise at the end of this chapter, and there are further examples in Chapter 7.

At this point, the *hello* eBPF program should be producing trace output every time a network packet is received. You can check this out by running `cat /sys/kernel/debug/tracing/trace_pipe`. This should show a lot of output that looks similar to this:

```
<idle>-0       [003] d.s.. 655370.944105: bpf_trace_printk: Hello World 4531
<idle>-0       [003] d.s.. 655370.944587: bpf_trace_printk: Hello World 4532
<idle>-0       [003] d.s.. 655370.944896: bpf_trace_printk: Hello World 4533
```

If you're struggling to remember the location of the trace pipe, you can get the same output using the command `bpftool prog tracelog`.

In comparison to the output you saw in Chapter 2, this time there is no command or process ID associated with each of these events; instead, you see `<idle>-0` at the start of each line of trace. In Chapter 2, each syscall event happened because a process executing a command in user space made a call to the syscall API. That process ID and command are part of the context in which the eBPF program was executed. But in the example here, the XDP event happens due to the arrival of a network packet. There is no user space process associated with this packet—at the point the *hello* eBPF program is triggered, the system hasn't done anything with the packet other than receive it in memory, and it has no idea what the packet is or where it's going.

You can see that the counter value that is traced out is being incremented by one each time, as expected. In the source code, `counter` is a global variable. Let's see how that is implemented in eBPF using a map.

Global Variables

As you learned in the previous chapter, an eBPF map is a data structure that can be accessed from an eBPF program or from user space. Since the same map can be accessed repeatedly by different runs of the same program, it can be used to hold state from one execution to the next. Multiple programs can also access the same map. Because of these characteristics, map semantics can be repurposed for use as global variables.

 Before support for global variables was added in 2019 (*https://oreil.ly/IDftt*), eBPF programmers had to write maps explicitly to perform the same task.

You saw earlier that `bpftool` shows this example program using two maps with the identities 165 and 166. (You will probably see different identities if you try this for yourself, as the identities are assigned when the maps are created in the kernel.) Let's explore what is in those maps.

The `bpftool` utility can show the maps loaded into the kernel. For clarity I will only show the entries 165 and 166 that relate to the example "Hello World" program:

```
$ bpftool map list
165: array  name hello.bss  flags 0x400
        key 4B  value 4B  max_entries 1  memlock 4096B
        btf_id 254
166: array  name hello.rodata  flags 0x80
        key 4B  value 15B  max_entries 1  memlock 4096B
        btf_id 254  frozen
```

A bss[6] section in an object file compiled from a C program typically holds global variables, and you can use `bpftool` to inspect its contents, like this:

```
$ bpftool map dump name hello.bss
[{
        "value": {
            ".bss": [{
                    "counter": 11127
                }
            ]
        }
    }
]
```

I could also have used `bpftool map dump id 165` to retrieve the same information. If I run either of these commands again, I'll see that the counter has increased, as the program has been run every time a network packet is received.

As you'll learn in Chapter 5, `bpftool` is able to pretty-print the field names from a map (here, the variable name `counter`) only if BTF information is available, and that information is included only if you compile with the `-g` flag. If you omitted that flag during the compilation step, you'd see something that looks more like this:

```
$ bpftool map dump name hello.bss
key: 00 00 00 00  value: 19 01 00 00
Found 1 element
```

Without BTF information, `bpftool` has no way of knowing what variable name was used in the source code. You can infer that since there is only one item in this map, the hex value `19 01 00 00` must be the current value of `counter` (281 in decimal, since the bytes are ordered starting with the least significant byte).

You've seen here that the eBPF program uses the semantics of a map to read and write to a global variable. Maps are also used to hold static data, as you can see by inspecting the other map.

---

6 Here, *bss* stands for "block started by symbol."

The fact that the other map is named `hello.rodata` gives a hint that this could be read-only data related to our *hello* program. You can dump the contents of this map to see that it holds the string used by the eBPF program for tracing:

```
$ bpftool map dump name hello.rodata
[{
        "value": {
            ".rodata": [{
                    "hello.____fmt": "Hello World %d"
                }
            ]
        }
    }
]
```

If you didn't compile the object with the `-g` flag, you'll see output that looks like this:

```
$ bpftool map dump id 166
key: 00 00 00 00   value: 48 65 6c 6c 6f 20 57 6f  72 6c 64 20 25 64 00
Found 1 element
```

There is one key–value pair in this map, and the value contains 12 bytes of data ending with a 0. It probably won't surprise you that those bytes are the ASCII representation of the string `"Hello World %d"`.

Now that we've finished inspecting this program and its maps, it's time to clean it up. We'll start by detaching it from the event that triggers it.

Detaching the Program

You can detach the program from the network interface like this:

```
$ bpftool net detach xdp dev eth0
```

There is no output if this command runs successfully, but you can confirm that the program is no longer attached by the lack of XDP entries in the output from `bpftool net list`:

```
$ bpftool net list
xdp:

tc:

flow_dissector:
```

However, the program is still loaded into the kernel:

```
$ bpftool prog show name hello
395: xdp  name hello  tag 9d0e949f89f1a82c  gpl
        loaded_at 2022-12-19T18:20:32+0000  uid 0
        xlated 48B  jited 108B  memlock 4096B  map_ids 4
```

Unloading the Program

There's no inverse of `bpftool prog load` (at least not at the time of this writing), but you can remove the program from the kernel by deleting the pinned pseudofile:

```
$ rm /sys/fs/bpf/hello
$ bpftool prog show name hello
```

There is no output from this `bpftool` command because the program is no longer loaded in the kernel.

BPF to BPF Calls

In the previous chapter you saw tail calls in action, and I mentioned that now there is also the ability to call functions from within an eBPF program. Let's take a look at a simple example, which, like the tail call example, can be attached to the `sys_enter` tracepoint, except this time it will trace out the opcode for the syscall. You'll find the code in *chapter3/hello-func.bpf.c*.

For illustrative purposes I have written a very simple function that extracts the syscall opcode from the tracepoint arguments:

```
static __attribute((noinline)) int get_opcode(struct bpf_raw_tracepoint_args
                                                                       *ctx) {
    return ctx->args[1];
}
```

Given the choice, the compiler would probably inline this very simple function that I'm only going to call from one place. Since that would defeat the point of this example, I have added `__attribute((noinline))` to force the compiler's hand. In normal circumstances you should probably omit this and allow the compiler to optimize as it sees fit.

The eBPF function that calls this function looks like this:

```
SEC("raw_tp")
int hello(struct bpf_raw_tracepoint_args *ctx) {
    int opcode = get_opcode(ctx);
    bpf_printk("Syscall: %d", opcode);
    return 0;
}
```

After compiling this to an eBPF object file, you can load it into the kernel and confirm that it is loaded with `bpftool`:

```
$ bpftool prog load hello-func.bpf.o /sys/fs/bpf/hello
$ bpftool prog list name hello
893: raw_tracepoint  name hello  tag 3d9eb0c23d4ab186  gpl
        loaded_at 2023-01-05T18:57:31+0000  uid 0
```

```
        xlated 80B   jited 208B   memlock 4096B   map_ids 204
        btf_id 302
```

The interesting part of this exercise is inspecting the eBPF bytecode to see the
get_opcode() function:

```
$ bpftool prog dump xlated name hello
int hello(struct bpf_raw_tracepoint_args * ctx):
; int opcode = get_opcode(ctx);                                    ❶
   0: (85) call pc+7#bpf_prog_cbacc90865b1b9a5_get_opcode
; bpf_printk("Syscall: %d", opcode);
   1: (18) r1 = map[id:193][0]+0
   3: (b7) r2 = 12
   4: (bf) r3 = r0
   5: (85) call bpf_trace_printk#-73584
; return 0;
   6: (b7) r0 = 0
   7: (95) exit
int get_opcode(struct bpf_raw_tracepoint_args * ctx):             ❷
; return ctx->args[1];
   8: (79) r0 = *(u64 *)(r1 +8)
; return ctx->args[1];
   9: (95) exit
```

❶   Here you can see the hello() eBPF program making a call to get_opcode(). The
    eBPF instruction at offset 0 is 0x85, which from the instruction set documenta-
    tion corresponds to "Function call." Instead of executing the next instruction,
    which would be at offset 1, execution will jump seven instructions ahead (pc+7),
    which means the instruction at offset 8.

❷   Here's the bytecode for get_opcode(), and as you might hope, the first instruc-
    tion is at offset 8.

The function call instruction necessitates putting the current state on the eBPF virtual
machine's stack so that when the called function exits, execution can continue in the
calling function. Since the stack size is limited to 512 bytes, BPF to BPF calls can't be
very deeply nested.

For a lot more detail on tail calls and BPF to BPF calls, there's an
excellent post by Jakub Sitnicki on Cloudflare's blog: "Assembly
within! BPF tail calls on x86 and ARM" (*https://oreil.ly/6kOp3*).

Summary

In this chapter you saw some example C source code transformed into eBPF bytecode and then compiled to machine code so that it's ready to be executed in the kernel. You also learned how to use bpftool to inspect programs and maps loaded into the kernel, and to attach to XDP events.

In addition, you saw examples of different types of eBPF programs triggered by different kinds of events. An XDP event is triggered by the arrival of a packet of data on a network interface, whereas kprobe and tracepoint events are triggered by hitting some particular point in kernel code. I'll discuss some other eBPF program types in Chapter 7.

You also learned how maps are used to implement global variables for eBPF programs, and you saw BPF to BPF function calls.

The next chapter goes into another level of detail as I show you what's happening at the system call level when bpftool—or any other user space code—loads programs and attaches them to events.

Exercises

Here are a few things to try if you want to explore BPF programs further:

1. Try using `ip link` commands like the following to attach and detach the XDP program:

   ```
   $ ip link set dev eth0 xdp obj hello.bpf.o sec xdp
   $ ip link set dev eth0 xdp off
   ```

2. Run any of the BCC examples from Chapter 2. While the program is running, use a second terminal window to inspect the loaded program using bpftool. Here's an example of what I saw by running the *hello-map.py* example:

   ```
   $ bpftool prog show name hello
   197: kprobe  name hello  tag ba73a317e9480a37  gpl
           loaded_at 2022-08-22T08:46:22+0000  uid 0
           xlated 296B  jited 328B  memlock 4096B  map_ids 65
           btf_id 179
           pids hello-map.py(2785)
   ```

   You can also use `bpftool prog dump` commands to see the bytecode and machine code versions of those programs.

3. Run *hello-tail.py* from the *chapter2* directory, and while it's running, take a look at the programs it loaded. You'll see that each tail call program is listed individually, like this:

```
$ bpftool prog list
...
120: raw_tracepoint  name hello  tag b6bfd0e76e7f9aac  gpl
        loaded_at 2023-01-05T14:35:32+0000  uid 0
        xlated 160B  jited 272B  memlock 4096B  map_ids 29
        btf_id 124
        pids hello-tail.py(3590)
121: raw_tracepoint  name ignore_opcode  tag a04f5eef06a7f555  gpl
        loaded_at 2023-01-05T14:35:32+0000  uid 0
        xlated 16B  jited 72B  memlock 4096B
        btf_id 124
        pids hello-tail.py(3590)
122: raw_tracepoint  name hello_exec  tag 931f578bd09da154  gpl
        loaded_at 2023-01-05T14:35:32+0000  uid 0
        xlated 112B  jited 168B  memlock 4096B
        btf_id 124
        pids hello-tail.py(3590)
123: raw_tracepoint  name hello_timer  tag 6c3378ebb7d3a617  gpl
        loaded_at 2023-01-05T14:35:32+0000  uid 0
        xlated 336B  jited 356B  memlock 4096B
        btf_id 124
        pids hello-tail.py(3590)
```

You could also use `bpftool prog dump xlated` to look at the bytecode instructions and compare them to what you saw in "BPF to BPF Calls" on page 54.

4. *Be careful with this one, as it may be best to simply think about why this happens rather than trying it!* If you return a 0 value from an XDP program, this corresponds to `XDP_ABORTED`, which tells the kernel to abort any further processing of this packet. This might seem a bit counterintuitive given that the 0 value usually indicates success in C, but that's how it is. So, if you try modifying the program to return 0 and attach it to a virtual machine's `eth0` interface, all network packets will get dropped. This will be somewhat unfortunate if you're using SSH to attach to that machine, and you'll likely have to reboot the machine to regain access!

You could run the program within a container so that the XDP program is attached to a virtual Ethernet interface that only affects that container and not the whole virtual machine. There's an example of doing this at *https://github.com/lizrice/lb-from-scratch*.

The bpf() System Call

As you saw in Chapter 1, when user space applications want the kernel to do something on their behalf, they make requests using the system call API. It therefore makes sense that if a user space application wants to load an eBPF program into the kernel, there must be some system calls involved. In fact, there's a system call named bpf(), and in this chapter I'll show you how it's used to load and interact with eBPF programs and maps.

It's worth noting that the eBPF code running in the kernel does not use syscalls to access maps. The syscall interface is only used by user space applications. Instead, eBPF programs use helper functions to read and write to maps; you already saw examples of this in the previous two chapters.

If you go on to write eBPF programs yourself, there's a good chance you won't directly call these bpf() system calls yourself. There are libraries that I'll discuss later in the book that offer higher-level abstractions to make things easier. That said, those abstractions generally map pretty directly to the underlying syscall commands you'll see in this chapter. Whatever library you're using, you'll need a grasp of the underlying operations—loading a program, creating and accessing maps, and so on—that you'll see in this chapter.

Before I show you examples of bpf() system calls, let's consider what the manpage for bpf() says (*https://oreil.ly/NJdIM*), which is that bpf() is used to "perform a command on an extended BPF map or program." It also tells us that bpf()'s signature is as follows:

```
int bpf(int cmd, union bpf_attr *attr, unsigned int size);
```

The first argument to bpf(), cmd, specifies which command to perform. The bpf() syscall doesn't just do one thing—there are lots of different commands that can be used to manipulate eBPF programs and maps. Figure 4-1 shows an overview of some of the common commands the user space code might use to load eBPF programs, create maps, attach programs to events, and access the key–value pairs in a map.

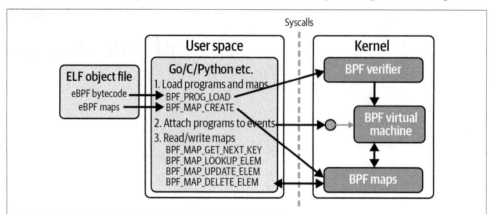

Figure 4-1. A userspace program interacts with eBPF programs and maps in the kernel using syscalls

The `attr` argument to the `bpf()` syscall holds whatever data is needed to specify the parameters for the command, and `size` indicates how many bytes of data there are in `attr`.

You already met `strace` in Chapter 1, when I used it to show how user space code makes many requests across the syscall API. In this chapter I'll use it to demonstrate how the `bpf()` syscall is used. The output from `strace` includes the arguments to each syscall, but to keep the example output in this chapter from being too cluttered, I'll omit lots of the details from the `attr` arguments unless they are particularly interesting.

 You'll find the code, along with instructions for setting up an environment to run it in, at *github.com/lizrice/learning-ebpf*. The code for this chapter is in the *chapter4* directory.

For this example I'm going to use a BCC program called *hello-buffer-config.py*, which builds on the examples you saw in Chapter 2. Like the *hello-buffer.py* example, this program sends a message to the perf buffer whenever it runs, conveying information from the kernel to user space about `execve()` syscall events. What's new in this version is that it allows for different messages to be configured for each user ID.

Here's the eBPF source code:

```
struct user_msg_t {                                            ❶
  char message[12];
};

BPF_HASH(config, u32, struct user_msg_t);                      ❷

BPF_PERF_OUTPUT(output);                                        ❸

struct data_t {                                                ❹
  int pid;
  int uid;
  char command[16];
  char message[12];
};

int hello(void *ctx) {                                         ❺
  struct data_t data = {};
  struct user_msg_t *p;
  char message[12] = "Hello World";

  data.pid = bpf_get_current_pid_tgid() >> 32;
  data.uid = bpf_get_current_uid_gid() & 0xFFFFFFFF;

  bpf_get_current_comm(&data.command, sizeof(data.command));

  p = config.lookup(&data.uid);                                ❻
  if (p != 0) {
    bpf_probe_read_kernel(&data.message, sizeof(data.message), p->message);
  } else {
    bpf_probe_read_kernel(&data.message, sizeof(data.message), message);
  }

  output.perf_submit(ctx, &data, sizeof(data));
  return 0;
}
```

❶ This line indicates that there's a structure definition, user_msg_t, for holding a 12-character message.

❷ The BCC macro BPF_HASH is used to define a hash table map called config. It will hold values of type user_msg_t, indexed by keys of type u32, which is the right size for a user ID. (If you don't specify the types for the keys and values, BCC defaults to u64 for both.)

❸ The perf buffer output is defined in exactly the same way as in Chapter 2. You can submit arbitrary data to a buffer, so there's no need to specify any data types here…

❹ …although in practice, in this example the program always submits a `data_t` structure. This is also unchanged from the Chapter 2 example.

❺ Most of the rest of the eBPF program is unchanged from the `hello()` version you saw earlier.

❻ The only difference is that having used a helper function to get the user ID, the code looks for an entry in the `config` hash map with that user ID as the key. If there is a matching entry, the value contains a message that gets used instead of the default "Hello World."

The Python code has two additional lines:

```
b["config"][ct.c_int(0)] = ct.create_string_buffer(b"Hey root!")
b["config"][ct.c_int(501)] = ct.create_string_buffer(b"Hi user 501!")
```

These define messages in the `config` hash table for user IDs 0 and 501, which correspond to the root user and my user ID on this virtual machine. This code uses Python's `ctypes` package to ensure that the key and value have the same types as those used in the C definition of `user_msg_t`.

Here's some illustrative output from this example, along with the commands I ran in a second terminal to obtain it:

```
Terminal 1                          Terminal 2
$ ./hello-buffer-config.py
37926 501 bash Hi user 501!         ls
37927 501 bash Hi user 501!         sudo ls
37929 0 sudo Hey root!
37931 501 bash Hi user 501!         sudo -u daemon ls
37933 1 sudo Hello World
```

Now that you've got an idea of what this program does, I'd like to show you the `bpf()` system calls that are used when it runs. I'll run it again using `strace`, specifying `-e bpf` to indicate that I am only interested in seeing the `bpf()` syscall:

```
$ strace -e bpf ./hello-buffer-config.py
```

The output you'll see if you try this yourself shows several calls to this syscall. For each, you'll see the command indicating what the `bpf()` syscall should do. The broad outline looks like this:

```
bpf(BPF_BTF_LOAD, ...) = 3
bpf(BPF_MAP_CREATE, {map_type=BPF_MAP_TYPE_PERF_EVENT_ARRAY…) = 4
bpf(BPF_MAP_CREATE, {map_type=BPF_MAP_TYPE_HASH...) = 5
bpf(BPF_PROG_LOAD, {prog_type=BPF_PROG_TYPE_KPROBE,...prog_name="hello",...) = 6
bpf(BPF_MAP_UPDATE_ELEM, ...}
...
```

Let's examine them one by one. Neither you, the reader, nor I have infinite patience, so I won't discuss every single argument to every single call! I'll focus on the parts that I think really help to tell the story of what's happening when a user space program interacts with an eBPF program.

Loading BTF Data

The first call to `bpf()` that I see looks like this:

```
bpf(BPF_BTF_LOAD, {btf="\237\353\1\0..."}, 128) = 3
```

In this case the command you can see in the output is `BPF_BTF_LOAD`. This is just one of a set of valid commands that are (at least at the time of this writing) most comprehensively documented within the kernel source code.[1]

It's possible that you won't see a call with this command if you're using a relatively old Linux kernel, as it relates to BTF, or BPF Type Format.[2] BTF allows eBPF programs to be portable across different kernel versions so that you can compile a program on one machine and use it on another, which might be using a different kernel version and hence have different kernel data structures. I'll discuss this in more detail in Chapter 5.

This call to `bpf()` is loading a blob of BTF data into the kernel, and the return code from the `bpf()` system call (3 in my example) is a file descriptor that refers to that data.

 A *file descriptor* is an identifier for an open file (or file-like object). If you open a file (with the `open()` or `openat()` system call) the return code is a file descriptor, which is then passed as an argument to other syscalls such as `read()` or `write()` to perform operations on that file. Here the blob of data isn't exactly a file, but it is given a file descriptor as an identifier that can be used for future operations that refer to it.

Creating Maps

The next `bpf()` creates the `output` perf buffer map:

```
bpf(BPF_MAP_CREATE, {map_type=BPF_MAP_TYPE_PERF_EVENT_ARRAY, , key_size=4,
value_size=4, max_entries=4, ... map_name="output", ...}, 128) = 4
```

---

1 If you want to see the full set of BPF commands, they're documented in the *linux/bpf.h* (*https://oreil.ly/Pyy7U*) header file.

2 BTF was introduced upstream in the 5.1 kernel, but it has been back-ported on some Linux distributions, as you can see from this discussion (*https://oreil.ly/LjcPN*).

You can probably guess from the command name BPF_MAP_CREATE that this call creates an eBPF map. You can see that the type of this map is PERF_EVENT_ARRAY and it is called output. The keys and values in this perf event map are 4 bytes long. There's also a limit of four key–value pairs that can be held in this map, defined by the field max_entries; I'll explain why there are four entries in this map later in this chapter. The return value of 4 is the file descriptor for the user space code to access the output map.

The next bpf() system call in the output creates the config map:

```
bpf(BPF_MAP_CREATE, {map_type=BPF_MAP_TYPE_HASH, key_size=4, value_size=12,
    max_entries=10240... map_name="config", ...btf_fd=3,...}, 128) = 5
```

This map is defined to be a hash table map, with keys that are 4 bytes long (which corresponds to a 32-bit integer that can be used to hold a user ID) and values that are 12 bytes long (which matches the length of the msg_t structure). I didn't specify the size of the table, so it has been given BCC's default size of 10,240 entries.

This bpf() system call also returns a file descriptor, 5, which will be used to refer to this config map in future syscalls.

You can also see the field btf_fd=3, which tells the kernel to use the BTF file descriptor 3 that was obtained earlier. As you'll see in Chapter 5, BTF information describes the layout of data structures, and including this in the definition of the map means there's information about the layout of the key and value types used in this map. This is used by tools like bpftool to pretty-print map dumps, making them human readable—you saw an example of this in Chapter 3.

Loading a Program

So far you have seen the example program using syscalls to load BTF data into the kernel and create some eBPF maps. The next thing it does is load the eBPF program being loaded into the kernel with the following bpf() syscall:

```
bpf(BPF_PROG_LOAD, {prog_type=BPF_PROG_TYPE_KPROBE, insn_cnt=44,
    insns=0xffffa836abe8, license="GPL", ... prog_name="hello", ...
    expected_attach_type=BPF_CGROUP_INET_INGRESS, prog_btf_fd=3,...}, 128) = 6
```

Quite a few of the fields here are interesting:

- The prog_type field describes the program type, which here indicates that it's intended to be attached to a kprobe. You'll learn more about program types in Chapter 7.

- The insn_cnt field means "instruction count." This is the number of bytecode instructions in the program.

- The bytecode instructions that make up this eBPF program are held in memory at the address specified in the insns field.

- This program was specified as GPL licensed so that it can use GPL-licensed BPF helper functions.

- The program name is hello.

- The expected_attach_type of BPF_CGROUP_INET_INGRESS might seem surprising, because that sounds like something to do with ingress network traffic, but you know this eBPF program is going to be attached to a kprobe. In fact, the expected_attach_type field is only used for some program types, and BPF_PROG_TYPE_KPROBE isn't one of them. BPF_CGROUP_INET_INGRESS just happens to be the first in the list of BPF attachment types,[3] so it has the value 0.

- The prog_btf_fd field tells the kernel which blob of previously loaded BTF data to use with this program. The value 3 here corresponds to the file descriptor you saw returned from the BPF_BTF_LOAD syscall (and it's the same blob of BTF data used for the config map).

If the program had failed verification (which I'll discuss in Chapter 6), this syscall would have returned a negative value, but here you can see it returned the file descriptor 6. To recap, at this point the file descriptors have the meanings shown in Table 4-1.

Table 4-1. File descriptors when running hello-buffer-config.py after loading the program

File descriptor	Represents
3	BTF data
4	output perf buffer map
5	config hash table map
6	hello eBPF program

Modifying a Map from User Space

You already saw the line in the Python user space source code that configures special messages that will be displayed for the root user with user ID 0, and for the user with ID 501:

```
b["config"][ct.c_int(0)] = ct.create_string_buffer(b"Hey root!")
b["config"][ct.c_int(501)] = ct.create_string_buffer(b"Hi user 501!")
```

You can see these entries being defined in the map through syscalls like this:

---

3 These are defined in the bpf_attach_type enumerator in *linux/bpf.h* (*https://oreil.ly/AO1rc*).

```
bpf(BPF_MAP_UPDATE_ELEM, {map_fd=5, key=0xffffa7842490, value=0xffffa7a2b410,
flags=BPF_ANY}, 128) = 0
```

The `BPF_MAP_UPDATE_ELEM` command updates the key–value pair in a map. The `BPF_ANY` flag indicates that if the key doesn't already exist in this map, it should be created. There are two of these calls, corresponding to the two entries configured for two different user IDs.

The `map_fd` field identifies which map is being operated on. You can see that in this case it's 5, which is the file descriptor value returned earlier when the `config` map was created.

File descriptors are assigned by the kernel for a particular process, so this value of 5 is only valid for this particular user space process in which the Python program is running. However, multiple user space programs (and multiple eBPF programs in the kernel) can all access the same map. Two user space programs that access the same map structure in the kernel might very well be assigned different file descriptor values; equally, two user space programs might have the same file descriptor value for entirely different maps.

Both the key and the value are pointers, so you can't tell the numeric value of either the key or the value from this `strace` output. You could, however, use `bpftool` to view the map's contents and see something like this:

```
$ bpftool map dump name config
[{
        "key": 0,
        "value": {
            "message": "Hey root!"
        }
    },{
        "key": 501,
        "value": {
            "message": "Hi user 501!"
        }
    }
]
```

How does `bpftool` know how to format this output? For example, how does it know the value is a structure, with a field called `message` that contains a string? The answer is that it uses the definitions in the BTF information included on the `BPF_MAP_CREATE` syscall that defined this map. You'll see more details on how BTF conveys this information in the next chapter.

You've now seen how user space interacts with the kernel to load programs and maps and to update the information in a map. In the sequence of syscalls you have seen up to this point, the program hasn't yet been attached to an event. This step has to happen; otherwise, the program will never be triggered.

Fair warning: different types of eBPF programs get attached to different events in a variety of different ways! Later in this chapter I'll show you the syscalls used in this example to attach to the kprobe event, and in this case it doesn't involve bpf(). In contrast, in the exercises at the end of this chapter I will show you another example where a bpf() syscall is used to attach a program to a raw tracepoint event.

Before we get to those details, I'd like to discuss what happens when you quit running the program. You'll find that the program and maps are automatically unloaded, and this happens because the kernel is keeping track of them using *reference counts*.

BPF Program and Map References

You know that loading a BPF program into the kernel with the bpf() syscall returns a file descriptor. Within the kernel, this file descriptor is a *reference* to the program. The user space process that made the syscall owns this file descriptor; when that process exits, the file descriptor gets released, and the reference count to the program is decremented. When there are no references left to a BPF program, the kernel removes the program.

An additional reference is created when you *pin* a program to the filesystem.

Pinning

You already saw pinning in action in Chapter 3, with the following command:

```
bpftool prog load hello.bpf.o /sys/fs/bpf/hello
```

 These pinned objects aren't real files persisted to disk. They are created on a *pseudo filesystem*, which behaves like a regular disk-based filesystem with directories and files. But they are held in memory, which means they will not remain in place over a system reboot.

If bpftool were to allow you to load the program without pinning it, that would be pointless, because the file descriptor gets released when bpftool exits, and if there are zero references, the program would get deleted, so nothing useful would have been achieved. But pinning it to the filesystem means there is an additional reference to the program, so the program remains loaded after the command completes.

The reference counter also gets incremented when a BPF program is attached to a hook that will trigger it. The behavior of these reference counts depends on the BPF program type. You'll learn more about these program types in Chapter 7, but there are some that relate to tracing (like kprobes and tracepoints) and are always associated with a user space process; for these types of eBPF programs, the kernel's reference count gets decremented when that process exits. Programs that are attached within the network stack or cgroups (short for "control groups") aren't associated with any user space process, so they stay in place even after the user space program that loads them exits. You already saw an example of this when loading an XDP program with the `ip link` command:

```
ip link set dev eth0 xdp obj hello.bpf.o sec xdp
```

The `ip` command has completed, and there is no definition of a pinned location, but nevertheless, `bpftool` will show you that the XDP program is loaded in the kernel:

```
$ bpftool prog list
…
1255: xdp  name hello  tag 9d0e949f89f1a82c  gpl
        loaded_at 2022-11-01T19:21:14+0000  uid 0
        xlated 48B  jited 108B  memlock 4096B  map_ids 612
```

The reference count for this program is nonzero, because of the attachment to the XDP hook that persisted after the `ip link` command completed.

eBPF maps also have reference counters, and they get cleaned up when their reference count drops to zero. Each eBPF program that uses a map increments the counter, as does each file descriptor that user space programs might hold to the map.

It's possible that the source code for an eBPF program might define a map that the program doesn't actually reference. Suppose you wanted to store some metadata about a program; you could define it as a global variable, and as you saw in the previous chapter, this information gets stored in a map. If the eBPF program doesn't do anything with that map, there won't automatically be a reference count from the program to the map. There's a `BPF(BPF_PROG_BIND_MAP)` syscall that associates a map with a program so that the map doesn't get cleaned up as soon as the user space loader program exits and is no longer holding a file descriptor reference to the map.

Maps can also be pinned to the filesystem, and user space programs can gain access to the map by knowing the path to the map.

> Alexei Starovoitov wrote a good description of BPF reference counters and file descriptors in his blog post "Lifetime of BPF Objects" (*https://oreil.ly/vofxH*).

Another way to create a reference to a BPF program is with a BPF link.

BPF Links

BPF links provide a layer of abstraction between an eBPF program and the event it's attached to. A BPF link itself can be pinned to the filesystem, which creates an additional reference to the program. This means the user space process that loaded the program into the kernel can terminate, leaving the program loaded. The file descriptor for the user space loader program gets freed up, decreasing the count of references to the program, but the reference count will be nonzero because of the BPF link.

You'll get an opportunity to see BPF links in action if you follow the exercises at the end of this chapter. For now, let's get back to the sequence of bpf() syscalls used by *hello-buffer-config.py*.

Additional Syscalls Involved in eBPF

To recap, so far you have seen bpf() syscalls that add the BTF data, program and maps, and map data to the kernel. The next thing the strace output shows relates to setting up the perf buffer.

 The rest of this chapter dives relatively deeply into the syscall sequences involved when using perf buffers, ring buffers, kprobes, and map iterations. Not all eBPF programs need to do these things, so if you're in a hurry or you're finding it a bit too detailed, feel free to skip to the chapter summary. I won't be offended!

Initializing the Perf Buffer

You have seen the bpf(BPF_MAP_UPDATE_ELEM) calls that add entries into the config map. Next, the output shows some calls that look like this:

```
bpf(BPF_MAP_UPDATE_ELEM, {map_fd=4, key=0xffffa7842490, value=0xffffa7a2b410,
flags=BPF_ANY}, 128) = 0
```

These look very similar to the calls that defined the config map entries, except in this case the map's file descriptor is 4, which represents the output perf buffer map.

As before, the key and the value are pointers, so you can't tell the numeric value of either the key or the value from this strace output. I see this syscall repeated four times with identical values for all the parameters, though there's no way of knowing whether the values the pointers hold have changed between each call. Looking at these BPF_MAP_UPDATE_ELEM bpf() calls leaves some unanswered questions about how the buffer is set up and used:

- Why are there four calls to BPF_MAP_UPDATE_ELEM? Does this relate to the fact that the output map was created with a maximum of four entries?

- After these four instances of BPF_MAP_UPDATE_ELEM, no more bpf() syscalls appear in the strace output. That might seem a little odd, because the map is there so that the eBPF program can write data every time it is triggered, and you've seen data being displayed by the user space code. That data is clearly not being retrieved from the map with `bpf()` syscalls, so how is it obtained?

You've also yet to see any evidence of how the eBPF program is getting attached to the kprobe event that triggers it. To get the explanation for all these concerns, I need `strace` to show a few more syscalls when running this example, like this:

```
$ strace -e bpf,perf_event_open,ioctl,ppoll ./hello-buffer-config.py
```

For brevity, I'm going to ignore calls to `ioctl()` that aren't specifically related to the eBPF functionality of this example.

Attaching to Kprobe Events

You've seen that file descriptor 6 was assigned to represent the eBPF program *hello* once it was loaded into the kernel. To attach the eBPF program to an event, you also need a file descriptor representing that particular event. The following line from the `strace` output shows the creation of the file descriptor for the `execve()` kprobe:

```
perf_event_open({type=0x6 /* PERF_TYPE_??? */, ...},...) = 7
```

According to the manpage for the `perf_event_open()` syscall (*https://oreil.ly/xpRJs*), it "creates a file descriptor that allows measuring performance information." You can see from the output that `strace` doesn't know how to interpret the type parameter with the value 6, but if you examine that manpage further, it describes how Linux supports dynamic types of Performance Measurement Unit:

> …there is a subdirectory per PMU instance under */sys/bus/event_source/devices*. In each subdirectory there is a type file whose content is an integer that can be used in the type field.

Sure enough, if you look under that directory, you'll find a *kprobe/type* file:

```
$ cat /sys/bus/event_source/devices/kprobe/type
6
```

From this, you can see that the call to `perf_event_open()` has a type set to the value 6 to indicate that it's a kprobe type of perf event.

Unfortunately, `strace` doesn't output the details that would conclusively show that the kprobe is attached to the `execve()` syscall, but I hope there is enough evidence here to convince you that that's what the file descriptor returned here represents.

The return code from `perf_event_open()` is 7, and this represents the file descriptor for the kprobe's perf event, and you know that file descriptor 6 represents the *hello* eBPF program. The manpage for `perf_event_open()` also explains how to use `ioctl()` to create the attachment between the two:

PERF_EVENT_IOC_SET_BPF [...] allows attaching a Berkeley Packet Filter (BPF) program to an existing kprobe tracepoint event. The argument is a BPF program file descriptor that was created by a previous bpf(2) system call.

This explains the following ioctl() syscall that you'll see in the strace output, with arguments referring to the two file descriptors:

```
ioctl(7, PERF_EVENT_IOC_SET_BPF, 6)      = 0
```

There is also another ioctl() call that turns the kprobe event on:

```
ioctl(7, PERF_EVENT_IOC_ENABLE, 0)       = 0
```

With this in place, the eBPF program should be triggered whenever execve() is run on this machine.

Setting Up and Reading Perf Events

I already mentioned that I see four calls to bpf(BPF_MAP_UPDATE_ELEM) related to the output perf buffer. With the additional syscalls being traced, the strace output shows four sequences, like this:

```
perf_event_open({type=PERF_TYPE_SOFTWARE, size=0 /* PERF_ATTR_SIZE_??? */,
config=PERF_COUNT_SW_BPF_OUTPUT, ...}, -1, X, -1, PERF_FLAG_FD_CLOEXEC) = Y

ioctl(Y, PERF_EVENT_IOC_ENABLE, 0)       = 0

bpf(BPF_MAP_UPDATE_ELEM, {map_fd=4, key=0xffffa7842490, value=0xffffa7a2b410,
flags=BPF_ANY}, 128) = 0
```

I've used X to indicate where the output shows values 0, 1, 2, and 3 in the four instances of this call. Referring to the manpage for the perf_event_open() syscall, you'll see that this is the cpu, and the field before it is pid or process ID. From the manpage:

pid == -1 and cpu >= 0

This measures all processes/threads on the specified CPU.

The fact that this sequence happens four times corresponds to there being four CPU cores in my laptop. This, at last, is the explanation for why there are four entries in the "output" perf buffer map: there is one for each CPU core. It also explains the "array" part of the map type name BPF_MAP_TYPE_PERF_EVENT_ARRAY, as the map doesn't just represent one perf ring buffer but an array of buffers, one for each core.

If you write eBPF programs, you won't need to worry about details like handling the number of cores, as this will be taken care of for you by any of the eBPF libraries discussed in Chapter 10, but I think it's an interesting aspect of the syscalls you see when you use strace on this program.

The `perf_event_open()` calls each return a file descriptor, which I've represented as Y; these have the values 8, 9, 10, and 11. The `ioctl()` syscalls enable the perf output for each of these file descriptors. The `BPF_MAP_UPDATE_ELEM bpf()` syscalls set the map entry to point to the perf ring buffer for each CPU core to indicate where it can submit data.

User space code can then use `ppoll()` on all four of these output stream file descriptors so that it can get the data output, whichever core happens to run the eBPF program *hello* for any given `execve()` kprobe event. Here's the syscall to `ppoll()`:

```
ppoll([{fd=8, events=POLLIN}, {fd=9, events=POLLIN}, {fd=10, events=POLLIN},
{fd=11, events=POLLIN}], 4, NULL, NULL, 0) = 1 ([{fd=8, revents=POLLIN}])
```

As you'll see if you try running the example program yourself, these `ppoll()` calls block until there is something to read from one of the file descriptors. You won't see the return code written to the screen until something triggers `execve()`, which causes the eBPF program to write data that user space retrieves using this `ppoll()` call.

In Chapter 2 I mentioned that if you have a kernel of version 5.8 or above, BPF ring buffers are now preferred over perf buffers.[4] Let's take a look at a modified version of the same example code that uses a ring buffer.

Ring Buffers

As discussed in the kernel documentation (*https://oreil.ly/RN_RA*), ring buffers are preferred over perf buffers partly for performance reasons, but also to ensure that the ordering of data is preserved, even if the data is submitted by different CPU cores. There is just one buffer, shared across all cores.

There aren't many changes needed to convert *hello-buffer-config.py* to use a ring buffer. In the accompanying GitHub repo you'll find this example as *chapter4/hello-ring-buffer-config.py*. Table 4-2 shows the differences.

Table 4-2. Differences between example BCC code using a perf buffer and a ring buffer

hello-buffer-config.py	hello-ring-buffer-config.py
`BPF_PERF_OUTPUT(output);`	`BPF_RINGBUF_OUTPUT(output, 1);`
`output.perf_submit(ctx, &data,` `sizeof(data));`	`output.ringbuf_output(&data,` `sizeof(data), 0);`
`b["output"].` `open_perf_buffer(print_event)`	`b["output"].` `open_ring_buffer(print_event)`
`b.perf_buffer_poll()`	`b.ring_buffer_poll()`

---

4 A reminder that for more information on the difference, read Andrii Nakryiko's "BPF ring buffer" (*https://oreil.ly/XkpUF*) blog post.

As you'd expect, since these changes relate only to the output buffer, the syscalls related to loading the program and the config map and attaching the program to the kprobe event all remain unchanged.

The bpf() syscall that creates the output ring buffer map looks like this:

```
bpf(BPF_MAP_CREATE, {map_type=BPF_MAP_TYPE_RINGBUF, key_size=0, value_size=0,
max_entries=4096, ... map_name="output", ...}, 128) = 4
```

The major difference in the strace output is that there is no sign of the series of four different perf_event_open(), ioctl(), and bpf(BPF_MAP_UPDATE_ELEM) system calls that you observed during the setup of a perf buffer. For a ring buffer, there's just the one file descriptor shared across all CPU cores.

At the time of this writing, BCC is using the ppoll mechanism I showed earlier for perf buffers, but it uses the newer epoll mechanism to wait for data from the ring buffer. Let's use this as an opportunity to understand the difference between ppoll and epoll.

In the perf buffer example, I showed *hello-buffer-config.py* generating a ppoll() syscall, like this:

```
ppoll([{fd=8, events=POLLIN}, {fd=9, events=POLLIN}, {fd=10, events=POLLIN},
{fd=11, events=POLLIN}], 4, NULL, NULL, 0) = 1 ([{fd=8, revents=POLLIN}])
```

Notice that this passes in the set of file descriptors 8, 9, 10, and 11 from which the user space process wants to retrieve data. Every time this poll event returns data, another call has to be made to ppoll() to set up the same set of file descriptors all over again. When using epoll, the file descriptor set is managed in a kernel object.

You can see this in the following sequence of epoll-related system calls made when *hello-ring-buffer-config.py* is setting up access to the output ring buffer.

First, the user space program asks for a new epoll instance to be created in the kernel:

```
epoll_create1(EPOLL_CLOEXEC) = 8
```

This returns file descriptor 8. Then there is a call to epoll_ctl(), which tells the kernel to add file descriptor 4 (the output buffer) to the set of file descriptors in that epoll instance:

```
epoll_ctl(8, EPOLL_CTL_ADD, 4, {events=EPOLLIN, data={u32=0, u64=0}}) = 0
```

The user space program uses epoll_pwait() to wait until data is available in the ring buffer. This call only returns when data is available:

```
epoll_pwait(8, [{events=EPOLLIN, data={u32=0, u64=0}}], 1, -1, NULL, 8) = 1
```

Of course, if you're writing code using a framework like BCC (or *libbpf* or any of the other libraries I'll describe later in this book), you really don't need to know these underlying details about how your user space application gets information from the kernel via perf or ring buffers. I hope you've found it interesting to get a peek under the covers to see how these things work.

However, you might well find yourself writing code that accesses a map from user space, and it might be helpful to see an example of how this is achieved. Earlier in this chapter, I used bpftool to examine the contents of the config map. Since it's a utility that runs in user space, let's use strace to see what syscalls it's making to retrieve this information.

Reading Information from a Map

The following command shows an extract of the bpf() syscalls that bpftool makes while reading the contents of the config map:

```
$ strace -e bpf bpftool map dump name config
```

As you'll see, the sequence consists of two main steps:

- Iterate through all the maps, looking for any with the name config.
- If a matching map is found, iterate through all the elements in that map.

Finding a Map

The output starts with a repeated sequence of similar calls, as bpftool walks through all the maps looking for any with the name config:

```
bpf(BPF_MAP_GET_NEXT_ID, {start_id=0,...}, 12) = 0          ❶
bpf(BPF_MAP_GET_FD_BY_ID, {map_id=48...}, 12) = 3           ❷
bpf(BPF_OBJ_GET_INFO_BY_FD, {info={bpf_fd=3, ...}}, 16) = 0  ❸

bpf(BPF_MAP_GET_NEXT_ID, {start_id=48, ...}, 12) = 0        ❹
bpf(BPF_MAP_GET_FD_BY_ID, {map_id=116, ...}, 12) = 3
bpf(BPF_OBJ_GET_INFO_BY_FD, {info={bpf_fd=3...}}, 16) = 0
```

❶ BPF_MAP_GET_NEXT_ID gets the ID of the next map after the value specified in start_id.

❷ BPF_MAP_GET_FD_BY_ID returns the file descriptor for the specified map ID.

❸ BPF_OBJ_GET_INFO_BY_FD retrieves information about the object (in this case, the map) referred to by the file descriptor. This information includes its name so bpftool can check whether this is the map it is looking for.

❹ The sequence repeats, getting the ID of the next map after the one in step 1.

There's a group of these three syscalls for each map loaded into the kernel, and you should also see that the values used for start_id and map_id match the IDs of those maps. The repeated pattern ends when there are no more maps left to look at, which results in BPF_MAP_GET_NEXT_ID returning a value of ENOENT, like this:

```
bpf(BPF_MAP_GET_NEXT_ID, {start_id=133,...}, 12) = -1 ENOENT (No such file or
directory)
```

If a matching map has been found, bpftool holds its file descriptor so that it can read the elements out of that map.

Reading Map Elements

At this point bpftool has a file descriptor reference to the map(s) it's going to read from. Let's look at the syscall sequence for reading that information:

```
bpf(BPF_MAP_GET_NEXT_KEY, {map_fd=3, key=NULL,              ❶
next_key=0xaaaaf7a63960}, 24) = 0
bpf(BPF_MAP_LOOKUP_ELEM, {map_fd=3, key=0xaaaaf7a63960,    ❷
value=0xaaaaf7a63980, flags=BPF_ANY}, 32) = 0
[{                                                          ❸
        "key": 0,
        "value": {
            "message": "Hey root!"
        }
bpf(BPF_MAP_GET_NEXT_KEY, {map_fd=3, key=0xaaaaf7a63960,   ❹
next_key=0xaaaaf7a63960}, 24) = 0
bpf(BPF_MAP_LOOKUP_ELEM, {map_fd=3, key=0xaaaaf7a63960,
value=0xaaaaf7a63980, flags=BPF_ANY}, 32) = 0
    },{
        "key": 501,
        "value": {
            "message": "Hi user 501!"
        }
bpf(BPF_MAP_GET_NEXT_KEY, {map_fd=3, key=0xaaaaf7a63960,   ❺
next_key=0xaaaaf7a63960}, 24) = -1 ENOENT (No such file or directory)
    }                                                      ❻
]
+++ exited with 0 +++
```

❶ First, the application needs to find a valid key that is present in the map. It does this with the BPF_MAP_GET_NEXT_KEY flavor of the bpf() syscall. The key argument is a pointer to a key, and the syscall will return the next valid key *after* this one. By passing in a NULL pointer, the application is requesting the first valid key in the map. The kernel writes the key into the location specified by the next_key pointer.

❷ Given a key, the application requests the associated value, which gets written to the memory location specified by value.

❸ At this point, bpftool has the contents of the first key–value pair, and it writes this information to the screen.

❹ Here, bpftool moves on to the next key in the map, retrieves its value, and writes out this key–value pair to the screen.

❺ The next call to BPF_MAP_GET_NEXT_KEY returns ENOENT to indicate that there are no more entries in the map.

❻ Here, bpftool finalizes the output written to screen and exits.

Notice that here, bpftool has been assigned file descriptor 3 to correspond to the config map. This is the same map that *hello-buffer-config.py* refers to with file descriptor 4. As I've mentioned already, file descriptors are process specific.

This analysis of how bpftool behaves shows how a user space program can iterate through the available maps and through the key–value pairs stored in a map.

Summary

In this chapter you saw how user space code uses the bpf() syscall to load eBPF programs and maps. You saw programs and maps being created using the BPF_PROG_LOAD and BPF_MAP_CREATE commands.

You learned that the kernel keeps track of the number of references to eBPF programs and maps, releasing them when the reference count drops to zero. You were also introduced to the concepts of pinning BPF objects to a filesystem and using BPF links to create additional references.

You saw an example of BPF_MAP_UPDATE_ELEM being used to create entries in a map from user space. There are similar commands—BPF_MAP_LOOKUP_ELEM and BPF_MAP_DELETE_ELEM—for retrieving and deleting values from a map. There is also the command BPF_MAP_GET_NEXT_KEY for finding the next key that's present in a map. You can use this to iterate through all the valid entries.

You saw examples of user space programs making use of perf_event_open() and ioctl() for attaching eBPF programs to kprobe events. The attachment method can be very different for other types of eBPF programs, and some of them even use the bpf() system call. For example, there's a bpf(BPF_PROG_ATTACH) syscall that can be used to attach cgroup programs, and bpf(BPF_RAW_TRACEPOINT_OPEN) for raw tracepoints (see Exercise 5 at the end of this chapter).

I also showed how you can use BPF_MAP_GET_NEXT_ID, BPF_MAP_GET_FD_BY_ID, and BPF_OBJ_GET_INFO_BY_FD to locate map (and other) objects held by the kernel.

There are some other `bpf()` commands that I haven't covered in this chapter, but what you have seen here is enough to get a good overview.

You also saw some BTF data being loaded into the kernel, and I mentioned that `bpftool` uses this information to understand the format of data structures so that it can print them out nicely. I didn't explain yet what BTF data looks like or how it's used to make eBPF programs portable across kernel versions. That's coming up in the next chapter.

Exercises

Here are a few things you can try if you'd like to explore the `bpf()` syscall further:

1. Confirm that the `insn_cnt` field from a `BPF_PROG_LOAD` system call corresponds to the number of instructions that are output if you dump the translated eBPF bytecode for that program using `bpftool`. (This is as documented on the man-page for the `bpf()` system call (*https://oreil.ly/NJdIM*).)

2. Run two instances of the example program so that there are two maps called `config`. If you run `bpftool map dump name config`, the output will include information about the two different maps as well as their contents. Run this under `strace`, and follow the use of different file descriptors through the syscall output. Can you see where it's retrieving information about a map and where it's retrieving the key–value pairs stored within it?

3. Use `bpftool map update` to modify the `config` map while one of the example programs is running. Use `sudo -u username` to check that these configuration changes are picked up by the eBPF program.

4. While *hello-buffer-config.py* is running, use `bpftool` to pin the program to the BPF filesystem, like this:

   ```
   bpftool prog pin name hello /sys/fs/bpf/hi
   ```

   Quit the running program, and check that the *hello* program is still loaded in the kernel using `bpftool prog list`. You can clean up the link by removing the pin with `rm /sys/fs/bpf/hi`.

5. Attaching to a raw tracepoint is considerably more straightforward at the syscall level than attaching to a kprobe, as it simply involves a `bpf()` syscall. Try converting *hello-buffer-config.py* to attach to the raw tracepoint for `sys_enter`, using BCC's `RAW_TRACEPOINT_PROBE` macro (if you did the exercises in Chapter 2, you'll already have a suitable program you can use). You won't need to explicitly attach the program in the Python code, as BCC will take care of it for you. Running this under `strace`, you should see a syscall similar to this:

```
bpf(BPF_RAW_TRACEPOINT_OPEN, {raw_tracepoint={name="sys_enter",
prog_fd=6}}, 128) = 7
```

The tracepoint in the kernel has the name sys_enter, and the eBPF program
with file descriptor 6 is being attached to it. From now on, whenever execution in
the kernel reaches that tracepoint, it will trigger the eBPF program.

6. Run the opensnoop application from BCC's set of *libbpf tools* (*https://oreil.ly/D31R4*). This tool sets up some BPF links that you can see with `bpftool`, like this:

```
$ bpftool link list
116: perf_event  prog 1849
        bpf_cookie 0
        pids opensnoop(17711)
117: perf_event  prog 1851
        bpf_cookie 0
        pids opensnoop(17711)
```

Confirm that the program IDs (1849 and 1851 in my example output here)
match the output from listing the loaded eBPF programs:

```
$ bpftool prog list
...
1849: tracepoint  name tracepoint__syscalls__sys_enter_openat
        tag 8ee3432dcd98ffc3  gpl run_time_ns 95875 run_cnt 121
        loaded_at 2023-01-08T15:49:54+0000  uid 0
        xlated 240B  jited 264B  memlock 4096B  map_ids 571,568
        btf_id 710
        pids opensnoop(17711)
1851: tracepoint  name tracepoint__syscalls__sys_exit_openat
        tag 387291c2fb839ac6  gpl run_time_ns 8515669 run_cnt 120
        loaded_at 2023-01-08T15:49:54+0000  uid 0
        xlated 696B  jited 744B  memlock 4096B  map_ids 568,571,569
        btf_id 710
        pids opensnoop(17711)
```

7. While opensnoop is running, try pinning one of these links with `bpftool link pin id 116 /sys/fs/bpf/mylink` (using one of the link IDs you see output from `bpftool link list`). You should see that even after you terminate opensnoop, both the link and the corresponding program remain loaded in the kernel.

8. If you skip ahead to the example code for Chapter 5, you'll find a version of *hello-buffer-config.py* written using the *libbpf* library. This library automatically sets up a BPF link to the program that it loads into the kernel. Use `strace` to inspect the `bpf()` system calls that it makes, and see `bpf(BPF_LINK_CREATE)` system calls.

CO-RE, BTF, and Libbpf

In the previous chapter you encountered BTF (BPF Type Format) for the first time. This chapter discusses why it exists and how it's used to make eBPF programs portable across different versions of the kernel. It's a key part of BPF's compile once, run everywhere (CO-RE) approach, which solves the problem of making eBPF programs portable across different kernel versions.

Many eBPF programs access kernel data structures, and an eBPF programmer would need to include relevant Linux header files so that their eBPF code can correctly locate fields within those data structures. However, the Linux kernel is under continuous development, which means internal data structures can change between different kernel versions. If you were to take an eBPF object file compiled on one machine[1] and load it onto a machine with a different kernel version, there would be no guarantee that the data structures would be the same.

The CO-RE approach is a huge step forward in addressing this portability issue in an efficient way. It allows eBPF programs to include information about the data structure layouts they were compiled with, and it provides a mechanism for adjusting how fields are accessed if the data structure layout is different on the target machine where they run. Provided the program doesn't want to access a field or data structure that simply doesn't exist in the target machine's kernel, the program is portable across different kernel versions.

---

1 Strictly speaking, the data structure definitions come from kernel header files, and you could choose to compile based on a set of these header files that is different from what was used to build the kernel running on that machine. To work correctly (without the CO-RE mechanisms described in this chapter), the kernel headers have to be compatible with the kernel on the target machine where the eBPF program will run.

But before we dive into the details of how CO-RE works, let's discuss why it was so desirable, by looking at the previous approach to kernel portability as originally implemented in the BCC project.

BCC's Approach to Portability

In Chapter 2 I used BCC (*https://oreil.ly/ReUtn*) to show a basic "Hello World" example of an eBPF program. The BCC project was the first popular project for implementing eBPF programs, providing a framework for both the user space and kernel aspects that's relatively accessible to programmers without much kernel experience. To address portability across kernels, BCC took the approach of compiling eBPF code at runtime, in situ on the destination machine. There are a number of issues with this approach:

- The compilation toolchain needs to be installed on every destination machine where you want the code to run, as well as the kernel header files (which aren't always present by default).

- You have to wait for the compilation to complete before the tool starts, which could mean a delay of several seconds, every time the tool is launched.

- If you're running the tool on a large fleet of identical machines, repeating the compilation on each machine is a waste of compute resources.

- Some BCC-based projects package their eBPF source code and the toolchain into a container image, which makes distribution to each machine easier. But it doesn't solve the problem of ensuring that the kernel headers are present, and it can even mean more duplication if several of these BCC containers are installed on each machine.

- Embedded devices might not have sufficient memory resources to run the compilation step.

Because of these issues, if you're planning to embark on developing a significant new eBPF project, I would not recommend using this legacy BCC approach for it, especially if you're planning to distribute it for others to use. In this book I've given some examples based on BCC because it's a good approach for learning about the basic concepts of eBPF, particularly because the Python user space code is so compact and easy to read. It's also a perfectly good choice if you're more comfortable with it and you want to put something together quickly. But it's not the best approach for serious modern eBPF development.

The CO-RE approach offers a much better solution to the problem of cross-kernel portability for eBPF programs.

The BCC project at *github.com/iovisor/bcc* (*https://oreil.ly/ReUtn*) includes a wide range of command-line tools for observing all sorts of information about how a Linux machine is behaving. The original versions located in the *tools* (*https://oreil.ly/fI4w_*) directory are mostly implemented in Python using this legacy approach to portability that I have described in this section.

In BCC's *libbpf-tools* (*https://oreil.ly/ke7yq*) directory, you'll find updated versions of these tools written in C that take advantage of *libbpf* and CO-RE and that don't suffer from the problems I've just listed. They are an incredibly useful set of utilities!

CO-RE Overview

The CO-RE approach consists of a few elements:[2,3]

BTF

BTF (*https://oreil.ly/iRCuI*) is a format for expressing the layout of data structures and function signatures. In CO-RE it's used to determine any differences between the structures used at compilation time and at runtime. BTF is also used by tools like `bpftool` to dump data structures in human-readable formats. Linux kernels from 5.4 onward support BTF.

Kernel headers

The Linux kernel source code includes header files that describe the data structures it uses, and these headers can change between versions of Linux. eBPF programmers can choose to include individual header files, or, as you'll see in this chapter, you can use `bpftool` to generate a header file called *vmlinux.h* from a running system, containing all the data structure information about a kernel that a BPF program might need.

Compiler support

The Clang compiler was enhanced (*https://oreil.ly/6xFJm*) so that when it compiles eBPF programs with the `-g` flag, it includes what are known as *CO-RE relocations*, derived from the BTF information describing the kernel data structures. The GCC compiler also added CO-RE support for BPF targets in version 12 (*https://oreil.ly/_6PEE*).

---

2 Part of this section is adapted from "What Is eBPF?" by Liz Rice. Copyright © 2022 O'Reilly Media. Used with permission.

3 A small and unscientific survey suggests that most people pronounce this the same as the word *core* rather than in two syllables.

Library support for data structure relocations

At the point where a user space program loads an eBPF program into the kernel, the CO-RE approach requires the bytecode to be adjusted to compensate for any differences between the data structures present when it was compiled, and what's on the destination machine where it's about to run, based on the CO-RE relocation information compiled into the object. There are a few libraries that will take care of this: *libbpf* (*https://oreil.ly/E742u*) was the original C library that includes this relocation capability, the Cilium eBPF library provides the same capability for Go programmers, and Aya does it for Rust.

Optionally, a BPF skeleton

A skeleton can be auto-generated from a compiled BPF object file, containing handy functions that user space code can call to manage the lifecycle of BPF programs—loading them into the kernel, attaching them to events, and so on. If you're writing the user space code in C, you can generate the skeleton with `bpftool gen skeleton`. These functions are higher-level abstractions that can be more convenient for the developer than using the underlying library (*libbpf*, *cilium/ebpf*, etc.) directly.

 Andrii Nakryiko wrote an excellent blog post (*https://oreil.ly/aeQJo*) that describes the background of CO-RE, as well as laying out how it works and how to use it. He also wrote the canonical BPF CO-RE Reference Guide (*https://oreil.ly/lbW_T*), so please do read that if you're embarking on writing code yourself. His *libbpf-bootstrap* guide (*https://oreil.ly/_jet-*) to building an eBPF app from scratch with CO-RE + *libbpf* + skeletons is another must-read.

Now that you have an overview of the elements of CO-RE, let's dig in to see how they work, starting with an exploration of BTF.

BPF Type Format

BTF information describes how data structures and code are laid out in memory. This information can be put to a variety of different uses.

BTF Use Cases

The main reason for discussing BTF in this chapter on CO-RE is that knowing the differences between a structure's layout where an eBPF program was compiled and where it is about to run allows for the appropriate adjustments to be made as the program is loaded into the kernel. I'll discuss the relocation process later in this chapter, but for now, let's also consider some of the other uses to which BTF information can be put.

Knowing how a structure is laid out, and the type of every field in that structure, makes it possible to pretty-print a structure's contents in human-readable form. For example, a string is just a series of bytes from the computer's point of view, but converting those bytes into characters makes the string much easier for humans to understand. You already saw an example of this in the previous chapter, where bpftool used BTF information to format the output of map dumps.

BTF information also includes the line and function information that enables bpftool to interleave source code within the output from translated or JITed program dumps, as you saw in Chapter 3. When you come to Chapter 6, you'll also see the source code information interleaved with the verifier log output, and again this comes from the BTF information.

BTF information is also required for BPF spin locks. *Spin locks* are used to stop two CPU cores from simultaneously accessing the same map values. The lock has to be part of the map's value structure, like this:

```
struct my_value {
    ... <other fields>
    struct bpf_spin_lock lock;
... <other fields>
};
```

Within the kernel, eBPF programs use bpf_spin_lock() and bpf_spin_unlock() helper functions to acquire and release a lock. These helpers can be used only if BTF information is available to describe where the lock field is within the structure.

 Spin lock support was added in kernel version 5.1. There are lots of restrictions on the use of spin locks: they can only be used on hash or array map types, and they can't be used in tracing or socket filter type eBPF programs. Read more about spin locks in the lwn.net article on concurrency management in BPF (*https://oreil.ly/ kAyAU*).

Now that you know why BTF information is useful, let's make it more concrete by looking at some examples.

Listing BTF Information with bpftool

As with programs and maps, you can use the bpftool utility to show BTF information. The following command lists all the BTF data loaded into the kernel:

```
bpftool btf list
1: name [vmlinux]  size 5843164B
2: name [aes_ce_cipher]  size 407B
3: name [cryptd]  size 3372B
...
```

```
149: name <anon>  size 4372B  prog_ids 319  map_ids 103
        pids hello-buffer-co(7660)
155: name <anon>  size 37100B
        pids bpftool(7784)
```

(I've omitted many entries from the results for brevity.)

The first entry in the list is vmlinux, and it corresponds to the *vmlinux* file I mentioned earlier that holds the BTF information about the currently running kernel.

 Some of the examples early in this chapter reuse the programs from Chapter 4, and then later in this chapter you'll find new examples for which the source is in the *chapter5* directory at *github.com/lizrice/learning-ebpf*.

To obtain this example output I ran this command while the hello-buffer-config example from Chapter 4 was running. You can see the entry describing the BTF information that this process is using, on the line that starts with 149::

```
149: name <anon>  size 4372B  prog_ids 319  map_ids 103
        pids hello-buffer-co(7660)
```

Here's what that line is telling us:

- This chunk of BTF information has ID 149.
- It's an anonymous blob of around 4 KB of BTF information.
- It's used by the BPF program with prog_id 319 and the BPF map with map_id 103.
- It's also used by the process with ID 7660 (shown within parentheses) running the hello-buffer-config executable (whose name has been truncated to 15 characters).

These program, map, and BTF identifiers match with the following output that bpftool shows about hello-buffer-config's program called hello:

```
bpftool prog show name hello
319: kprobe  name hello  tag a94092da317ac9ba  gpl
        loaded_at 2022-08-28T14:13:35+0000  uid 0
        xlated 400B  jited 428B  memlock 4096B  map_ids 103,104
        btf_id 149
        pids hello-buffer-co(7660)
```

The only thing that doesn't appear to match completely between these two sets of information is that the program refers to an extra map_id, 104. That's the perf event buffer map, and it doesn't use BTF information; hence, it doesn't appear in the BTF-related output.

Much like `bpftool` can dump the contents of programs and maps, it can also be used to view the BTF type information contained in a blob of data.

BTF Types

Knowing the ID of the BTF information, you can inspect its contents with the command `bpftool btf dump id <id>`. When I ran this using the ID 149 that I obtained earlier, I got 69 lines of output, each of which is a type definition. I'll just describe the first few lines, which should give you a good idea of how to interpret the rest. The BTF information from these first few lines relates to the `config` hash map, which was defined in the source code like this:

```
struct user_msg_t {
  char message[12];
};

BPF_HASH(config, u32, struct user_msg_t);
```

This hash table has keys of type `u32` and values of type `struct user_msg_t`. That structure holds a 12-byte `message` field. Let's see how these types are defined in the corresponding BTF information.

The first three lines of the BTF output are as follows:

```
[1] TYPEDEF 'u32' type_id=2
[2] TYPEDEF '__u32' type_id=3
[3] INT 'unsigned int' size=4 bits_offset=0 nr_bits=32 encoding=(none)
```

The number in square brackets at the start of each line is the type ID (so the first line, starting with `[1]`, defines `type_id` 1, etc.). Let's dive into these three types in more detail:

- Type 1 defines a type named `u32` and its type, defined by `type_id` 2, that is, the type defined in the line that starts with `[2]`. As you know, the keys in the hash table have this type `u32`.

- Type 2 has the name `__u32` and the type defined by `type_id` 3.

- Type 3 is an integer type with the name `unsigned int`, which is 4 bytes long.

All three of these types are synonyms for a 32-bit unsigned integer type. In C, the lengths of integers are platform dependent, so Linux defines types like `u32` to explicitly define integers of specific lengths. On this machine, `u32` corresponds to an unsigned integer. User space code that refers to these should use the synonym prefixed with underscores, as in `__u32`.

The next few types in the BTF output look like this:

```
[4] STRUCT 'user_msg_t' size=12 vlen=1
        'message' type_id=6 bits_offset=0
[5] INT 'char' size=1 bits_offset=0 nr_bits=8 encoding=(none)
[6] ARRAY '(anon)' type_id=5 index_type_id=7 nr_elems=12
[7] INT '__ARRAY_SIZE_TYPE__' size=4 bits_offset=0 nr_bits=32 encoding=(none)
```

These relate to the user_msg_t structure used for values in the config map:

- Type 4 is the user_msg_t structure itself, and in total it is 12 bytes long. It contains one field named message, which is defined by type 6. The vlen field indicates how many fields there are in this definition.

- Type 5 is named char and is a 1-byte integer—exactly the definition a C programmer would expect for a type called "char."

- Type 6 defines the type for that message field as an array with 12 elements. Each element has type 5 (it's a char), and the array is indexed by type 7.

- Type 7 is a 4-byte integer.

With these definitions, you can build a complete picture of how the user_msg_t structure is laid out in memory, as illustrated in Figure 5-1.

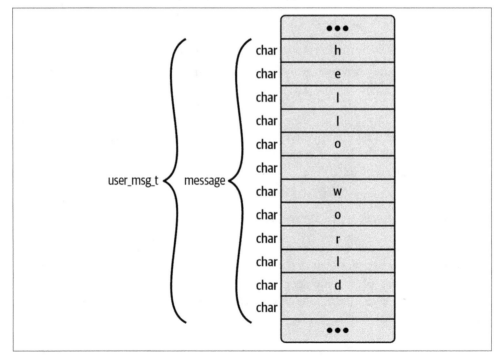

Figure 5-1. A user_msg_t structure takes 12 bytes of memory

So far, all the entries have `bits_offset` set to 0, but the next line of output has a structure with more than one field:

```
[8] STRUCT '____btf_map_config' size=16 vlen=2
        'key' type_id=1 bits_offset=0
        'value' type_id=4 bits_offset=32
```

This is a structure definition for the key–value pairs stored in the map called `config`. I didn't define this `____btf_map_config` type myself in the source code, but it has been generated by BCC. The key is of type `u32`, and the value is the `user_msg_t` structure. These correspond to the types 1 and 4 that you saw earlier.

The other important part of the BTF information about this structure is that the `value` field starts 32 bits after the start of the structure. That completely makes sense because the first 32 bits are needed to hold the `key` field.

In C, structure fields get automatically aligned to boundaries, so you can't simply assume that one field always follows directly after the previous one in memory. For example, consider a structure like this:

```
struct something {
    char letter;
    u64 number;
}
```

There would be 7 bytes of unused memory after the field called `let ter` before the `number` field so that the 64-bit number can be aligned to a memory location divisible by 8.

It's possible in some circumstances to turn on compiler packing to avoid this unused space, but it generally results in lower performance and—at least in my experience—it's unusual to do so. More often, C programmers will design structures by hand to make efficient use of space.

Maps with BTF Information

You've just seen the BTF information associated with a map. Now let's see how this BTF data is passed to the kernel when the map is created.

You saw in Chapter 4 that maps are created using the `bpf(BPF_MAP_CREATE)` syscall. This takes a `bpf_attr` structure as a parameter, defined in the kernel (*https://oreil.ly/PLrYG*) like this (some details omitted):

```
struct { /* anonymous struct used by BPF_MAP_CREATE command */
    __u32   map_type;               /* one of enum bpf_map_type */
    __u32   key_size;               /* size of key in bytes */
    __u32   value_size;             /* size of value in bytes */
    __u32   max_entries;            /* max number of entries in a map */
```

```
...
char      map_name[BPF_OBJ_NAME_LEN];
...
__u32     btf_fd;                /* fd pointing to a BTF type data */
__u32     btf_key_type_id;       /* BTF type_id of the key */
__u32     btf_value_type_id;     /* BTF type_id of the value */
...
};
```

Before the introduction of BTF, the `btf_*` fields weren't present in this `bpf_attr` structure, and the kernel had no knowledge of the structure of keys or values. The `key_size` and `value_size` fields defined how much memory was required for them, but they were just treated as so many bytes. By additionally passing in the BTF information defining the types of the keys and values, the kernel can introspect them, and utilities like bpftool can retrieve the type information for pretty-printing, as discussed earlier. However, it's interesting to note that separate BTF `type _ids` are passed in for the key and the value. The `____btf_map_config` structure that you just saw defined isn't used by the kernel for the map definition; it's just used by BCC on the user space side.

BTF Data for Functions and Function Prototypes

So far the BTF data in this example output has related to data types, but the BTF data also contains information about functions and function prototypes. Here's the information from the same BTF data blob that describes the `hello` function:

```
[31] FUNC_PROTO '(anon)' ret_type_id=23 vlen=1
        'ctx' type_id=10
[32] FUNC 'hello' type_id=31 linkage=static
```

In type 32 you can see the function named `hello` is defined as having the type defined in the previous line. That's a *function prototype*, which returns a value of type ID 23 and takes a single parameter (`vlen=1`) called `ctx` with type ID `10`. For completeness, here are the definitions of those types from earlier in the output:

```
[10] PTR '(anon)' type_id=0
```

```
[23] INT 'int' size=4 bits_offset=0 nr_bits=32 encoding=SIGNED
```

Type 10 is an anonymous pointer with the default type of 0, which isn't explicitly included in the BTF output but is defined as a void pointer.[4]

---

4 See the kernel documentation at *https://docs.kernel.org/bpf/btf.html#type-encoding*.

The return value with type 23 is a 4-byte integer, and `encoding=SIGNED` indicates that it's a signed integer; that is, it can have either a positive or negative value. This corresponds to the function definition in the source code of *hello-buffer-config.py*, which looks like this:

```
int hello(void *ctx)
```

The example BTF information I've shown so far comes from listing the contents of a blob of BTF data. Let's see how to obtain just the BTF information that relates to a particular map or program.

Inspecting BTF Data for Maps and Programs

If you want to inspect the BTF types associated with a particular map, `bpftool` makes that easy. For example, here's the output for the `config` map:

```
bpftool btf dump map name config
[1] TYPEDEF 'u32' type_id=2
[4] STRUCT 'user_msg_t' size=12 vlen=1
        'message' type_id=6 bits_offset=0
```

Similarly, you can inspect the BTF information related to a particular program with `bpftool btf dump prog <prog identity>`. I'll leave you to check out the manpage (*https://oreil.ly/lCoV5*) for additional details.

> If you'd like to better understand how the BTF type data is generated and de-duplicated, there is another excellent blog post from Andrii Nakryiko (*https://oreil.ly/0-a9g*) on the subject.

By this stage you should have an understanding of how BTF describes the format of data structures and functions. An eBPF program written in C needs header files that define the types and structures. Let's see how easy it is to generate a header file for any kernel data types that an eBPF program might need.

Generating a Kernel Header File

If you run `bpftool btf list` on a BTF-enabled kernel, you'll see lots of preexisting blobs of BTF data that look like this:

```
$ bpftool btf list
1: name [vmlinux]  size 5842973B
2: name [aes_ce_cipher]  size 407B
3: name [cryptd]  size 3372B
...
```

The first item in this list, with ID 1 and named vmlinux, is the BTF information about all the data types, structures, and function definitions used by the kernel that's running on this (virtual) machine.[5]

An eBPF program needs the definitions of any kernel data structures and types that it is going to refer to. Before the days of CO-RE, you'd typically have to figure out which of the many individual header files in the Linux kernel source held the definition for the structures you were interested in, but now there is a much easier way, as BTF-enabled tools can generate an appropriate header file from the BTF information included with the kernel.

This header file is conventionally called *vmlinux.h*, and you can generate it with bpftool like this:

```
bpftool btf dump file /sys/kernel/btf/vmlinux format c > vmlinux.h
```

This file defines all the kernel's data types, so including this generated *vmlinux.h* file in your eBPF program source supplies the definitions of any Linux data structures you might need. When you compile the source into an eBPF object file, that object will include BTF information that matches the definitions used in this header file. Later, when the program is run on a target machine, the user space program that loads it into the kernel will make adjustments to account for differences between this build-time BTF information and the BTF information for the kernel that's running on that target machine.

BTF information in the form of the */sys/kernel/btf/vmlinux* file has been included in the Linux kernel since version 5.4,[6] but raw BTF data that *libbpf* can make use of can also be generated for older kernels. In other words, if you want to run a CO-RE–enabled eBPF program on a target machine that doesn't have BTF information already, you might be able to provide the BTF data for that target yourself. There's information on how to generate BTF files, and an archive of files for a variety of Linux distributions, on the BTFHub (*https://oreil.ly/mPSO0*).

> The BTFHub repo also includes further reading about BTF internals (*https://oreil.ly/CfyQh*) should you want to dive deeper into this topic.

Next, let's look at how this and other tactics are used to write eBPF programs to be portable across kernels using CO-RE.

---

5 The kernel needs to have been built with the CONFIG_DEBUG_INFO_BTF option enabled.

6 Which is the oldest Linux kernel version that can support BTF? See *https://oreil.ly/HML9m*.

CO-RE eBPF Programs

You'll recall that eBPF programs run in the kernel. Later in this chapter I'll show some user space code that will interact with the code running in the kernel, but in this section I'm concentrating on the kernel side.

As you've already seen, eBPF programs are compiled to eBPF bytecode, and (at least at the time of this writing) the compilers that support this are Clang or gcc for compiling C code, and the Rust compiler. I'll discuss some of your options for using Rust in Chapter 10, but for the purposes of this chapter I'll assume you're writing in C and using Clang, along with the *libbpf* library.

For the remainder of this chapter, let's consider an example application called *hello-buffer-config*. It's very similar to the *hello-buffer-config.py* example from the previous chapter that used the BCC framework, but this version is written in C to use *libbpf* and CO-RE.

If you have BCC-based eBPF code that you want to migrate to *libbpf*, check out the excellent and comprehensive guide by Andrii Nakryiko on his website (*https:// oreil.ly/iWDcv*). BCC provides some convenient shortcuts that aren't handled in quite the same way using *libbpf*; conversely, *libbpf* provides its own set of macros and library functions to make life easier for the eBPF programmer. As I walk through the example, I will point out a few differences between the BCC and *libbpf* approaches.

 You'll find the example C eBPF program to accompany this section in the *chapter5* directory of the *github.com/lizrice/learning-ebpf* repo.

First let's look at *hello-buffer-config.bpf.c*, which implements the eBPF program that runs in the kernel. Later in the chapter I'll show you the user space code in *hello-buffer-config.c* that loads the program and displays output, much as the Python code did in the BCC implementation of this example in Chapter 4.

Like any C program, an eBPF program will need to include some header files.

Header Files

The first few lines of *hello-buffer-config.bpf.c* specify the header files that it needs:

```
#include "vmlinux.h"
#include <bpf/bpf_helpers.h>
#include <bpf/bpf_tracing.h>
#include <bpf/bpf_core_read.h>
#include "hello-buffer-config.h"
```

These five files are the *vmlinux.h* file, a few headers from *libbpf*, and an application-specific header file that I wrote myself. Let's see why this is a typical pattern for the header files needed for a *libbpf* program.

Kernel header information

If you're writing an eBPF program that refers to any kernel data structures or types, the easiest option is to include the *vmlinux.h* file described earlier in this chapter. Alternatively, it's possible to include individual header files from the Linux source, or to define the types by hand in your own code if you really want to go to that trouble. If you're going to use any BPF helper functions from *libbpf*, you'll need to include either *vmlinux.h* or *linux/types.h* to get the definitions for types like u32, u64, and so on, that the BPF helper source refers to.

The *vmlinux.h* file is derived from the kernel source headers, but it doesn't include #define'd values from them. For example, if your eBPF program parses Ethernet packets, you'll probably need the constant definitions that tell you what protocol the packet contains (such as 0x0800 to indicate that it's an IP packet, or 0x0806 for an ARP packet). There is a series of constant values that you'll need to duplicate in your own code, if you don't include the *if_ether.h* file (*https://oreil.ly/hoZzP*) that defines these values for the kernel. I didn't need any of these value definitions for *hello-buffer-config*, but you'll see another example in Chapter 8 where this is relevant.

Headers from libbpf

To use any BPF helper functions in your eBPF code, you'll need to include the header files from *libbpf* that give you their definitions.

> One thing that can be slightly confusing about *libbpf* is that it's not just a user space library. You'll find yourself including header files from *libbpf* in both user space and eBPF C code.

At the time of this writing, it is common to see eBPF projects including *libbpf* as a submodule and building/installing from source—this is what I have done in the example repository for this book. If you include it as a submodule, you'll simply need to run make install from the *libbpf/src* directory. I don't think it will be long before it's more common to see *libbpf* widely available as a package on common Linux distributions, particularly since *libbpf* has now passed the milestone of a version 1.0 release (*https://oreil.ly/8BFq6*).

Application-specific headers

It's very common to have an application-specific header file that defines any structures that are used by both the user space and eBPF parts of your app. In my example, the *hello-buffer-config.h* header file defines the `data_t` structure that I'm using to pass event data from the eBPF program to user space. It's almost the same structure you saw in the BCC version of this code, and it looks like this:

```
struct data_t {
  int pid;
  int uid;
  char command[16];
  char message[12];
  char path[16];
};
```

The only difference from the version you saw before is that I have added a field called `path`.

The reason to pull this structure definition into a separate header file is that I will also refer to it from the user space code in *hello-buffer-config.c*. In the BCC version, the kernel and user space code were both defined in a single file, and BCC did some work behind the scenes to make the structure available to the Python user space code.

Defining Maps

After including the header files, the next few lines of the source code in *hello-buffer-config.bpf.c* define the structures used for maps, like this:

```
struct {
    __uint(type, BPF_MAP_TYPE_PERF_EVENT_ARRAY);
    __uint(key_size, sizeof(u32));
    __uint(value_size, sizeof(u32));
} output SEC(".maps");

struct user_msg_t {
  char message[12];
};

struct {
    __uint(type, BPF_MAP_TYPE_HASH);
    __uint(max_entries, 10240);
    __type(key, u32);
    __type(value, struct user_msg_t);
} my_config SEC(".maps");
```

This requires more lines of code than I needed in the equivalent BCC example! With BCC, the map called `config` was created with the following macro:

```
BPF_HASH(config, u64, struct user_msg_t);
```

This macro isn't available when you're not using BCC, so in C you have to write it out longhand. You'll see that I have used __uint and __type. These are defined in *bpf/bpf_helpers_def.h* (*https://oreil.ly/2FgjB*) along with __array, like this:

```
#define __uint(name, val) int (*name)[val]
#define __type(name, val) typeof(val) *name
#define __array(name, val) typeof(val) *name[]
```

These macros generally seem to be used by convention in *libbpf*-based programs, and I think they make the map definitions a little easier to read.

 The name "config" clashed with a definition in *vmlinux.h*, so I renamed the map "my_config" for this example.

eBPF Program Sections

Use of *libbpf* requires each eBPF program to be marked with a SEC() macro that defines the program type, like this:

```
SEC("kprobe")
```

This results in a section called kprobe in the compiled ELF object, so *libbpf* knows to load this as a BPF_PROG_TYPE_KPROBE. We'll discuss different program types further in Chapter 7.

Depending on the program type, you can also use the section name to specify what event the program will be attached to. The *libbpf* library will use this information to set up the attachment automatically, rather than leaving you to do it explicitly in your user space code. So, for example, to auto-attach to the kprobe for the execve syscall on an ARM-based machine, you could specify the section like this:

```
SEC("kprobe/__arm64_sys_execve")
```

This requires you to know the function name for the syscall on that architecture (or figure it out, perhaps by looking at the */proc/kallsyms* file on your target machine, which lists all the kernel symbols, including its function names). But *libbpf* can make life even easier for you with the k(ret)syscall section name, which tells the loader to attach to the kprobe in the architecture-specific function automatically:

```
SEC("ksyscall/execve")
```

The valid section names and formats are listed in the *libbpf* documentation (*https://oreil.ly/FhHrm*). In the past, the requirements for section names were much looser, so you may come across eBPF programs written before *libbpf 1.0* with section names that don't match the valid set. Don't let them confuse you!

The section definition declares where the eBPF program should be attached, and then the program itself follows. As before, the eBPF program itself is written as a C function. In the example code it's called hello(), and it's extremely similar to the hello() function you saw in Chapter 4. Let's consider the differences between that previous version and the version here:

```
SEC("ksyscall/execve")
int BPF_KPROBE_SYSCALL(hello, const char *pathname)          ❶
{
  struct data_t data = {};
  struct user_msg_t *p;

  data.pid = bpf_get_current_pid_tgid() >> 32;
  data.uid = bpf_get_current_uid_gid() & 0xFFFFFFFF;

  bpf_get_current_comm(&data.command, sizeof(data.command));
  bpf_probe_read_user_str(&data.path, sizeof(data.path), pathname);   ❷

  p = bpf_map_lookup_elem(&my_config, &data.uid);             ❸
  if (p != 0) {
     bpf_probe_read_kernel(&data.message, sizeof(data.message), p->message);
  } else {
     bpf_probe_read_kernel(&data.message, sizeof(data.message), message);
  }

  bpf_perf_event_output(ctx, &output, BPF_F_CURRENT_CPU,       ❹
                        &data, sizeof(data));
  return 0;
}
```

❶ I've taken advantage of a BPF_KPROBE_SYSCALL (*https://oreil.ly/pgI1B*) macro defined in *libbpf* that makes it easy to access the arguments to a syscall by name. For execve(), the first argument is the pathname for the program that's going to be executed. The eBPF program name is hello.

❷ Since the macro has made it so easy to access that pathname argument to exe cve(), I'm including it in the data sent to the perf buffer output. Notice that copying memory requires the use of a BPF helper function.

❸ Here, `bpf_map_lookup_elem()` is the BPF helper function for looking up values in a map, given a key. BCC's equivalent of this would be `p = my_con fig.lookup(&data.uid)`. BCC rewrites this to use the underlying `bpf_map_lookup_elem()` function before it passes the C code to the compiler. When you're using *libbpf*, there is no rewriting of the code before compilation,[7] so you have to write directly to the helper functions.

❹ Here's another similar example where I have written directly to the helper function `bpf_perf_event_output()`, where BCC gave me the convenient equivalent `output.perf_submit(ctx, &data, sizeof(data))`.

The only other difference is that in the BCC version, I defined the message string as a local variable within the `hello()` function. BCC doesn't (at least at the time of this writing) support global variables. In this version I have defined it as a global variable, like this:

```
char message[12] = "Hello World";
```

In *chapter4/hello-buffer-config.py* the `hello` function was defined rather differently, like this:

```
int hello(void *ctx)
```

The `BPF_KPROBE_SYSCALL` macro is one of the convenient additions from *libbpf* that I mentioned. You're not required to use the macro, but it makes life easier. It does all the heavy lifting to provide named arguments for all the parameters passed to a syscall. In this case, it supplies a `pathname` argument that points to a string holding the path of the executable that is about to be run, which is the first argument to the `execve()` syscall.

If you're paying very close attention you might notice that the `ctx` variable isn't visibly defined in my source code for *hello-buffer-config.bpf.c*, but nevertheless, I've been able to use it when submitting data to the output perf buffer, like this:

```
bpf_perf_event_output(ctx, &output, BPF_F_CURRENT_CPU, &data, sizeof(data));
```

The `ctx` variable does exist, hidden within the `BPF_KPROBE_SYSCALL` macro definition inside *bpf/bpf_tracing.h* (*https://oreil.ly/pgI1B*), in *libbpf*, where you'll also find some commentary about this. It can be slightly confusing to use a variable that's not visibly defined, but it's very helpful that it can be accessed.

---

7 Well, normal C preprocessing applies so that you can do things like `#define`. But there's no *special* rewriting like there is when you use BCC.

Memory Access with CO-RE

eBPF programs for tracing have restricted access to memory, via a BPF helper function from the `bpf_probe_read_*()` family.[8] (There is also a `bpf_probe_write_user()` helper function, but it's only "meant for experiments" (*https://oreil.ly/ibcy1*)). The problem is that, as you'll see in the next chapter, the eBPF verifier generally won't let you simply read memory through a pointer as you usually can in C (e.g., x = p->y).[9]

The *libbpf* library provides CO-RE wrappers around the `bpf_probe_read_*()` helpers to take advantage of the BTF information and make memory access calls portable across different kernel versions. Here's an example of one of those wrappers, as defined in the *bpf_core_read.h* header file (*https://oreil.ly/XWWyc*):

```
#define bpf_core_read(dst, sz, src)                       \
    bpf_probe_read_kernel(dst, sz,                        \
                          (const void *)__builtin_preserve_access_index(src))
```

As you can see, `bpf_core_read()` calls directly to `bpf_probe_read_kernel()`, the only difference being that it wraps the `src` field with `__builtin_pre serve_access_index()`. This tells Clang to emit a CO-RE relocation entry along with the eBPF instruction that accesses this address in memory.

 This `__builtin_preserve_access_index()` instruction is an extension to "regular" C code, and adding it to eBPF also required changes to the Clang compiler to support it and emit these CO-RE relocation entries. Extensions like these are examples of why some C compilers cannot (today, at least) generate eBPF bytecode. Read more about the Clang changes required for eBPF CO-RE support on the LLVM mailing list (*https://oreil.ly/jHTHE*).

As you'll see later in this chapter, the CO-RE relocation entry tells *libbpf* to rewrite the address, as it's loading the eBPF program into the kernel, to take account of any BTF differences. If the offset of `src` within its containing structure is different on the target kernel, the rewritten instruction will take that into account.

The *libbpf* library provides a `BPF_CORE_READ()` macro so that you can write several `bpf_core_read()` calls in a single line rather than needing a separate helper function call for every pointer dereference. For example, if you wanted to do something like d = a->b->c->d, you could write the following code:

---

8 eBPF programs handling network packets don't get to use this helper function and can only access the network packet memory.

9 It is permitted in certain BTF-enabled program types such as `tp_btf`, `fentry`, and `fexit`.

```
struct b_t *b;
struct c_t *c;

bpf_core_read(&b, 8, &a->b);
bpf_core_read(&c, 8, &b->c);
bpf_core_read(&d, 8, &c->d);
```

But it's much more compact to use:

```
d = BPF_CORE_READ(a, b, c, d);
```

You can then read from point d using the `bpf_probe_read_kernel()` helper function.

There's a good description of this in Andrii's guide (*https://oreil.ly/tU0Gb*).

License Definition

As you already know from Chapter 3, the eBPF program has to declare its license. The example code does it like this:

```
char LICENSE[] SEC("license") = "Dual BSD/GPL";
```

You've now seen all the code in the *hello-buffer-config.bpf.c* example. Now let's compile it into an object file.

Compiling eBPF Programs for CO-RE

In Chapter 3 you saw an extract from a Makefile that compiles C to eBPF bytecode. Let's dig into the options used and see why they are necessary for CO-RE/*libbpf* programs.

Debug Information

You have to pass the -g flag to Clang so that it includes debug information, which is necessary for BTF. However, the -g flag also adds DWARF debugging information to the output object file, but that's not needed by eBPF programs, so you can reduce the size of the object by running the following command to strip it out:

```
llvm-strip -g <object file>
```

Optimization

The -02 optimization flag (level 2 or higher) is required for Clang to produce BPF bytecode that will pass the verifier. One example of this being necessary is that, by default, Clang will output `callx <register>` to call helper functions, but eBPF doesn't support calling addresses from registers.

Target Architecture

If you're using certain macros defined by *libbpf*, you'll need to specify the target architecture at compile time. The *libbpf* header file *bpf/bpf_tracing.h* defines several macros that are platform specific, such as BPF_KPROBE and BPF_KPROBE_SYSCALL that I've used in this example. The BPF_KPROBE macro can be used for eBPF programs that are being attached to kprobes, and BPF_KPROBE_SYSCALL is a variant specifically for syscall kprobes.

The argument to a kprobe is a pt_regs structure that holds a copy of the contents of the CPU registers. Since registers are architecture specific, the pt_regs structure definition depends on the architecture you're running on. This means that if you want to use these macros, you'll need to also tell the compiler what the target architecture is. You can do this by setting -D __TARGET_ARCH_($ARCH) where $ARCH is an architecture name like arm64, amd64, and so on.

Also note that if you didn't use the macro, you'd need architecture-specific code to access the register information anyway for a kprobe.

Perhaps "compile once *per architecture*, run everywhere" would have been a bit of a mouthful!

Makefile

The following is an example Makefile instruction for compiling CO-RE objects (taken from the Makefile in the *chapter5* directory of the GitHub repo for this book):

```
hello-buffer-config.bpf.o: %.o: %.c
    clang \
        -target bpf \
        -D __TARGET_ARCH_$(ARCH) \
        -I/usr/include/$(shell uname -m)-linux-gnu \
        -Wall \
        -O2 -g \
        -c $< -o $@
    llvm-strip -g $@
```

If you're using the example code, you should be able to build the eBPF object file *hello-buffer-config.bpf.o* (and its companion user space executable that I'll describe shortly) by running make in the *chapter5* directory. Let's inspect that object file to see that it includes BTF information.

BTF Information in the Object File

The kernel documentation for BTF (*https://oreil.ly/5QrBy*) describes how BTF data is encoded in an ELF object file in two sections: *.BTF*, which contains the data and string information, and *.BTF.ext*, which covers function and line information. You can use `readelf` to see that these sections have been added to the object file, like this:

```
$ readelf -S hello-buffer-config.bpf.o | grep BTF
  [10] .BTF              PROGBITS        0000000000000000  000002c0
  [11] .rel.BTF          REL             0000000000000000  00000e50
  [12] .BTF.ext          PROGBITS        0000000000000000  00000b18
  [13] .rel.BTF.ext      REL             0000000000000000  00000ea0
```

The `bpftool` utility lets us examine the BTF data from an object file, like this:

```
bpftool btf dump file hello-buffer-config.bpf.o
```

The output looks just like the output you get from dumping BTF info from loaded programs and maps, as you saw earlier in this chapter.

Let's see how this BTF information can be used to allow the program to run on another machine with a different kernel version and different data structures.

BPF Relocations

The *libbpf* library adapts eBPF programs to work with the data structure layout on the target kernel where they run, even if this layout is different from the kernel where the code was compiled. To do this, *libbpf* needs the BPF CO-RE relocation information generated by Clang as part of the compilation process.

You can learn more about how the relocations work from the definition of `struct bpf_core_relo` in the *linux/bpf.h* header file:

```
struct bpf_core_relo {
    __u32 insn_off;
    __u32 type_id;
    __u32 access_str_off;
    enum bpf_core_relo_kind kind;
};
```

The CO-RE relocation data for an eBPF program consists of one of these structures for each instruction that needs relocation. Suppose the instruction is setting a register to the value of a field within a structure. The `bpf_core_relo` structure for that instruction (identified by the `insn_off` field) encodes the BTF type of that structure (the `type_id` field) and also indicates how the field is accessed relative to that structure (`access_str_off`).

As you've just seen, the relocation data for the kernel data structures is generated automatically by Clang and encoded in the ELF object file. It's the following line, which you'll find near the start of the *vmlinux.h* file, that causes Clang to do this:

```
#pragma clang attribute push (__attribute__((preserve_access_index)), \
                                                   apply_to = record)
```

The `preserve_access_index` attribute tells Clang to generate BPF CO-RE relocations for a type definition. The `clang attribute push` part says that this attribute should be applied to all definitions until a `clang attribute pop`, which appears at the end of the file. That means Clang generates the relocation information for all the types defined in *vmlinux.h*.

You can see the relocations taking place when you load a BPF program, by using bpftool and turning on the debug information with the -d flag, like this:

```
bpftool -d prog load hello.bpf.o /sys/fs/bpf/hello
```

This generates a lot of output, but the parts relating to relocation look like this:

```
libbpf: CO-RE relocating [24] struct user_pt_regs: found target candidate [205]
struct user_pt_regs in [vmlinux]
libbpf: prog 'hello': relo #0: <byte_off> [24] struct user_pt_regs.regs[0]
(0:0:0 @ offset 0)
libbpf: prog 'hello': relo #0: matching candidate #0 <byte_off> [205] struct
user_pt_regs.regs[0] (0:0:0 @ offset 0)
libbpf: prog 'hello': relo #0: patched insn #1 (LDX/ST/STX) off 0 -> 0
```

In this example you can see that type ID 24 from the `hello` program's BTF information refers to the structure called `user_pt_regs`. The *libbpf* library has matched this against a kernel structure, also called `user_pt_regs`, that has type ID 205 in the *vmlinux* BTF data set. In practice, because I compiled and loaded the program on the same machine, the type definitions are identical, so in this example the offset of 0 from the start of the structure remains unchanged, and the "patch" to instruction #1 leaves it unchanged.

In many applications you won't want to ask users to run `bpftool` to load an eBPF program. Instead, you'll want to build this functionality into a dedicated user space program that you supply as an executable. Let's consider how to write this user space code.

CO-RE User Space Code

There are a few different frameworks in different programming languages that support CO-RE by implementing the relocations as they load eBPF programs into the kernel. In this chapter I'll show C code that uses *libbpf*; other options include the Go packages *cilium/ebpf* and *libbpfgo*, and Aya for Rust. I'll discuss those options further in Chapter 10.

The Libbpf Library for User Space

The *libbpf* library is a user space library you can use directly if you're writing the user space part of your application in C. If you want to, you can use this library without using CO-RE. There's an example of this in Andrii Nakryiko's excellent blog post on *libbpf-bootstrap* (*https://oreil.ly/b3v7B*).

This library provides functions that wrap the bpf() and related syscalls that you met in Chapter 4 to perform operations like loading programs into the kernel and attaching them to events, or accessing map information from user space. The conventional and easiest way to use these abstractions is through auto-generated BPF skeleton code.

BPF Skeletons

You can use bpftool to auto-generate this skeleton code from existing eBPF objects in ELF file format, like this:

```
bpftool gen skeleton hello-buffer-config.bpf.o > hello-buffer-config.skel.h
```

Look into this skeleton header and you'll see that it contains structure definitions for the eBPF programs and maps, as well as several functions that all start with the name hello_buffer_config_bpf__ (based on the name of the object file). These functions manage the lifecycle of the eBPF programs and maps. You don't have to use the skeleton code—you can make calls to *libbpf* directly if you prefer—but the auto-generated code will typically save you some typing.

Toward the end of the generated skeleton file you'll see a function called hello_buffer_config_bpf__elf_bytes that returns the byte contents of the ELF object file *hello-buffer-config.bpf.o*. Once the skeleton has been generated, we don't really need that object file anymore. You can test this by running make to generate the hello-buffer-config executable and then deleting the *.o* file; the executable has the eBPF bytecode contained within it.

 If you prefer, you can use the *libbpf* function bpf_object__open_file to load the eBPF programs and maps from an ELF file rather than using the bytes from a skeleton file.

Here's the outline of the user space code that manages the lifecycle of the eBPF program and maps for this example, using the generated skeleton code. I have omitted some of the details and error handling for clarity, but you'll find the full source code in *chapter5/hello-buffer-config.c*.

```
... [other #includes]
#include "hello-buffer-config.h"                                  ❶
#include "hello-buffer-config.skel.h"

... [some callback functions]

int main()
{
    struct hello_buffer_config_bpf *skel;
    struct perf_buffer *pb = NULL;
    int err;

    libbpf_set_print(libbpf_print_fn);                            ❷

    skel = hello_buffer_config_bpf__open_and_load();              ❸
...
    err = hello_buffer_config_bpf__attach(skel);                  ❹
...
    pb = perf_buffer__new(bpf_map__fd(skel->maps.output), 8, handle_event,
                                          lost_event, NULL, NULL);
                                                                  ❺
...
    while (true) {                                                ❻
        err = perf_buffer__poll(pb, 100);
...}

    perf_buffer__free(pb);                                        ❼
    hello_buffer_config_bpf__destroy(skel);
    return -err;
}
```

❶ This file includes the auto-generated skeleton header, as well as the header file I wrote manually for data structures shared between the user space and kernel code.

❷ This code sets a callback function that will print any log messages generated by *libbpf*.

❸ Here a skel structure is created that represents all the maps and programs defined in the ELF bytes and loads them into the kernel.

❹ Programs are auto-attached to the appropriate events.

❺ This function creates a structure for handling the perf buffer output.

❻ Here that perf buffer is continuously polled.

❼ This is the clean-up code.

Let's dive into some of those steps in more detail.

Loading programs and maps into the kernel

The first call to an auto-generated function is this one:

```
skel = hello_buffer_config_bpf__open_and_load();
```

As its name suggests, this function covers two phases: opening and loading. The "open" phase involves reading the ELF data and converting its sections into structures that represent eBPF programs and maps. The "load" phase loads those maps and programs into the kernel, performing any CO-RE fixups as necessary.

These two phases can easily be handled separately, as the skeleton code provides separate name__open() and name__load() functions. This gives you the option to manipulate the eBPF information before loading it. This is commonly done to configure a program before loading it. For example, I could initialize a counter global variable c to some value, like this:

```
skel = hello_buffer_config_bpf__open();
if (!skel) {
    // Error ...
}
skel->data->c = 10;
err = hello_buffer_config_bpf__load(skel);
```

The data type returned by hello_buffer_config_bpf__open(), and also by hello_buffer_config_bpf__load(), is a structure called hello_buffer_config_bpf defined in the skeleton header to include information about all the maps, programs, and data defined in the object file.

> The skeleton object (hello_buffer_config_bpf in this example) is just a user space representation of information from the ELF bytes. Once it has been loaded into the kernel, if you change a value in the object, it won't have any effect on the kernel-side data. So, for example, changing skel->data->c after loading will not have any effect.

Accessing existing maps

By default, *libbpf* will also create any maps that are defined in the ELF bytes, but sometimes you might want to write an eBPF program that reuses an existing map. You already saw an example of this in the previous chapter, where you saw bpftool iterating through all the maps, looking for the one that matched a specified name. Another common reason to use a map is to share information between two different eBPF programs, so only one program should create the map. The bpf_map__set_autocreate() function allows you to override *libbpf*'s auto-creation.

So how do you access an existing map? Maps can be pinned, and if you know the pinned path, you can get a file descriptor to an existing map with bpf_obj_get(). Here's a very simple example (available in the GitHub repository as *chapter5/find-map.c*):

```
struct bpf_map_info info = {};
unsigned int len = sizeof(info);

int findme = bpf_obj_get("/sys/fs/bpf/findme");
if (findme <= 0) {
    printf("No FD\n");
} else {
    bpf_obj_get_info_by_fd(findme, &info, &len);
    printf("Name: %s\n", info.name);
}
```

To try this out you can create a map using bpftool, like this:

```
$ bpftool map create /sys/fs/bpf/findme type array key 4 value 32 entries 4
name findme
```

Running the find-map executable will print out:

```
Name: findme
```

Let's get back to the *hello-buffer-config* example and the skeleton code.

Attaching to events

The next skeleton function in the example attaches the program to the execve syscall function:

```
err = hello_buffer_config_bpf__attach(skel);
```

The *libbpf* library automatically takes the attachment point from the SEC() definition for this program. If you didn't define the attachment point fully, there are a whole series of *libbpf* functions, such as bpf_program__attach_kprobe, bpf_program__attach_xdp, and so on, for attaching different program types.

Managing an event buffer

Setting up the perf buffer uses a function defined in *libbpf* itself, rather than in the skeleton:

```
pb = perf_buffer__new(bpf_map__fd(skel->maps.output), 8, handle_event,
                                                lost_event, NULL, NULL);
```

You can see the perf_buffer__new() function takes the file descriptor for the "output" map as the first argument. The handle_event argument is a callback function that gets called when new data arrives in the perf buffer, and lost_event gets called if there isn't enough room in the perf buffer for the kernel to write a data entry. In my example these functions just write messages to the screen.

Finally, the program has to poll the perf buffer repeatedly:

```
while (true) {
    err = perf_buffer__poll(pb, 100);
    ...
}
```

The 100 is a timeout in milliseconds. The callback functions previously set up will get called as appropriate when data arrives or when the buffer is full.

Finally, to clean up I free the perf buffer and destroy the eBPF programs and maps in the kernel, like this:

```
perf_buffer__free(pb);
hello_buffer_config_bpf__destroy(skel);
```

There are a whole set of `perf_buffer_*-` and `ring_buffer_*`-related functions in *libbpf* to help you manage event buffers.

If you make and run this example `hello-buffer-config` program, you'll see the following output (that's very similar to what you saw in Chapter 4):

```
23664  501    bash        Hello World
23665  501    bash        Hello World
23667  0      cron        Hello World
23668  0      sh          Hello World
```

Libbpf Code Examples

There are lots of great examples of *libbpf*-based eBPF programs available that you can use as inspiration and guidance for writing your own:

- The *libbpf-bootstrap* (*https://oreil.ly/zB0Co*) project is intended to help you get off the ground with a set of example programs.
- The BCC project has many of the original BCC-based tools migrated to a *libbpf* version. You'll find them in the *libbpf-tools* directory (*https://oreil.ly/Z9xDX*).

Summary

CO-RE enables eBPF programs that can run on kernel versions different from the versions on which they were built. This massively improves the portability of eBPF and makes life much easier for tool developers who want to deliver production-ready tooling to their users and customers.

In this chapter you saw how CO-RE achieves this by encoding type information into the compiled object file and using relocations to rewrite instructions as they are loaded into the kernel. You also had an introduction to writing code in C that uses *libbpf*: both the eBPF programs that run in the kernel and the user space programs that manage the lifecycle of those programs, based on auto-generated BPF skeleton code. In the next chapter you'll learn how the kernel verifies that eBPF programs are safe to run.

Exercises

Here are a few things you can do to further explore BTF, CO-RE, and *libbpf*:

1. Experiment with `bpftool btf dump map` and `bpftool btf dump prog` to see the BTF information associated with maps and programs, respectively. Remember that you can specify individual maps and programs in more than one way.

2. Compare the output from `bpftool btf dump file` and `bpftool btf dump prog` for the same program in its ELF object file form and after it has been loaded into the kernel. They should be identical.

3. Examine the debug output from *bpftool -d prog load hello-buffer-config.bpf.o /sys/fs/bpf/hello*. You'll see each section being loaded, checks on the license, and relocations taking place, as well as output describing each BPF program instruction.

4. Try building a BPF program against a different *vmlinux* header file from BTFHub, and look in the debug output from `bpftool` for relocations that change offsets.

5. Modify the *hello-buffer-config.c* program so that you can configure different messages for different user IDs using the map (similar to the *hello-buffer-config.py* example in Chapter 4).

6. Try changing the section name in the `SEC();`, perhaps to your own name. When you come to load the program into the kernel you should see an error because *libbpf* doesn't recognize the section name. This illustrates how *libbpf* uses the section name to work out what kind of BPF program this is. You could try writing your own attachment code to explicitly attach to an event of your choice rather than relying on *libbpf*'s auto-attachment.

CHAPTER 6

The eBPF Verifier

I've mentioned the verification step a few times, so you already know that when you load an eBPF program into the kernel, this verification process ensures that the program is safe. In this chapter we'll dive into how the verifier works to achieve this goal.

Verification involves checking every possible execution path through the program and ensuring that every instruction is safe. The verifier also makes some updates to the bytecode to ready it for execution. In this chapter I'll show some examples of verification failures, by starting from an example that works and making modifications that render that code invalid to the verifier.

 The example code for this chapter is in the *chapter6* directory of the repository at *github.com/lizrice/learning-ebpf*.

This chapter doesn't attempt to cover every possible check the verifier makes. It's intended to be an overview, with illustrative examples that will help you deal with verification errors that you might run into when writing your own eBPF code.

One thing to bear in mind is that the verifier works on eBPF bytecode, not directly on the source. That bytecode depends on the output from the compiler. Because of things like compiler optimization, a change in the source code might not always result in exactly what you expect in the bytecode, so correspondingly it might not give you the result you expect in the verifier's verdict. For example, the verifier will reject unreachable instructions, but the compiler might optimize them away before the verifier sees them.

The Verification Process

The verifier analyzes the program to assess all possible execution paths. It steps through the instructions in order, evaluating them rather than actually executing them. As it goes along it keeps track of the state of each register in a structure called bpf_reg_state. (The registers I'm referring to here are the registers from the eBPF virtual machine that you met in Chapter 3.) This structure includes a field called bpf_reg_type, which describes what type of value is held in that register. There are several possible types, including these:

- NOT_INIT, indicating that the register has not yet been set to a value.

- SCALAR_VALUE, indicating that the register has been set to a value that doesn't represent a pointer.

- Several PTR_TO_* types, indicating that the register holds a pointer to something. That something could be, for example:

  — PTR_TO_CTX: The register holds a pointer to the context passed as the argument to a BPF program.

  — PTR_TO_PACKET: The register points to a network packet (held in the kernel as skb->data).

  — PTR_TO_MAP_KEY or PTR_TO_MAP_VALUE: I'm sure you can guess what these mean.

There are several other PTR_TO_* types, and you can find the full set enumerated in the *linux/bpf.h* header file (*https://oreil.ly/aWb50*).

The bpf_reg_state structure also keeps track of the range of possible values the register might hold. This information is used by the verifier to determine when invalid actions are being attempted.

Each time the verifier comes to a branch, where a decision has to be made on whether to carry on in sequence or jump to a different instruction, the verifier pushes a copy of the current state of all the registers onto a stack and explores one of the possible paths. It continues evaluating the instructions until it reaches the return at the end of the program (or reaches the limit on the number of instructions it will process, which is currently one million instructions[1]), at which point it pops a branch off the stack to evaluate next. If it finds an instruction that could result in an invalid operation, it fails verification.

---

1 For a long time the limit was 4,096 instructions, which imposed significant restrictions on the complexity of eBPF programs. This limit still applies to unprivileged users running BPF programs.

Verifying every single possibility could get computationally expensive, so in practice there are optimizations called *state pruning* that avoid reevaluating paths through the program that are essentially equivalent. As it works through the program, the verifier records the state of all the registers at certain instructions within the program. If it later arrives at the same instruction with registers in a matching state, there is no need to continue to verify the rest of that path, as it's already known to be valid.

Lots of work has gone into optimizing the verifier (*https://oreil.ly/pQDES*) and its pruning process. The verifier used to store pruning state before and after each jump instruction, but analysis showed that this results in storing state on average every four instructions or so, and the vast majority of these pruning states would never get matched. It turned out that it's more efficient to store pruning state every 10 instructions, regardless of branching.

You can read more details on how verification works in the kernel documentation (*https://oreil.ly/atNda*).

The Verifier Log

When the verification of a program fails, the verifier generates a log showing how it reached the conclusion that the program is invalid. If you're using `bpftool prog load`, the verifier log gets output to stderr. When you're writing a program with *libbpf*, you can use the function `libbpf_set_print()` to set a handler that will display (or do something else useful with) any errors. (You'll see an example of this in the *hello-verifier.c* source code for this chapter.)

If you really want to dig into what the verifier is doing, you can get it to generate the log on success as well as on failure. There is a basic example of this in the *hello-verifier.c* file too. It involves passing a buffer that will hold verifier log contents into the *libbpf* call that loads the program into the kernel and then writing the contents of that log to screen.

The verifier log includes a summary of how much work the verifier did, which looks something like this:

```
processed 61 insns (limit 1000000) max_states_per_insn 0 total_states 4
peak_states 4 mark_read 3
```

In this example, the verifier processed 61 instructions, including potentially processing the same instruction multiple times by arriving at it through different paths. Note that the complexity limit of one million is an upper bound on the number of instructions in a program; in practice, if there are branches in the code, the verifier will process some instructions more than once.

The total number of states stored was four, which for this simple program matches the peak number of stored states. If some of the states had been pruned, the peak number might be lower than the total.

The log output includes the BPF instructions the verifier has analyzed, along with the corresponding C source code lines (if the object file was built with the -g flag to include debug information) and summaries of verifier state information. Here is an example extract of the verifier log relating to the first few lines of the program in *hello-verifier.bpf.c*:

```
0: (bf) r6 = r1
; data.counter = c;                                              ❶
1: (18) r1 = 0xffff800008178000
3: (61) r2 = *(u32 *)(r1 +0)
 R1_w=map_value(id=0,off=0,ks=4,vs=16,imm=0) R6_w=ctx(id=0,off=0,imm=0)
 R10=fp0                                                         ❷
; c++;
4: (bf) r3 = r2
5: (07) r3 += 1
6: (63) *(u32 *)(r1 +0) = r3
 R1_w=map_value(id=0,off=0,ks=4,vs=16,imm=0) R2_w=inv(id=1,umax_value=4294967295,
 var_off=(0x0; 0xffffffff)) R3_w=inv(id=0,umin_value=1,umax_value=4294967296,
 var_off=(0x0; 0x1ffffffff)) R6_w=ctx(id=0,off=0,imm=0) R10=fp0  ❸
```

❶ The log includes source code lines to make it easier to understand how the output relates to the source. This source code is available because the -g flag was used to build in debug information during the compilation step.

❷ Here's an example of some register state information being output in the log. It tells us that at this stage Register 1 contains a map value, Register 6 holds the context, and Register 10 is the frame (or stack) pointer where local variables are held.

❸ This is another example of register state information. Here you can see not only the types of values that are held in each (initialized) register, but also the range of possible values for Register 2 and Register 3.

Let's dig further into the details of this. I said that Register 6 holds the context, and the verifier log indicates this with R6_w=ctx(id=0,off=0,imm=0). This was set up in the very first line of the bytecode, where Register 1 was copied to Register 6. When an eBPF program is called, Register 1 always holds the context argument passed to the program. Why copy it to Register 6? Well, when a BPF helper function is called, the arguments to that call are passed in Registers 1 through 5. Helper functions don't modify the contents of Registers 6 through 9, so saving the context off into Register 6 means the code can call a helper function without losing access to the context.

Register 0 is used for the return value from a helper function and also for the return value from an eBPF program. Register 10 always holds a pointer to the eBPF stack frame (and the eBPF program can't modify it).

Let's look at the register state information for Registers 2 and 3 after instruction 6:

```
R2_w=inv(id=1,umax_value=4294967295,var_off=(0x0; 0xffffffff))
R3_w=inv(id=0,umin_value=1,umax_value=4294967296,var_off=(0x0; 0x1ffffffff))
```

Register 2 doesn't have a minimum value, and the umax_value shown here in decimal corresponds to 0xFFFFFFFF, which is the largest value that can be held in an 8-byte register. In other words, at this point the register could hold any of its possible values.

In instruction 4, the contents of Register 2 are copied into Register 3, and then instruction 5 adds one to that value. Therefore, Register 3 could have any value that's 1 or greater. You can see this in the state information for Register 3, which has umin_value set to 1, and a umax_value of 0xFFFFFFFF.

The verifier uses the information about not just the states of each register, but also the range of values each can contain, to determine the possible paths through the program. This is also used for the state pruning that I mentioned before: if the verifier has been in the same position in the code, with the same types and possible ranges of values for each register, there's no need to evaluate this path further. What's more, if the current state is a subset of a state that was seen earlier, it can also be pruned.

Visualizing Control Flow

The verifier explores all the possible paths through the eBPF program, and if you're trying to debug an issue, it can be helpful to see those paths for yourself. The bpftool utility can help with this by producing a control flow graph of the program in DOT format (*https://oreil.ly/V-1WN*), which you can then convert into an image format, like this:

```
$ bpftool prog dump xlated name kprobe_exec visual > out.dot
$ dot -Tpng out.dot > out.png
```

This produces a visual representation of the control flow like that shown in Figure 6-1.

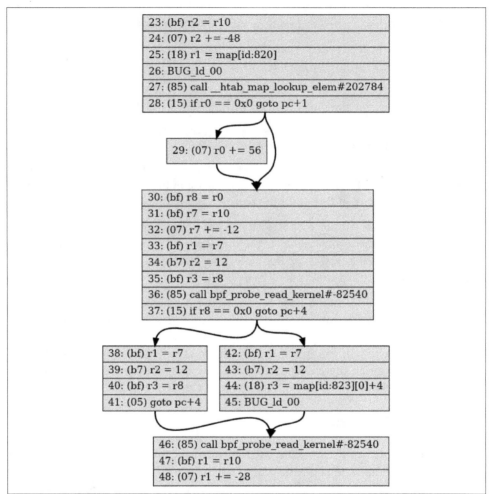

Figure 6-1. Extract from control flow graph (the full image can be found as chapter6/kprobe_exec.png in the GitHub repo for this book)

Validating Helper Functions

You're not allowed to call directly from eBPF programs to any kernel function (unless it has been registered as a kfunc, which you'll meet in the next chapter), but eBPF provides a number of helper functions that enable programs to access information from the kernel. There's a bpf-helpers manpage (*https://oreil.ly/pdLGW*) that attempts to document them all.

Different helper functions are valid for different BPF program types. For example, the helper function `bpf_get_current_pid_tgid()` retrieves the current user space process ID and thread ID, but it doesn't make sense to call this from an XDP program that is triggered by the receipt of a packet at a network interface, because there is no user space process involved. You can see an example of this by changing the SEC() definition for the *hello* eBPF program in *hello-verifier.bpf.c* from kprobe to xdp. On attempting to load this program the verifier output gives the following message:

```
...
16: (85) call bpf_get_current_pid_tgid#14
unknown func bpf_get_current_pid_tgid#14
```

The `unknown func` doesn't mean the function is completely unknown, just that it is unknown *for this BPF program type*. (BPF program types are a topic for the next chapter; for now you can just think of them as being programs that are suitable for attaching to different types of event.)

Helper Function Arguments

If you look, for example, in *kernel/bpf/helpers.c* (*https://oreil.ly/tjjVR*),[2] you'll find that each helper function has a `bpf_func_proto` structure similar to this example for the helper function `bpf_map_lookup_elem()`:

```
const struct bpf_func_proto bpf_map_lookup_elem_proto = {
    .func       = bpf_map_lookup_elem,
    .gpl_only = false,
    .pkt_access       = true,
    .ret_type = RET_PTR_TO_MAP_VALUE_OR_NULL,
    .arg1_type = ARG_CONST_MAP_PTR,
    .arg2_type = ARG_PTR_TO_MAP_KEY,
};
```

This structure defines the constraints for arguments to and return values from the helper function. Because the verifier is keeping track of the type of value held in each register, it can spot if you try to pass the wrong kind of argument to a helper function. For example, try changing the argument to the call to `bpf_map_lookup_elem()` in the *hello* program, like this:

```
p = bpf_map_lookup_elem(&data, &uid);
```

Instead of passing `&my_config`, which is a pointer to a map, this now passes `&data`, which is a pointer to a local variable structure. This is valid from the compiler's point of view, so you can build the BPF object file *hello-verifier.bpf.o*, but when you try to load the program into the kernel, you'll see an error like this in the verifier log:

---

2 Helper functions are also defined in some other places in the source code, for example, *kernel/trace/bpf_trace.c* (*https://oreil.ly/cY8y9*) and *net/core/filter.c* (*https://oreil.ly/qww-b*).

```
27: (85) call bpf_map_lookup_elem#1
R1 type=fp expected=map_ptr
```

Here, `fp` stands for *frame pointer*, and it's the area of memory on the stack where local variables are stored. Register 1 was loaded with the address of the local variable called `data`, but the function expects a pointer to a map (as indicated by the `arg1_type` field in the `bpf_func_proto` structure shown earlier). By tracking the types of value stored in each register, the verifier was able to spot this discrepancy.

Checking the License

The verifier also checks that if you are using a BPF helper function that's licensed under GPL, your program also has a GPL-compatible license. The last line in the Chapter 6 example code *hello-verifier.bpf.c* defines a "license" section that holds the string `Dual BSD/GPL`. If you remove this line, the output from the verifier will end like this:

```
...
37: (85) call bpf_probe_read_kernel#113
cannot call GPL-restricted function from non-GPL compatible program
```

That's because the `gpl_only` field is set to `true` for the `bpf_probe_read_kernel()` helper function. There are other helper functions called earlier in this eBPF program, but they are not GPL licensed, so the verifier doesn't object to their use.

The BCC project maintains a list of helper functions (*https://oreil.ly/mCpvB*), indicating whether they are GPL licensed or not. If you're interested in more details on how helper functions are implemented, there's a section on this in the BPF and XDP reference guide (*https://oreil.ly/kVd6j*).

Checking Memory Access

The verifier performs a number of checks to make sure BPF programs only access memory they are supposed to have access to.

For example, when processing a network packet, an XDP program is only permitted to access the memory locations that make up that network packet. Most XDP programs start with something very similar to the following:

```
SEC("xdp")
int xdp_load_balancer(struct xdp_md *ctx)
{
    void *data = (void *)(long)ctx->data;
    void *data_end = (void *)(long)ctx->data_end;
...
```

The `xdp_md` structure passed as the context to the program describes the network packet that has been received. The `ctx->data` field within that structure is the location in memory where the packet starts, and ctx->data_end is the last location in the packet. The verifier will ensure that the program doesn't exceed these bounds.

For example, the following program in *hello_verifier.bpf.c* is valid:

```
SEC("xdp")
int xdp_hello(struct xdp_md *ctx) {
    void *data = (void *)(long)ctx->data;
    void *data_end = (void *)(long)ctx->data_end;
    bpf_printk("%x", data_end);
    return XDP_PASS;
}
```

The variables data and data_end are very similar, but the verifier is smart enough to recognize that data_end relates to the end of a packet. Your program is required to check that any values read from the packet aren't from beyond that location, and it won't let you "cheat" by modifying the data_end value. Try adding the following line just before the bpf_printk() call:

```
data_end++;
```

The verifier will complain, like this:

```
; data_end++;
1: (07) r3 += 1
R3 pointer arithmetic on pkt_end prohibited
```

In another example, when accessing an array you need to make sure there's no possibility of accessing an index that is beyond the bounds of that array. In the example code there is a section that reads a character out of the message array, like this:

```
if (c < sizeof(message)) {
    char a = message[c];
    bpf_printk("%c", a);
}
```

This is fine because of the explicit check to ensure that the counter variable c is no bigger than the size of the message array. Making a simple "off by one" error like the following renders it invalid:

```
if (c <= sizeof(message)) {
    char a = message[c];
    bpf_printk("%c", a);
}
```

The verifier will fail this with an error message similar to this:

```
invalid access to map value, value_size=16 off=16 size=1
R2 max value is outside of the allowed memory range
```

It's fairly clear from this message that there is an invalid access to a map value because Register 2 might hold a value that's too large for indexing the map. If you were debugging this error, you'd want to dig into the log to see what line in the source code was responsible. The log ends like this just before emitting the error message (I have removed some of the state information for clarity):

```
; if (c <= sizeof(message)) {
30: (25) if r1 > 0xc goto pc+10                                           ❸
  R0_w=map_value_or_null(id=2,off=0,ks=4,vs=12,imm=0) R1_w=inv(id=0,
  umax_value=12,var_off=(0x0; 0xf)) R6=ctx(id=0,off=0,imm=0) ...
; char a = message[c];
31: (18) r2 = 0xffff800008e00004                                         ❷
33: (0f) r2 += r1
last_idx 33 first_idx 19
regs=2 stack=0 before 31: (18) r2 = 0xffff800008e00004
regs=2 stack=0 before 30: (25) if r1 > 0xc goto pc+10
regs=2 stack=0 before 29: (61) r1 = *(u32 *)(r8 +0)
34: (71) r3 = *(u8 *)(r2 +0)                                             ❶
  R0_w=map_value_or_null(id=2,off=0,ks=4,vs=12,imm=0) R1_w=invP(id=0,
  umax_value=12,var_off=(0x0; 0xf)) R2_w=map_value(id=0,off=4,ks=4,vs=16,
  umax_value=12,var_off=(0x0; 0xf),s32_max_value=15,u32_max_value=15)
  R6=ctx(id=0,off=0,imm=0) ...
```

❶ Working backward from the error, the last register state information shows that Register 2 could have a maximum value of 12.

❷ At instruction 31, Register 2 is set to an address in memory and then is incremented by the value of Register 1. The output shows that this corresponds to the line of code accessing message[c], so it stands to reason that Register 2 is set to point to the message array and then to be incremented by the value of c, which is held in the Register 1 register.

❸ Working further back to find the value of Register 1, the log shows that it has a maximum value of 12 (which is hex 0x0c). However, message is defined as a 12-byte character array, so only indexes 0 through 11 are within its bounds. From this, you can see that the error springs from the source code testing for c <= sizeof(message).

At step 2, I have inferred the relationship between some registers and the source code variables they represent, from the lines of source code the verifier has helpfully included in the log. You could work back through the verifier log to check that this is true, and indeed you might have to if the code was compiled without debug information. Given the debug information is present, it makes sense to use it.

The message array is declared as a global variable, and you might recall from Chapter 3 that global variables are implemented using maps. This explains why the error message talks about "invalid access to a map value."

Checking Pointers Before Dereferencing Them

One easy way to make a C program crash is to dereference a pointer when the pointer has a zero value (also known as *null*). Pointers indicate where in memory a value is being held, and zero is not a valid memory location. The eBPF verifier requires all pointers to be checked before they are dereferenced so that this type of crash can't happen.

The example code in *hello-verifier.bpf.c* looks for a custom message that might exist in the my_config hash table map for a user, with the following line:

```
p = bpf_map_lookup_elem(&my_config, &uid);
```

If there's no entry in this map corresponding to uid, this will set p (which is a pointer to the message structure msg_t) to zero. Here's a little bit of additional code that attempts to dereference this potentially null pointer:

```
char a = p->message[0];
bpf_printk("%c", a);
```

This compiles fine, but the verifier rejects it as follows:

```
; p = bpf_map_lookup_elem(&my_config, &uid);
25: (18) r1 = 0xffff263ec2fe5000
27: (85) call bpf_map_lookup_elem#1
28: (bf) r7 = r0                              ❶
; char a = p->message[0];
29: (71) r3 = *(u8 *)(r7 +0)                  ❷
R7 invalid mem access 'map_value_or_null'
```

 The return value from a helper function call gets stored in Register 0. Here, that value is being stored in Register 7. This means Register 7 now holds the value of the local variable p.

 This instruction attempts to dereference the pointer value p. The verifier has been keeping track of the state of Register 7 and knows that it may hold a pointer to a map value, or it might be null.

The verifier rejects this attempt to dereference a null pointer, but the program will pass if there is an explicit check, like this:

```
if (p != 0) {
    char a = p->message[0];
    bpf_printk("%d", cc);
}
```

Some helper functions incorporate the pointer check for you. For example, if you look at the manpage for bpf-helpers, you'll find the function signature for `bpf_probe_read_kernel()` is as follows:

```
long bpf_probe_read_kernel(void *dst, u32 size, const void *unsafe_ptr)
```

The third argument to this function is called `unsafe_ptr`. This is an example of a BPF helper function that helps programmers write safe code by handling checks for you. You're allowed to pass a potentially null pointer—but only as the third argument called `unsafe_ptr`—and the helper function will check that it's not null before attempting to deference it.

Accessing Context

Every eBPF program is passed some context information as an argument, but depending on the program and attachment type, it may be allowed to access only some of that context information. For example, tracepoint programs (*https://oreil.ly/6RFFI*) receive a pointer to some tracepoint data. The format of that data depends on the particular tracepoint, but they all start with some common fields—yet those common fields are not accessible to eBPF programs. Only the tracepoint-specific fields that follow can be accessed. Attempting to read or write the wrong fields leads to an `invalid bpf_context access` error. There is an example of this in the exercises at the end of this chapter.

Running to Completion

The verifier ensures that the eBPF program will run to completion; otherwise, there is a risk that it might consume resources indefinitely. It does this by having a limit on the total number of instructions that it will process, which, as I mentioned earlier, is set at one million instructions at the time of this writing. That limit is hard-coded into the kernel (*https://oreil.ly/IucYm*); it's not a configurable option. If the verifier hasn't reached the end of the BPF program before it has processed this many instructions, it rejects the program.

One easy way to create a program that never completes is to write a loop that never ends. Let's see how loops can be created in eBPF programs.

Loops

To guarantee completion, until kernel version 5.3 there was a restriction on loops.[3] Looping through the same instructions requires a jump backward to earlier instructions, and it used to be the case that the verifier would not permit this. eBPF programmers worked around this by using the `#pragma unroll` compiler directive to tell the compiler to write out a set of identical (or very similar) bytecode instructions for each time around the loop. This saved the programmer typing in the same lines many times, but you would see repeated instructions in the emitted bytecode.

From version 5.3 onward the verifier follows branches backward as well as forward as part of its process of checking all the possible execution paths. This means it can accept some loops, provided the execution path remains within the limit of one million instructions.

You can see an example of a loop in the example *xdp_hello* program. A version of the loop that passes verification looks like this:

```
for (int i=0; i < 10; i++) {
    bpf_printk("Looping %d", i);
}
```

The (successful) verifier log will show that it has followed the execution path around this loop 10 times. In doing so, it doesn't hit the complexity limit of one million instructions. In the exercises for this chapter, there's another version of this loop that will hit that limit and will fail verification.

In version 5.17 a new helper function, `bpf_loop()`, was introduced that makes it much easier for the verifier not only to accept loops but also to do it in a much more efficient way. This helper takes the maximum number of iterations as its first argument, and it is also passed a function that is called for each iteration. The verifier only has to validate the BPF instructions in that function once, however many times it might be called. That function can return a nonzero value to indicate that there is no need to call it again, which is used to terminate a loop early once the desired result is achieved.

There's also a helper function `bpf_for_each_map_elem()` (*https://oreil.ly/Yg_oQ*) that calls a provided callback function for each item in a map.

---

3 This release brought a number of significant optimizations and improvements to the BPF verifier, which are summarized nicely in the LWN article "Bounded loops in BPF for the 5.3 kernel" (*https://oreil.ly/50BoD*).

Checking the Return Code

The return code from an eBPF program is stored in Register 0 (R0). If the program leaves R0 uninitialized, the verifier will fail, like this:

```
R0 !read_ok
```

You can try this by commenting out all the code in a function; for example, modify the xdp_hello example to be like this:

```
SEC("xdp")
int xdp_hello(struct xdp_md *ctx) {
 void *data = (void *)(long)ctx->data;
 void *data_end = (void *)(long)ctx->data_end;

 // bpf_printk("%x", data_end);
 // return XDP_PASS;
}
```

This will fail the verifier. However, if you put the line with the helper function bpf_printf() back in, the verifier won't complain, even though there's no explicit return value set by the source code!

This is because Register 0 is also used to hold the return code from a helper function. After returning from a helper function in an eBPF program, Register 0 is no longer uninitialized.

Invalid Instructions

As you know from the discussion of the eBPF (virtual) machine in Chapter 3, eBPF programs consist of a set of bytecode instructions. The verifier checks that the instructions in a program are valid bytecode instructions—for example, using only known opcodes.

It would be considered a bug in the compiler if it emitted invalid bytecode, so you're not likely to see this kind of verifier error unless you choose (for some reason best known to yourself) to write eBPF bytecode by hand. However, there have been some instructions added more recently, such as the atomic operations. If your compiled bytecode uses these instructions, they would fail verification on an older kernel.

Unreachable Instructions

The verifier also rejects programs that have unreachable instructions. Oftentimes, these will get optimized out by the compiler anyway.

Summary

When I first got interested in eBPF, getting code through the verifier seemed like a dark art, where seemingly valid code would get rejected, throwing up what seemed to be arbitrary errors. Over time there have been *lots* of improvements to the verifier, and in this chapter you've seen several examples where the verifier log gives hints to help you figure out what the problem is.

These hints are more helpful when you have a mental model of how the eBPF (virtual) machine works, using a set of registers for temporary value storage as it steps through an eBPF program. The verifier keeps track of the types and possible range of values for each register to ensure that eBPF programs are safe to run.

If you try writing some eBPF code of your own, you might find yourself needing assistance to resolve verifier errors. The eBPF community Slack channel (*http://ebpf.io/slack*) is a good place to ask for help, and lots of people have also found advice on StackOverflow (*https://oreil.ly/nu_0v*).

Exercises

Here are some more ways to cause a verifier error. See if you can correlate the verifier log output to the errors you get:

1. In "Checking Memory Access" on page 116, you saw the verifier rejecting access beyond the end of the global `message` array. In the example code there's a section that accesses the local variable `data.message` in a similar way:

   ```
   if (c < sizeof(data.message)) {
       char a = data.message[c];
       bpf_printk("%c", a);
   }
   ```

   Try adjusting the code to make the same out-by-one mistake by replacing the `<` with `<=`, and you'll see an error message about `invalid variable-offset read from stack R2`.

2. Find the commented-out loops in *xdp_hello* in the example code. Try adding in the first loop that looks like this:

   ```
   for (int i=0; i < 10; i++) {
       bpf_printk("Looping %d", i);
   }
   ```

   You should see in the verifier log a repeated series of lines that look something like this:

   ```
   42: (18) r1 = 0xffff800008e10009
   44: (b7) r2 = 11
   45: (b7) r3 = 8
   ```

```
46: (85) call bpf_trace_printk#6
 R0=inv(id=0) R1_w=map_value(id=0,off=9,ks=4,vs=26,imm=0) R2_w=inv11
 R3_w=inv8 R6=pkt_end(id=0,off=0,imm=0) R7=pkt(id=0,off=0,r=0,imm=0)
 R10=fp0
last_idx 46 first_idx 42
regs=4 stack=0 before 45: (b7) r3 = 8
regs=4 stack=0 before 44: (b7) r2 = 11
```

From the log, work out which register is tracking the loop variable i.

3. Now try adding in a loop that will fail, which looks like this:

```
for (int i=0; i < c; i++) {
    bpf_printk("Looping %d", i);
}
```

You should see that the verifier tries to explore this loop to its conclusion, but it reaches the instruction complexity limit before it completes (because there is no upper bound on the global variable c).

4. Write a program that attaches to a tracepoint. (You may have done this already for the exercises in Chapter 4.) Looking ahead to "Tracepoints" on page 131, you can see a structure definition for the context argument that starts with these fields:

```
unsigned short common_type;
unsigned char common_flags;
unsigned char common_preempt_count;
int common_pid;
```

Create your own version of a structure that starts like this, and make the context argument in your program a pointer to this structure. In the program, try accessing any of these fields and see that the verifier fails with invalid bpf_context access.

CHAPTER 7

eBPF Program and Attachment Types

In the preceding chapters you saw lots of examples of eBPF programs, and you probably spotted the fact that they are attached to different types of events. Some of the
examples I've shown attach to kprobes, but in other examples I've demonstrated XDP
programs that handle a newly arrived network packet. These are just two of the many
attachment points within the kernel. In this chapter we'll take a deeper look at different program types and how they can be attached to different events.

> You can build and run the examples from this chapter using the
> code and instructions at *github.com/lizrice/learning-ebpf*. The code
> for this chapter is in the *chapter7* directory.
>
> At the time of this writing, some of the examples are not supported
> on ARM processors. Check out the *README* file in the *chapter7*
> directory for more details and advice.

There are currently around 30 program types enumerated in *uapi/linux/bpf.h* (*https://
oreil.ly/6dNIW*), and more than 40 attachment types. The attachment type defines
more specifically where the program gets attached; for lots of program types, the
attachment type can be inferred from the program type, but some program types can
be attached to multiple different points in the kernel, so an attachment type has to be
specified as well.

As you know, this book isn't intended to be a reference manual, so I won't cover every
single eBPF program type. There's a good chance that new types will have been added
by the time you read this book anyway!

Program Context Arguments

All eBPF programs take a context argument that is a pointer, but the structure it points to depends on the type of event that triggered it. eBPF programmers need to write programs that accept the appropriate type of context; there is no point in pretending that the context argument points to a network packet if the event is, say, a tracepoint. Defining different types of programs allows the verifier to ensure that the contextual information is handled appropriately and to enforce rules about what helper functions are permissible.

 To dive into the details of the context data passed to different BPF program types, check out this post by Alan Maguire on Oracle's blog (*https://oreil.ly/6dNIW*).

Helper Functions and Return Codes

As you saw in the previous chapter, the verifier checks that all helper functions used by a program are compatible with its program type. The example in the previous chapter demonstrated that the `bpf_get_current_pid_tgid()` helper function isn't permitted in an XDP program. There is no user space process or thread involved at the point where a packet is received and the XDP hook is triggered, so a call to discover the current process and thread ID doesn't make sense in that context.

The program type also determines the meaning of the return code from the program. Again using XDP as an example, the return code value tells the kernel what to do with the packet once the eBPF program has finished processing it—which could involve passing it to the network stack, dropping it, or redirecting it to a different interface. These return codes wouldn't make any sense when an eBPF program is triggered by, say, hitting a particular tracepoint, where there is no network packet involved.

There is a manpage for helper functions (*https://oreil.ly/e8K73*) (with, quite reasonably, disclaimers that it might not be complete due to the ongoing development of the BPF subsystem).

You can get a list of which helper functions are available for each program type in your version of the kernel with the `bpftool feature` command. This shows the system configuration and lists all the available program types and map types, and even lists all the helper functions that are supported for each program type.

Helper functions are considered part of the *UAPI*, the Linux kernel's external, stable interface. As such, once a helper function has been defined in the kernel, it shouldn't change in the future, even though the kernel's internal functions and data structures can change.

Despite the risk of changes between kernel versions, there was demand from eBPF programmers to be able to access some internal functions from eBPF programs. This can be achieved using the mechanism called *BPF kernel functions*, or *kfuncs* (*https://oreil.ly/gKSEx*).

Kfuncs

Kfuncs allow internal kernel functions to be registered with the BPF subsystem so that the verifier will allow them to be called from eBPF programs. There is a registration for each eBPF program type that is permitted to call a given kfunc.

Unlike helper functions, kfuncs don't provide compatibility guarantees, so an eBPF programmer has to consider the possibility of changes between kernel versions.

There is a set of "core" BPF kfuncs (*https://oreil.ly/06qoi*), which at the time of this writing consists of functions that allow eBPF programs to obtain and release kernel references to tasks and cgroups.

To recap, the type of an eBPF program determines what events it can be attached to, which in turn defines the type of context information it receives. The program type also defines the set of helper functions and kfuncs it can call.

Program types are broadly considered to fall into two categories: tracing (or perf) program types and networking-related program types. Let's look at some examples.

Tracing

Programs that attach to kprobes, tracepoints, raw tracepoints, fentry/fexit probes, and perf events were all designed to provide an efficient way for eBPF programs in the kernel to report tracing information about events into user space. These tracing-related types weren't expected to influence the way the kernel behaves in response to the events they are attached to (although, as you'll see in Chapter 9, there have been some innovations in this area!).

These are sometimes referred to as "perf-related" programs. For example, the `bpftool perf` subcommand lets you view programs attached to perf-related events like this:

```
$ sudo bpftool perf show
pid 232272  fd 16: prog_id 392  kprobe  func __x64_sys_execve  offset 0
pid 232272  fd 17: prog_id 394  kprobe  func do_execve  offset 0
pid 232272  fd 19: prog_id 396  tracepoint  sys_enter_execve
pid 232272  fd 20: prog_id 397  raw_tracepoint  sched_process_exec
pid 232272  fd 21: prog_id 398  raw_tracepoint  sched_process_exec
```

The preceding output is what I see when running example code from the *hello.bpf.c* file in the *chapter7* directory, which attaches different programs to a variety of events that are all related to execve(). I'll discuss all of these types in this section, but as an overview, these programs are:

- A kprobe attached to the entry point to the execve() system call.
- A kprobe attached to a kernel function, do_execve().
- A tracepoint placed at the entry to the execve() syscall.
- Two versions of a raw tracepoint called during the processing of execve(). One of these, as you'll see in this section, is a BTF-enabled version.

You'll need CAP_PERFMON and CAP_BPF or CAP_SYS_ADMIN capabilities to use any of the tracing-related eBPF program types.

Kprobes and Kretprobes

I discussed the concept of kprobes in Chapter 1. You can attach kprobe programs almost anywhere in the kernel.[1] Commonly, they are attached using kprobes to the entry to a function and kretprobes to the exit of a function, but you can use kprobes to attach to an instruction that is some specified offset after the entry to the function. If you choose to do this,[2] you'd need to be confident that the kernel version you're running on has the instruction you want to attach to where you think it is! Attaching to kernel function entry and exit points can be relatively stable, but arbitrary lines of code might easily be modified from one release to the next.

 In the example output from bpftool perf list, you can see that there is an offset of 0 for both of the kprobes.

When the kernel is compiled, there's also the possibility that the compiler chooses to "inline" any given kernel function; that is, rather than jump from where the function is called, the compiler might emit the machine code to implement whatever the function does within the calling functions. If a function happens to get inlined, there won't be a kprobe entry point for your eBPF program to attach to.

---

[1] Except for a few parts of the kernel where kprobes aren't permitted for security reasons. These are listed in /sys/kernel/debug/kprobes/blacklist.

[2] The only example I have seen so far is in the cilium/ebpf test suite (*https://oreil.ly/rL5E8*).

Attaching kprobes to syscall entry points

The first example eBPF program for this chapter is called `kprobe_sys_execve`, and it is a kprobe attached to the `execve()` syscall. The function and its section definition look like this:

```
SEC("ksyscall/execve")
int BPF_KPROBE_SYSCALL(kprobe_sys_execve, char *pathname)
```

This is the same as what you saw in Chapter 5.

One reason to attach to syscalls is that they are stable interfaces that won't change between kernel versions (the same is true of tracepoints, which we'll come to shortly). However, syscall kprobes shouldn't be relied on for security tooling, for reasons I'll cover in detail in Chapter 9.

Attaching kprobes to other kernel functions

You can find lots of examples where eBPF-based tools use kprobes to attach to system calls, but, as mentioned earlier, kprobes can also be attached to any noninlined function in the kernel. I've provided an example in *hello.bpf.c* that attaches a kprobe to the function `do_execve()`, and it's defined like this:

```
SEC("kprobe/do_execve")
int BPF_KPROBE(kprobe_do_execve, struct filename *filename)
```

Because `do_execve()` isn't a system call, there are a few differences between this and the previous example:

- The format of the SEC name is identical to the previous version attached to the syscall entry point, but there is no need to define platform-specific variants because `do_execve()`, like most kernel functions, is common to all platforms.

- I used the `BPF_KPROBE` macro rather than `BPF_KPROBE_SYSCALL`. The intent is exactly the same, just that the latter handles syscall parameters.

- There is another important difference: the `pathname` parameter to the syscall is a pointer to a string (`char *`), but for this function the parameter is called `file name`, and it's a pointer to a `struct filename`, which is a data structure used within the kernel.

You might well be wondering how I knew to use this type for this parameter. I'll show you. The `do_execve()` function in the kernel has the following signature:

```
int do_execve(struct filename *filename,
    const char __user *const __user *__argv,
    const char __user *const __user *__envp)
```

I chose to ignore the `do_execve()` parameters `__argv` and `__envp`, and only declare the `filename` argument, using the type `struct filename *` to match the kernel function's definition. Given the way arguments are laid out sequentially in memory, it's OK to ignore the last *n* parameters, but you can't ignore an earlier argument in the list if you want to use a later one.

This `filename` structure is defined internal to the kernel, and it's an illustration of how eBPF programming is kernel programming: I had to look up the definition of `do_execve()` to find its arguments, and the definition of `struct filename`. The name of the executable that is about to be run is pointed to by `filename->name`. I'm retrieving this name in the example code with the following lines:

```
const char *name = BPF_CORE_READ(filename, name);
bpf_probe_read_kernel(&data.command, sizeof(data.command), name);
```

So to recap: the context parameter to a syscall kprobe is a structure representing the values passed by user space into the syscall. The context parameter to a "regular" (nonsyscall) kprobe is a structure representing the parameters passed to the called function by whatever kernel code is calling it, so the structure depends on the function definition.

Kretprobes are very similar to kprobes, except that they are triggered when a function returns and can access the return value instead of the arguments.

Kprobes and kretprobes are a reasonable way to hook into kernel functions, but there's a newer option you should consider if you're running on recent kernels.

Fentry/Fexit

A more efficient mechanism for tracing the entry to and exit from kernel functions was introduced along with the idea of *BPF trampoline* in kernel version 5.5 (on x86 processors; BPF trampoline support doesn't arrive for ARM processors until Linux 6.0 (*https://oreil.ly/ccuz1*)). If you're using a recent enough kernel, fentry/fexit is now the preferred method for tracing the entry to or exit from a kernel function. You can write the same code inside a kprobe or fentry type program.

There's an example fentry program called `fentry_execve()` in *chapter7/hello.bpf.c*. I declared the eBPF program for this kprobe using *libbpf*'s macro `BPF_PROG`, which is another convenient wrapper giving access to typed parameters rather than the generic context pointer, but this version is used for fentry, fexit, and tracepoint program types. The definition looks like this:

```
SEC("fentry/do_execve")
int BPF_PROG(fentry_execve, struct filename *filename)
```

The section name tells *libbpf* to attach to the fentry hook at the start of the do_execve() kernel function. Just as in the kprobe example, the context parameters reflect the parameters passed to the kernel function where you want to attach this eBPF program.

Fentry and fexit attachment points were designed to be more efficient than kprobes, but there's another advantage when you want to generate an event at the end of a function: the fexit hook has access to the input parameters to the function, which kretprobe does not. You can see an example of this in *libbpf-bootstrap*'s examples (*https://oreil.ly/6HDh_*). Both *kprobe.bpf.c* and *fentry.bpf.c* are equivalent examples that hook into the do_unlinkat() kernel function. The eBPF program attached to the kretprobe has the following signature:

```
SEC("kretprobe/do_unlinkat")
int BPF_KRETPROBE(do_unlinkat_exit, long ret)
```

The BPF_KRETPROBE macro expands to make this a kretprobe program on exit from do_unlinkat(). The only parameter the eBPF program receives is ret, which holds the return value from do_unlinkat(). Compare this to the fexit version:

```
SEC("fexit/do_unlinkat")
int BPF_PROG(do_unlinkat_exit, int dfd, struct filename *name, long ret)
```

In this version the program gets access not just to the return value ret, but also to the input parameters to do_unlinkat(), which are dfd and name.

Tracepoints

Tracepoints (*https://oreil.ly/yXk_L*) are marked locations in the kernel code (we'll come to user space tracepoints later in this chapter). They're not by any means exclusive to eBPF and have long been used to generate kernel trace output and by tools like SystemTap (*https://oreil.ly/bLmQL*). Unlike attaching to arbitrary instructions using kprobes, tracepoints are stable between kernel releases (although an older kernel might not have the full set of tracepoints that have been added into a newer one).

You can see the available set of tracing subsystems on your kernel by looking at */sys/kernel/tracing/available_events*, as follows:

```
$ cat /sys/kernel/tracing/available_events
tls:tls_device_offload_set
tls:tls_device_decrypted
...
syscalls:sys_exit_execveat
syscalls:sys_enter_execveat
syscalls:sys_exit_execve
syscalls:sys_enter_execve
...
```

My 5.15 version of the kernel has more than 1,400 tracepoints defined in this list. The section definition for a tracepoint eBPF program should match one of these items so that *libbpf* can automatically attach it to the tracepoint. The definition is in the form SEC("tp/tracing subsystem/tracepoint name").

You'll find an example in the *chapter7/hello.bpf.c* files that matches the sys calls:sys_enter_execve tracepoint that gets hit when the kernel starts processing an execve() call. The section definition tells *libbpf* that this is a tracepoint program, and where it should be attached, like this:

```
SEC("tp/syscalls/sys_enter_execve")
```

What about the context parameter to a tracepoint? As I'll come to shortly, BTF can help us here, but first let's consider what is needed when BTF isn't available. Each tracepoint has a format describing the fields that get traced out from it. As an example, here's the format for the tracepoint at the entry to the execve() syscall:

```
$ cat /sys/kernel/tracing/events/syscalls/sys_enter_execve/format
name: sys_enter_execve
ID: 622
format:
    field:unsigned short common_type;        offset:0;   size:2; signed:0;
    field:unsigned char common_flags;        offset:2;   size:1; signed:0;
    field:unsigned char common_preempt_count; offset:3;  size:1; signed:0;
    field:int common_pid;                    offset:4;   size:4; signed:1;

    field:int __syscall_nr;                  offset:8;   size:4; signed:1;
    field:const char * filename;             offset:16;  size:8; signed:0;
    field:const char *const * argv;          offset:24;  size:8; signed:0;
    field:const char *const * envp;          offset:32;  size:8; signed:0;

print fmt: "filename: 0x%08lx, argv: 0x%08lx, envp: 0x%08lx",
((unsigned long)(REC->filename)), ((unsigned long)(REC->argv)),
((unsigned long)(REC->envp))
```

I used this information to define a matching structure called my_syscalls_enter_execve in *chapter7/hello.bpf.c*:

```
struct my_syscalls_enter_execve {
    unsigned short common_type;
    unsigned char common_flags;
    unsigned char common_preempt_count;
    int common_pid;

    long syscall_nr;
    long filename_ptr;
    long argv_ptr;
    long envp_ptr;
};
```

eBPF programs aren't allowed to access the first four of these fields. If you try to access them, the program will fail verification with an invalid bpf_context access error.

My example eBPF program that attaches to this tracepoint can use a pointer to this type as its context parameter, like this:

```
int tp_sys_enter_execve(struct my_syscalls_enter_execve *ctx) {
```

Then you can access the contents of this structure. For example, you can get the file-name pointer as follows:

```
bpf_probe_read_user_str(&data.command, sizeof(data.command), ctx->filename_ptr);
```

When you use a tracepoint program type, the structure passed to the eBPF program has already been mapped from a set of raw arguments. For better performance, you can directly access these raw arguments with a raw tracepoint eBPF program type. The section definition should start with raw_tp (or raw_tracepoint) instead of tp. You'll need to convert the arguments from __u64 to whatever type the tracepoint structure uses (when the tracepoint is the entry to a system call, these arguments are dependent on the chip architecture).

BTF-Enabled Tracepoints

In the previous example I wrote a structure called my_syscalls_enter_execve to define the context parameter for my eBPF program. But when you define a structure in your eBPF code or parse the raw arguments, there's a risk that your code might not match the kernel it's running on. The good news is that BTF, which you met in Chapter 5, also solves this problem.

With BTF support, there will be a structure defined in *vmlinux.h* that matches the context structure passed to a tracepoint eBPF program. Your eBPF program should use the section definition SEC("tp_btf/*tracepoint name*") where the tracepoint name is one of the available events listed in */sys/kernel/tracing/available_events*. The example program in *chapter7/hello.bpf.c* looks like this:

```
SEC("tp_btf/sched_process_exec")
int handle_exec(struct trace_event_raw_sched_process_exec *ctx)
```

As you can see, the structure name matches the tracepoint name, prefixed with trace_event_raw_.

User Space Attachments

So far I have shown examples of eBPF programs attaching to events defined within the kernel's source code. There are similar attachment points within user space code: uprobes and uretprobes for attaching to the entry and exit of user space functions, and user statically defined tracepoints (USDTs) for attaching to specified tracepoints within application code or user space libraries. These all use the BPF_PROG_TYPE_KPROBE program type.

There are lots of public examples of programs attached to user space events. Here are a few from the BCC project:

- The bashreadline (*https://oreil.ly/gDkaQ*) and funclatency tools (*https://oreil.ly/zLT54*) attach to u(ret)probe.
- USDT sample (*https://oreil.ly/o894f*) in BCC.

If you're using *libbpf*, the SEC() macro lets you define the auto-attachment point for these user space probes. You'll find the format required for the section name in the *libbpf* documentation (*https://oreil.ly/o0CBQ*). For example, to attach a uprobe to the start of the SSL_write() function in OpenSSL, you would define the section for the eBPF program with the following:

```
SEC("uprobe/usr/lib/aarch64-linux-gnu/libssl.so.3/SSL_write")
```

There are a few gotchas to be aware of when instrumenting user space code:

- Notice that the path to this shared library in this example is architecture specific, so you may need corresponding architecture-specific definitions.
- Unless you control the machine you're running the code on, you can't know what user space libraries and applications will be installed.
- An application might be built as a standalone binary, so it won't hit any probes you might attach within shared libraries.
- Containers typically run with their own copy of a filesystem, with their own set of dependencies installed in it. The path to a shared library used by a container won't be the same as the path to a shared library on the host machine.
- Your eBPF program might need to be aware of the language in which an application was written. For example, in C the arguments to a function are generally passed using registers, but in Go they are passed using the stack,[3] so the pt_args structure holding register information may be of less use.

That said, there are lots of useful tools that instrument user space applications with eBPF. For example, you can hook into the SSL library to trace out decrypted versions of encrypted information—we'll explore this in more detail in the next chapter. Another example is continuous profiling of your applications, using tools such as Parca (*https://www.parca.dev*).

---

3 Up to Go version 1.17, when a new register-based calling convention was introduced. Nevertheless, I think there will be Go executables built with older versions circulating for some time to come.

LSM

BPF_PROG_TYPE_LSM programs are attached to the *Linux Security Module (LSM) API*, which is a stable interface within the kernel originally intended for kernel modules to use to enforce security policies. As you'll see in Chapter 9, where I'll discuss this in more detail, eBPF security tooling can now use this interface too.

BPF_PROG_TYPE_LSM programs are attached using bpf(BPF_RAW_TRACEPOINT_OPEN), and in many ways they are treated like tracing programs. One interesting characteristic of BPF_PROG_TYPE_LSM programs is that the return value affects the way the kernel behaves. A nonzero return code indicates that the security check wasn't passed, so the kernel won't proceed with whatever operation it was asked to complete. This is a significant difference from perf-related program types where the return code is ignored.

 The Linux kernel documentation covers LSM BPF programs (*https://oreil.ly/vcPHY*).

The LSM program type isn't the only one with a role to play in security. Many of the networking-related program types that you'll see in the next section can be used for network security to permit or deny networking traffic or networking-related operations. You'll also see more about eBPF being used for security purposes in Chapter 9.

So far in this chapter you have seen how a set of kernel and user space tracing program types enable visibility over the whole system. The next set of eBPF program types to consider are those that let us hook into the network stack, with the option not merely to observe but also to affect how it handles data being sent and received.

Networking

There are lots of different eBPF program types intended to process network messages as they pass through various points in the network stack. Figure 7-1 shows where some of the commonly used program types attach. These program types all require CAP_NET_ADMIN and CAP_BPF, or CAP_SYS_ADMIN, capabilities to be permitted.

The context passed to these types of programs is the network message in question, although the type of structure depends on the data the kernel has at the relevant point in the network stack. At the bottom of the stack, data is held in the form of Layer 2 network packets, which are essentially a series of bytes that have been or are ready to be transmitted "on the wire." At the top of the stack, applications use sockets, and the kernel creates socket buffers to handle data being sent and received from these sockets.

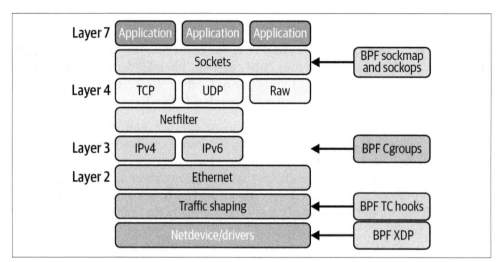

Figure 7-1. BPF program types hook into various points in the network stack

 The network layer model is beyond the scope of this book, but it's covered in many other books, posts, and training courses. I discussed it in Chapter 10 of *Container Security* (O'Reilly). For the purposes of this book, it's sufficient to know that Layer 7 covers formats intended for applications to use, such as HTTP, DNS, or gRPC; TCP is at Layer 4; IP is at Layer 3; and Ethernet and WiFi are at Layer 2. One of the roles of the networking stack is to convert messages between these different formats.

One big difference between the networking program types and the tracing-related types you saw earlier in this chapter is that they are generally intended to allow for the customization of networking behaviors. That involves two main characteristics:

1. Using a return code from the eBPF program to tell the kernel what to do with a network packet—which could involve processing it as usual, dropping it, or redirecting it to a different destination

2. Allowing the eBPF program to modify network packets, socket configuration parameters, and so on

You'll see some examples of how these characteristics are used to build powerful networking capabilities in the next chapter, but for now, here's an overview of the eBPF program types.

Sockets

At the top of the stack, a subset of these network-related program types relates to sockets and socket operations:

- `BPF_PROG_TYPE_SOCKET_FILTER` was the first program type to be added to the kernel. You probably guessed from the name that this is used for socket filtering, but what's less obvious is that this doesn't mean filtering data being sent to or from an application. It's used to filter a *copy* of socket data that can be sent to an observability tool such as tcpdump.

- A socket is specific to a Layer 4 (TCP) connection. `BPF_PROG_TYPE_SOCK_OPS` allows eBPF programs to intercept various operations and actions that take place on a socket, and to set for that socket parameters such as TCP timeout values. Sockets only exist at the endpoints for a connection, and not on any middleboxes that they might pass through.

- `BPF_PROG_TYPE_SK_SKB` programs are used in conjunction with a special map type that holds a set of references to sockets to provide what's known as *sockmap* operations (*https://oreil.ly/0Enuo*): redirecting traffic to different destinations at the socket layer.

Traffic Control

Further down the network stack comes "TC" or traffic control. There is a whole subsystem in the Linux kernel related to TC, and a glance at the manpage for the `tc` command (*https://oreil.ly/kfyg5*) will give you an idea of how complex it is and how important it is to computing in general to have deep levels of flexibility and configuration over the way network packets are handled.

eBPF programs can be attached to provide custom filters and classifiers for network packets for both ingress and egress traffic. This is one of the building blocks of the Cilium project, and I'll cover some examples in the next chapter. If you can't wait until then, there are some good examples on Quentin Monnet's blog (*https://oreil.ly/heQ2D*). This can be done programmatically, but you also have the option to use the `tc` command to manipulate these kinds of eBPF programs.

XDP

You briefly met XDP (eXpress Data Path) eBPF programs in Chapter 3. In that example I loaded the eBPF program and attached it to the `eth0` interface using the following commands:

```
bpftool prog load hello.bpf.o /sys/fs/bpf/hello
bpftool net attach xdp id 540 dev eth0
```

It's worth noting that XDP programs attach to a specific interface (or virtual interface), and you may very well have different XDP programs attached to different interfaces. In Chapter 8 you'll learn more about how XDP programs can be offloaded to network cards or executed by network drivers.

XDP programs are another example of programs that can be managed using Linux network utilities—in this case, the link subcommand of iproute2's ip (*https://oreil.ly/8Isau*). The roughly equivalent command for loading and attaching the program to eth0 would be this:

```
$ ip link set dev eth0 xdp obj hello.bpf.o sec xdp
```

This command reads the eBPF program marked as section xdp from the hello.bpf.o object and attaches it to the eth0 network interface. The ip link show command for this interface now includes some information about the XDP program that's attached to it:

```
2: eth0: <BROADCAST,MULTICAST,UP,LOWER_UP> mtu 1500 xdpgeneric qdisc fq_codel
state UP mode DEFAULT group default qlen 1000
    link/ether 52:55:55:3a:1b:a2 brd ff:ff:ff:ff:ff:ff
    prog/xdp id 1255 tag 9d0e949f89f1a82c jited
```

Removing the XDP program with ip link can be done like this:

```
$ ip link set dev eth0 xdp off
```

You'll see a lot more about XDP programs and their applications in the next chapter.

Flow Dissector

A flow dissector is used at various points in the network stack to extract details from a packet's headers. eBPF programs of type BPF_PROG_TYPE_FLOW_DISSECTOR can implement custom packet dissection. There's a nice write-up in this LWN article on writing network flow dissectors in BPF (*https://oreil.ly/nFKLV*).

Lightweight Tunnels

The family of BPF_PROG_TYPE_LWT_* program types can be used to implement network encapsulation in eBPF programs. These program types can also be manipulated using the ip command, but this time it's the route subcommand that's involved. In practice, these are used infrequently.

Cgroups

eBPF programs can be attached to cgroups (short for "control groups"). *Cgroups* are a concept in the Linux kernel that restricts the set of resources a given process or group of processes can have access to. Cgroups are one of the mechanisms that isolate one container (or one Kubernetes pod) from another. Attaching eBPF programs to a cgroup allows for custom behavior that only applies to that cgroup's processes. All processes are associated with a cgroup, including processes that are not running inside a container.

There are several cgroup-related program types, and even more hooks where they can be attached. At least at the time of this writing, they are nearly all networking related, although there is also a `BPF_CGROUP_SYSCTL` program type that can be attached to sysctl commands affecting a particular cgroup.

As an example, there are socket-related program types specific to cgroups `BPF_PROG_TYPE_CGROUP_SOCK` and `BPF_PROG_TYPE_CGROUP_SKB`. eBPF programs can determine whether a given cgroup is permitted to perform a requested socket operation or data transmission. This is useful for network security policy enforcement (which I'll cover in the next chapter). Socket programs can also trick the calling process into thinking they are connecting to a particular destination address.

Infrared Controllers

Programs of type BPF_PROG_TYPE_LIRC_MODE2 (*https://oreil.ly/AwG1C*) can be attached to the file descriptor for an infrared controller device to provide decoding for infrared protocols. At the time of this writing, this program type requires `CAP_NET_ADMIN`, but I think this illustrates that the division of program types into tracing related and networking related doesn't fully express the range of different applications that eBPF can address.

BPF Attachment Types

The attachment type offers more fine-grained control over where a program can be attached in the system. For some program types there is a one-to-one correlation to the type of hook that it can be attached to, so the attachment type is implicitly defined by the program type. For example, XDP programs are attached to XDP hooks in the network stack. For a few program types, an attachment type also has to be specified.

The attachment type is involved in deciding which helper functions are valid, and it also restricts access to parts of the context information in some cases. There was an example of this earlier in this chapter where the verifier gives an `invalid bpf_con text access` error.

You can also see which program types need an attachment type to be specified, and which attachment types are valid, in the kernel function bpf_prog_load_check_attach (*https://oreil.ly/0LqCQ*) (defined in *bpf/syscall.c* (*https://oreil.ly/7OrYS*)).

For example, here is the code that checks the attachment type for a program of type CGROUP_SOCK:

```
case BPF_PROG_TYPE_CGROUP_SOCK:
    switch (expected_attach_type) {
    case BPF_CGROUP_INET_SOCK_CREATE:
    case BPF_CGROUP_INET_SOCK_RELEASE:
    case BPF_CGROUP_INET4_POST_BIND:
    case BPF_CGROUP_INET6_POST_BIND:
        return 0;
    default:
        return -EINVAL;
    }
```

This program type can be attached in multiple places: at socket creation, at socket release, or after a bind is completed in IPv4 or IPv6.

Another place to find a listing of the valid attachment types for programs is the *libbpf* documentation (*https://oreil.ly/jraLh*), where you'll also find the section names that *libbpf* understands for each program and attachment type.

Summary

In this chapter you saw that various eBPF program types are used to attach into different hook points in the kernel. If you want to write code that responds to a particular event, you'll need to determine the program type(s) that are appropriate for hooking onto that event. The context passed into the program depends on the program type, and the kernel may also respond differently to the return code from your program, depending on its type.

The example code for this chapter mostly focused on perf-related (tracing) events. In the next two chapters you'll see more details on different eBPF program types used for networking and security applications.

Exercises

The example code for this chapter includes kprobe, fentry, tracepoint, raw tracepoint, and BTF-enabled tracepoint programs that are all attached to the entry to the same system call. As you know, eBPF tracing programs can be attached to many other places besides syscalls.

1. Run the example code using `strace` to capture the `bpf()` system calls, like this:

   ```
   strace -e bpf -o outfile ./hello
   ```

   This will record information about each `bpf()` syscall into a file called *outfile*. Look for the `BPF_PROG_LOAD` instructions in that file, and see how the `prog_type` file varies for different programs. You can identify which program is which by the prog_name field in the trace, and match them to the source code in *chapter7/ hello.bpf.c.*

2. The example user space code in *hello.c* loads all the program objects defined in hello.bpf.o. As an exercise in writing *libbpf* user space code, modify the example code load and attach just one of the eBPF programs (pick whichever one you like), without removing those programs from *hello.bpf.c.*

3. Write a kprobe and/or fentry program that is triggered when some other kernel function is called. You can find the available functions in your kernel version by looking at */proc/kallsyms.*

4. Write a regular, raw or BTF-enabled tracepoint program that attaches to some other kernel tracepoint. You can find the available tracepoints in /sys/kernel/ tracing/available_events.

5. Try to attach more than one XDP program to a given interface, and confirm that you can't! You should see an error that looks something like this:

```
libbpf: Kernel error message: XDP program already attached
Error: interface xdpgeneric attach failed: Device or resource busy
```

eBPF for Networking

As you saw in Chapter 1, the dynamic nature of eBPF allows us to customize the behavior of the kernel. In the world of networking, there is a huge range of desirable behavior that depends on the application. For example, a telecommunications operator might have to interface with telco-specific protocols like SRv6; a Kubernetes environment might need to be integrated with legacy applications; dedicated hardware load balancers can be replaced with XDP programs running on commodity hardware. eBPF allows programmers to build networking features to meet specific needs, without having to force them on all upstream kernel users.

Network tools based on eBPF are now widely used and have proven to be effective at prolific scale. The CNCF's Cilium project (*http://cilium.io*), for example, uses eBPF as a platform for Kubernetes networking, standalone load balancing, and much more, and it's used by cloud native adopters in every conceivable industry vertical.[1] Meta has been using eBPF at a vast scale—every packet to and from Facebook since 2017 has been through an XDP program. Another public and hyper-scaled example is Cloudflare's use of eBPF for DDoS (distributed denial-of-service) protection.

These are complex, production-ready solutions, and their details are far beyond the scope of this book, but by reading the examples in this chapter you can get a feel for how eBPF networking solutions like these are built.

---

1 At the time of this writing, around 100 organizations have publicly announced their use of Cilium in its *USERS.md* file (*https://oreil.ly/PC7-G*), though this number is growing quickly. Cilium has also been adopted by AWS, Google, and Microsoft.

The code examples for this chapter are in the *chapter8* directory of the repository at *github.com/lizrice/learning-ebpf*.

Packet Drops

There are several network security features that involve dropping certain incoming packets and allowing others. These features include firewalling, DDoS protection, and mitigating packet-of-death vulnerabilities:

- Firewalling involves deciding on a per-packet basis whether to allow a packet, based on the source and destination IP addresses and/or port numbers.

- DDoS protection adds some complexity, perhaps keeping track of the rate at which packets are arriving from a particular source and/or detecting certain characteristics of the packet contents to determine that an attacker or set of attackers is trying to flood the interface with traffic.

- A packet-of-death vulnerability is a class of kernel vulnerability in which the kernel fails to safely process a packet crafted in a particular way. An attacker who sends packets with this particular format can exploit the vulnerability, which could potentially cause the kernel to crash. Traditionally, when a kernel vulnerability like this is found, it requires installing a new kernel with the fix, which in turn requires machine downtime. But an eBPF program that detects and drops these malicious packets can be installed dynamically, instantly protecting that host without affecting any applications running on the machine.

The decision-making algorithms for features like these are beyond the scope of this book, but let's explore how eBPF programs attached to the XDP hook on a network interface drop certain packets, which is the basis for implementing these use cases.

XDP Program Return Codes

An XDP program is triggered by the arrival of a network packet. The program examines the packet, and when it's done, the return code gives a *verdict* that indicates what to do next with that packet:

- XDP_PASS indicates that the packet should be sent to the network stack in the normal way (as it would have done if there were no XDP program).

- XDP_DROP causes the packet to be discarded immediately.

- XDP_TX sends the packet back out of the same interface it arrived on.

- XDP_REDIRECT is used to send it to a different network interface.

- `XDP_ABORTED` results in the packet being dropped, but its use implies an error case or something unexpected, rather than a "normal" decision to discard a packet.

For some use cases (like firewalling), the XDP program simply has to decide between passing the packet on or dropping it. An outline for an XDP program that decides whether to drop packets looks something like this:

```
SEC("xdp")
int hello(struct xdp_md *ctx) {
    bool drop;

    drop = <examine packet and decide whether to drop it>;

    if (drop)
        return XDP_DROP;
    else
        return XDP_PASS;
}
```

An XDP program can also manipulate the packet contents, but I'll come to that later in this chapter.

XDP programs get triggered whenever an inbound network packet arrives on the interface to which it is attached. The `ctx` parameter is a pointer to an `xdp_md` structure, which holds metadata about the incoming packet. Let's see how you can use this structure to examine the packet's contents in order to reach a verdict.

XDP Packet Parsing

Here's the definition of the `xdp_md` structure:

```
struct xdp_md {
    __u32 data;
    __u32 data_end;
    __u32 data_meta;
    /* Below access go through struct xdp_rxq_info */
    __u32 ingress_ifindex; /* rxq->dev->ifindex */
    __u32 rx_queue_index;  /* rxq->queue_index  */

    __u32 egress_ifindex;  /* txq->dev->ifindex */
};
```

Don't be fooled by the `__u32` type for the first three fields, as they are really pointers. The `data` field indicates the location in memory where the packet starts, and `data_end` shows where it ends. As you saw in Chapter 6, to pass the eBPF verifier you will have to explicitly check that any reads or writes to the packet's contents are within the range `data` to `data_end`.

There is also an area in memory ahead of the packet, between `data_meta` and `data`, for storing metadata about this packet. This can be used for coordination between multiple eBPF programs that might process the same packet at various places on its journey through the stack.

To illustrate the basics of parsing a network packet, there is an XDP program called ping() in the example code, which will simply generate a line of trace whenever it detects a ping (ICMP) packet. Here's the code for that program:

```
SEC("xdp")
int ping(struct xdp_md *ctx) {
    long protocol = lookup_protocol(ctx);
    if (protocol == 1) // ICMP
    {
        bpf_printk("Hello ping");
    }
    return XDP_PASS;
}
```

You can see this program in action by following these steps:

1. Run make in the *chapter8* directory. This doesn't just build the code; it also attaches the XDP program to the loopback interface (called lo).

2. Run ping localhost in one terminal window.

3. In another terminal window, watch the output generated in the trace pipe by running cat /sys/kernel/tracing/trace_pipe.

You should see two lines of trace being generated approximately every second, and they should look like this:

```
ping-26622    [000] d.s11 276880.862408: bpf_trace_printk: Hello ping
ping-26622    [000] d.s11 276880.862459: bpf_trace_printk: Hello ping
ping-26622    [000] d.s11 276881.889575: bpf_trace_printk: Hello ping
ping-26622    [000] d.s11 276881.889676: bpf_trace_printk: Hello ping
ping-26622    [000] d.s11 276882.910777: bpf_trace_printk: Hello ping
ping-26622    [000] d.s11 276882.910930: bpf_trace_printk: Hello ping
```

There are two lines of trace per second because the loopback interface is receiving both the ping requests and the ping responses.

You can easily modify this code to drop ping packets by adding a line of code to return XDP_DROP when the protocol matches, like this:

```
if (protocol == 1) // ICMP
{
    bpf_printk("Hello ping");
    return XDP_DROP;
}
return XDP_PASS;
```

If you try this, you'll see that output resembling the following is only generated in the trace output once per second:

```
ping-26639   [002] d.s11 277050.589356: bpf_trace_printk: Hello ping
ping-26639   [002] d.s11 277051.615329: bpf_trace_printk: Hello ping
ping-26639   [002] d.s11 277052.637708: bpf_trace_printk: Hello ping
```

The loopback interface receives a ping request, and the XDP program drops it, so the request never gets far enough through the network stack to elicit a response.

Most of the work in this XDP program is being done in a function called lookup_pro tocol() that determines the Layer 4 protocol type. It's just an example, not a production-quality implementation of parsing a network packet! But it's sufficient to give you an idea of how parsing in eBPF works.

The network packet that has been received consists of a string of bytes that are laid out as shown in Figure 8-1.

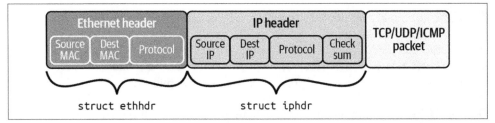

Figure 8-1. Layout of an IP network packet, starting with an Ethernet header, followed by an IP header, and then the Layer 4 data

The lookup_protocol() function takes the ctx structure that holds information about where this network packet is in memory and returns the protocol type that it finds in the IP header. The code is as follows:

```
unsigned char lookup_protocol(struct xdp_md *ctx)
{
    unsigned char protocol = 0;

    void *data = (void *)(long)ctx->data;                           ❶
    void *data_end = (void *)(long)ctx->data_end;
    struct ethhdr *eth = data;                                      ❷
    if (data + sizeof(struct ethhdr) > data_end)                    ❸
        return 0;

    // Check that it's an IP packet
    if (bpf_ntohs(eth->h_proto) == ETH_P_IP)                        ❹
    {
        // Return the protocol of this packet
        // 1 = ICMP
        // 6 = TCP
        // 17 = UDP
        struct iphdr *iph = data + sizeof(struct ethhdr);           ❺
        if (data + sizeof(struct ethhdr) + sizeof(struct iphdr) <= data_end) ❻
            protocol = iph->protocol;                               ❼
```

```
    }
    return protocol;
}
```

❶ The local variables data and data_end point to the start and end of the network packet.

❷ The network packet should start with an Ethernet header.

❸ But you can't simply assume this network packet is big enough to hold that Ethernet header! The verifier requires that you check this explicitly.

❹ The Ethernet header contains a 2-byte field that tells us the Layer 3 protocol.

❺ If the protocol type indicates that it's an IP packet, the IP header immediately follows the Ethernet header.

❻ You can't just assume there's enough room for that IP header in the network packet. Again the verifier requires that you check explicitly.

❼ The IP header contains the protocol byte the function will return to its caller.

The bpf_ntohs() function used by this program ensures that the two bytes are in the order expected on this host. Network protocols are big-endian, but most processors are little-endian, meaning they hold multibyte values in a different order. This function converts (if necessary) from network ordering to host ordering. You should use this function whenever you extract a value from a field in a network packet that's more than one byte long.

The simple example here shows how just a few lines of eBPF code can have a dramatic impact on networking functionality. It's not hard to imagine how more complex rules about which packets to pass and which packets to drop could result in the features I described at the start of this section: firewalling, DDoS protection, and packet-of-death vulnerability mitigation. Now let's consider how even more functionality can be provided given the power to modify network packets within eBPF programs.

Load Balancing and Forwarding

XDP programs aren't limited to inspecting the contents of a packet. They can also modify the packet's contents. Let's consider what's involved if you want to build a simple load balancer that takes packets sent to a given IP address and fans those requests to a number of backends that can fulfill the request.

There's an example of this in the GitHub repo.[2] The setup here is a set of containers that run on the same host. There's a client, a load balancer, and two backends, each running in their own container. As illustrated in Figure 8-2, the load balancer receives traffic from the client and forwards it to one of the two backend containers.

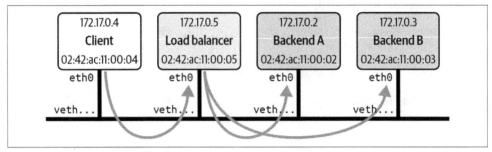

Figure 8-2. Example load balancer setup

The load balancing function is implemented as an XDP program attached to the load balancer's eth0 network interface. The return code from this program is XDP_TX, indicating that the packet should be sent back out of the interface it came in on. But before that happens, the program has to update the address information in the packet headers.

Although I think it's useful as a learning exercise, this example code is very, very far from being production ready; for example, it uses hard-coded addresses that assume the exact setup of IP addresses shown in Figure 8-2. It assumes that the only TCP traffic it will ever receive is requests from the client or responses to the client. It also cheats by taking advantage of the way Docker sets up virtual MAC addresses, using each container's IP address as the last four bytes of the MAC address for the virtual Ethernet interface for each container. That virtual Ethernet interface is called eth0 from the perspective of the container.

Here's the XDP program from the example load balancer code:

```
SEC("xdp_lb")
int xdp_load_balancer(struct xdp_md *ctx)
{
    void *data = (void *)(long)ctx->data;           ❶
    void *data_end = (void *)(long)ctx->data_end;

    struct ethhdr *eth = data;
    if (data + sizeof(struct ethhdr) > data_end)
        return XDP_ABORTED;
```

---

2 This example is based on a talk I gave at eBPF Summit 2021 called "A Load Balancer from scratch" (*https://oreil.ly/mQxtT*). Build an eBPF load balancer in just over 15 minutes!

```
        if (bpf_ntohs(eth->h_proto) != ETH_P_IP)
            return XDP_PASS;

        struct iphdr *iph = data + sizeof(struct ethhdr);
        if (data + sizeof(struct ethhdr) + sizeof(struct iphdr) > data_end)
            return XDP_ABORTED;

        if (iph->protocol != IPPROTO_TCP)                       ❷
            return XDP_PASS;

        if (iph->saddr == IP_ADDRESS(CLIENT))                   ❸
        {
            char be = BACKEND_A;                                ❹
            if (bpf_get_prandom_u32() % 2)
                be = BACKEND_B;

            iph->daddr = IP_ADDRESS(be);                        ❺
            eth->h_dest[5] = be;
        }
        else
        {
            iph->daddr = IP_ADDRESS(CLIENT);                    ❻
            eth->h_dest[5] = CLIENT;
        }
        iph->saddr = IP_ADDRESS(LB);                            ❼
        eth->h_source[5] = LB;

        iph->check = iph_csum(iph);                             ❽

        return XDP_TX;
    }
```

❶ The first part of this function is practically the same as in the previous example: it locates the Ethernet header and then the IP header in the packet.

❷ This time it will process only TCP packets, passing anything else it receives on up the stack as if nothing had happened.

❸ Here the source IP address is checked. If this packet didn't come from the client, I will assume it is a response going to the client.

❹ This code generates a pseudorandom choice between backends A and B.

❺ The destination IP and MAC addresses are updated to match whichever backend was chosen...

❻ ...or if this is a response from a backend (which is the assumption here if it didn't come from a client), the destination IP and MAC addresses are updated to match the client.

⓻ Wherever this packet is going, the source addresses need to be updated so that it looks as though the packet originated from the load balancer.

⓼ The IP header includes a checksum calculated over its contents, and since the source and destination IP addresses have both been updated, the checksum also needs to be recalculated and replaced in this packet.

 Since this is a book on eBPF and not networking, I haven't delved into details such as why the IP and MAC addresses need to be updated or what happens if they aren't. If you're interested, I cover this some more in my YouTube video of the eBPF Summit talk (*https://oreil.ly/mQxtT*) where I originally wrote this example code.

Much like the previous example, the Makefile includes instructions to not only build the code but also use `bpftool` to load and attach the XDP program to the interface, like this:

```
xdp: $(BPF_OBJ)
    bpftool net detach xdpgeneric dev eth0
    rm -f /sys/fs/bpf/$(TARGET)
    bpftool prog load $(BPF_OBJ) /sys/fs/bpf/$(TARGET)
    bpftool net attach xdpgeneric pinned /sys/fs/bpf/$(TARGET) dev eth0
```

This `make` instruction needs to be run *inside* the load balancer container so that eth0 corresponds to its virtual Ethernet interface. This leads to an interesting point: an eBPF program is loaded into the kernel, of which there is only one; yet the attachment point may be within a particular network namespace and visible only within that network namespace.[3]

XDP Offloading

The idea for XDP originated from a conversation speculating how useful it would be if you could run eBPF programs on a network card to make decisions about individual packets before they even reach the kernel's networking stack.[4] There are some network interface cards that support this full *XDP offload* capability where they can indeed run eBPF programs on inbound packets on their own processor. This is illustrated in Figure 8-3.

---

3 If you want to explore this, try CTF Challenge 3 from eBPF Summit 2022 (*https://oreil.ly/YIh_t*). I won't give spoilers here in the book, but you can see the solution in a walkthrough given by Duffie Cooley and me here (*https://oreil.ly/_51rC*).

4 See Daniel Borkmann's presentation "Little Helper Minions for Scaling Microservices" (*https://oreil.ly/_8ZuF*) that includes a history of eBPF, where he tells this anecdote.

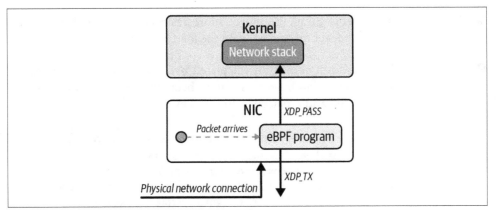

Figure 8-3. Network interface cards that support XDP offload can process, drop, and retransmit packets without any work required from the host CPU

This means a packet that gets dropped or redirected back out of the same physical interface—like the packet drop and load balancing examples earlier in this chapter—is never seen by the host's kernel, and no CPU cycles on the host machine are ever spent processing them, as all the work is done on the network card.

Even if the physical network interface card doesn't support full XDP offload, many NIC drivers support XDP hooks, which minimizes the memory copying required for an eBPF program to process a packet.[5]

This can result in significant performance benefits and allows functionality like load balancing to run very efficiently on commodity hardware.[6]

You've seen how XDP can be used to process inbound network packets, accessing them as soon as possible as they arrive on a machine. eBPF can also be used to process traffic at other points in the network stack, in whatever direction it is flowing. Let's move on and think about eBPF programs attached within the TC subsystem.

---

5 Cilium maintains a list of drivers that support XDP (*https://oreil.ly/wCMjB*) within the BPF and XDP Reference Guide (*https://oreil.ly/eB7vL*).

6 Ceznam shared data about the performance boost its team saw when experimenting with an eBPF-based load balancer in this blog post (*https://oreil.ly/0cbCx*).

Traffic Control (TC)

I mentioned traffic control in the previous chapter. By the time a network packet reaches this point it will be in kernel memory in the form of an sk_buff (*https://oreil.ly/TKDCF*). This is a data structure that's used throughout the kernel's network stack. eBPF programs attached within the TC subsystem receive a pointer to the sk_buff structure as the context parameter.

 You might be wondering why XDP programs don't also use this same structure for their context. The answer is that the XDP hook happens before the network data reaches the network stack and before the sk_buff structure has been set up.

The TC subsystem is intended to regulate how network traffic is scheduled. For example, you might want to limit the bandwidth available to each application so that they all get a fair chance. But when you're looking at scheduling individual packets, *bandwidth* isn't a terribly meaningful term, as it's used for the average amount of data being sent or received. A given application might be very bursty, or another application might be very sensitive to network latency, so TC gives much finer control over the way packets are handled and prioritized.[7]

eBPF programs were introduced here to give custom control over the algorithms used within TC. But with the power to manipulate, drop, or redirect packets, eBPF programs attached within TC can also be used as the building blocks for complex network behaviors.

A given piece of network data in the stack flows in one of two directions: *ingress* (inbound from the network interface) or *egress* (outbound toward the network interface). eBPF programs can be attached in either direction and will affect traffic only in that direction. Unlike XDP, it's possible to attach multiple eBPF programs that will be processed in sequence.

Traditional traffic control is split into *classifiers*, which classify packets based on some rule, and separate *actions*, which are taken based on the output from a classifier and determine what to do with a packet. There can be a series of classifiers, all defined as part of a *qdisc* or queuing discipline.

---

7 For a more complete overview of TC and its concepts, I recommend Quentin Monnet's post "Understanding tc "direct action" mode for BPF" (*https://oreil.ly/7gU2A*).

eBPF programs are attached as a classifier, but they can also determine what action to take within the same program. The action is indicated by the program's return code (whose values are defined in *linux/pkt_cls.h*):

- TC_ACT_SHOT tells the kernel to drop the packet.
- TC_ACT_UNSPEC behaves as if the eBPF program hadn't been run on this packet (so it would be passed to the next classifier in the sequence, if there is one).
- TC_ACT_OK tells the kernel to pass the packet to the next layer in the stack.
- TC_ACT_REDIRECT sends the packet to the ingress or egress path of a different network device.

Let's take a look at a few simple examples of programs that can be attached within TC. The first simply generates a line of trace and then tells the kernel to drop the packet:

```
int tc_drop(struct __sk_buff *skb) {
  bpf_trace_printk("[tc] dropping packet\n");
  return TC_ACT_SHOT;
}
```

Now let's consider how to drop only a subset of packets. This example drops ICMP (ping) request packets and is very similar to the XDP example you saw earlier in this chapter:

```
int tc(struct __sk_buff *skb) {
  void *data = (void *)(long)skb->data;
  void *data_end = (void *)(long)skb->data_end;

  if (is_icmp_ping_request(data, data_end)) {
    struct iphdr *iph = data + sizeof(struct ethhdr);
    struct icmphdr *icmp = data + sizeof(struct ethhdr) + sizeof(struct iphdr);
    bpf_trace_printk("[tc] ICMP request for %x type %x\n", iph->daddr,
                     icmp->type);
    return TC_ACT_SHOT;
  }
  return TC_ACT_OK;
}
```

The sk_buff structure has pointers to the start and end of the packet data, very much like the xdp_md structure, and packet parsing proceeds in very much the same way. Again, to pass verification you have to explicitly check that any access to data is within the range between data and data_end.

You might be wondering why you would want to implement something like this at the TC layer when you have already seen the same kind of functionality implemented with XDP. One good reason is that you can use TC programs for egress traffic, where XDP can only process ingress traffic. Another is that because XDP is triggered as soon as the packet arrives, there is no sk_buff kernel data structure related to the packet at that point. If the eBPF program is interested in or wants to manipulate the sk_buff the kernel creates for this packet, the TC attachment point is suitable.

 To better understand the differences between XDP and TC eBPF programs, read the "Program Types" section in the BPF and XDP Reference Guide (*https://oreil.ly/MWAJL*) from the Cilium project.

Now let's consider an example that doesn't just drop certain packets. This example identifies a ping request being received and responds with a ping response:

```
int tc_pingpong(struct __sk_buff *skb) {
  void *data = (void *)(long)skb->data;
  void *data_end = (void *)(long)skb->data_end;

  if (!is_icmp_ping_request(data, data_end)) {         ❶
    return TC_ACT_OK;
  }

  struct iphdr *iph = data + sizeof(struct ethhdr);
  struct icmphdr *icmp = data + sizeof(struct ethhdr) + sizeof(struct iphdr);

  swap_mac_addresses(skb);                             ❷
  swap_ip_addresses(skb);

  // Change the type of the ICMP packet to 0 (ICMP Echo Reply)
  // (was 8 for ICMP Echo request)
  update_icmp_type(skb, 8, 0);                         ❸

  // Redirecting a clone of the modified skb back to the interface
  // it arrived on
  bpf_clone_redirect(skb, skb->ifindex, 0);            ❹

  return TC_ACT_SHOT;                                  ❺
}
```

❶ The is_icmp_ping_request() function parses the packet and checks not only that it's an ICMP message, but also that it's an echo (ping) request.

❷ Since this function is going to send a response to the sender, the source and destination addresses need to be swapped. (You can read the example code if you want to see the nitty-gritty details of this, which also includes updating the IP header checksum.)

❸ This is converted to an echo response by changing the type field in the ICMP header.

❹ This helper function sends a clone of the packet back through the interface (`skb->ifindex`) on which it was received.

❺ Since the helper function cloned the packet before sending out the response, the original packet should be dropped.

In normal circumstances, a ping request would be handled later by the kernel's network stack, but this small example demonstrates how network functionality more generally can be replaced by an eBPF implementation.

Lots of networking capabilities today are handled by user space services, but where they can be replaced by eBPF programs, it's likely to be great for performance. A packet that's processed within the kernel doesn't have to complete its journey through the rest of the stack; there is no need for it to transition to user space for processing, and the response doesn't require a transition back into the kernel. What's more, the two could run in parallel—an eBPF program can return `TC_ACT_OK` for any packet that requires complex processing that it can't handle so that it gets passed up to the user space service as normal.

For me, this is an important aspect of implementing network functionality in eBPF. As the eBPF platform develops (e.g., more recent kernels allowing programs of one million instructions), it's possible to implement increasingly complex aspects of networking in the kernel. The parts that are not yet implemented in eBPF can still be handled either by the traditional stack within the kernel or in user space. Over time, more and more features can be moved from user space into the kernel, with the flexibility and dynamic nature of eBPF meaning you won't have to wait for them to be part of the kernel distribution itself. You can load eBPF implementations immediately, just as I discussed in Chapter 1.

I'll return to the implementation of networking features in "eBPF and Kubernetes Networking" on page 160. But first, let's consider another use case that eBPF enables: inspecting the decrypted contents of encrypted traffic.

Packet Encryption and Decryption

If an application uses encryption to secure data it sends or receives, there will be a point before it's encrypted or after it's decrypted where the data is in the clear. Recall that eBPF can attach programs pretty much anywhere on a machine, so if you can hook into a point where data is being passed and isn't yet encrypted, or just after it has been decrypted, that would allow your eBPF program to observe that data in the clear. There's no need to supply any certificates to decrypt the traffic, as you would in a traditional SSL inspection tool.

In many cases an application will encrypt data using a library like OpenSSL or BoringSSL that lives in user space. In this case the traffic will already be encrypted by the time it reaches the socket, which is the user space/kernel boundary for network traffic. If you want to trace out this data in its unencrypted form, you can use an eBPF program attached to the right place in the user space code.

User Space SSL Libraries

One common way to trace out the decrypted content of encrypted packets is to hook into calls made to user space libraries like OpenSSL or BoringSSL. An application using OpenSSL sends data to be encrypted by making a call to a function called `SSL_write()` and retrieves cleartext data that was received over the network in encrypted form using `SSL_read()`. Hooking eBPF programs into these functions with uprobes allows an application to observe the data *from any application that uses this shared library* in the clear, before it is encrypted or after it has been decrypted. And there is no need for any keys, because those are already being provided by the application.

There is a fairly straightforward example called openssl-tracer in the Pixie project (*https://oreil.ly/puDp9*),[8] within which the eBPF programs are in a file called *openssl_tracer_bpf_funcs.c*. Here's the part of that code that sends data to user space, using a perf buffer (similar to examples you have seen earlier in this book):

```
static int process_SSL_data(struct pt_regs* ctx, uint64_t id, enum
ssl_data_event_type type, const char* buf) {
  ...
  bpf_probe_read(event->data, event->data_len, buf);
  tls_events.perf_submit(ctx, event, sizeof(struct ssl_data_event_t));

  return 0;
}
```

---

8 There is also a blog post that accompanies this example at *https://blog.px.dev/ebpf-openssl-tracing*.

You can see that data from buf gets read into an event structure using the helper function bpf_probe_read(), and then that event structure is submitted to a perf buffer.

If this data is being sent to user space, it's reasonable to assume this must be the data in unencrypted format. So where is this buffer of data obtained? You can work that out by seeing where the process_SSL_data() function is called. It's called in two places: one for data being read and one for data being written. Figure 8-4 illustrates what is happening in the case of reading data that arrives on this machine in encrypted form.

When you're reading data, you supply a pointer to a buffer to SSL_read(), and when the function returns, that buffer will contain the unencrypted data. Much like kprobes, the input parameters to a function—including that buffer pointer—are only available to a uprobe attached to the entry point, as the registers they're held in might well get overwritten during the function's execution. But the data won't be available in the buffer until the function exits, when you can read it using a uretprobe.

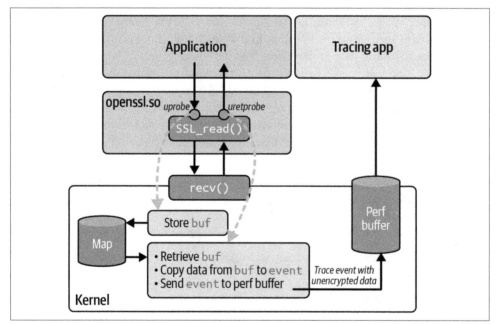

Figure 8-4. eBPF programs are hooked to uprobes at the entry to and exit from SSL_read() so that the unencrypted data can be read from the buffer pointer

So this example follows a common pattern for kprobes and uprobes, illustrated in Figure 8-4, where the entry probe temporarily stores input parameters using a map, from which the exit probe can retrieve them. Let's look at the code that does this, starting with the eBPF program attached to the start of SSL_read():

```
// Function signature being probed:
// int SSL_read(SSL *s, void *buf, int num)
int probe_entry_SSL_read(struct pt_regs* ctx) {
  uint64_t current_pid_tgid = bpf_get_current_pid_tgid();
  ...

  const char* buf = (const char*)PT_REGS_PARM2(ctx);          ❶

  active_ssl_read_args_map.update(&current_pid_tgid, &buf);   ❷
  return 0;
}
```

❶ As described in the comment for this function, the buffer pointer is the second parameter passed into the SSL_read() function to which this probe will be attached. The PT_REGS_PARM2 macro gets this parameter from the context.

❷ The buffer pointer is stored in a hash map, for which the key is the current process and thread ID, obtained at the start of the function using the helper bpf_get_current_pid_tgif().

Here's the corresponding program for the exit probe:

```
int probe_ret_SSL_read(struct pt_regs* ctx) {
  uint64_t current_pid_tgid = bpf_get_current_pid_tgid();

  ...
  const char** buf = active_ssl_read_args_map.lookup(&current_pid_tgid);   ❶
  if (buf != NULL) {
    process_SSL_data(ctx, current_pid_tgid, kSSLRead, *buf);               ❷
  }

  active_ssl_read_args_map.delete(&current_pid_tgid);                      ❸
  return 0;
}
```

❶ Having looked up the current process and thread ID, use this as the key to retrieve the buffer pointer from the hash map.

❷ If this isn't a null pointer, call process_SSL_data(), which is the function you saw earlier that sends the data from that buffer to user space using the perf buffer.

❸ Clean up the entry in the hash map, since every entry call should be paired with an exit.

This example shows how to trace out the cleartext version of encrypted data that gets sent and received by a user space application. The tracing itself is attached to a user space library, and there's no guarantee that every application will use a given SSL library. The BCC project includes a utility called *sslsniff* (*https://oreil.ly/tFT9p*) that also supports GnuTLS and NSS. But if someone's application uses some other encryption library (or even, heaven forbid, they chose to "roll their own crypto"), the uprobes simply won't have the right places to hook to and these tracing tools won't work.

There are even more common reasons why this uprobe-based approach might not be successful. Unlike the kernel (of which there is only one per [virtual] machine), there can be multiple copies of user space library code. If you're using containers, each one is likely to have its own set of all library dependencies. You can hook into uprobes in these libraries, but you'd have to identify the right copy for the particular container you want to trace. Another possibility is that rather than using a shared, dynamically linked library, an application might be statically linked so that it's a single standalone executable.

eBPF and Kubernetes Networking

Although this book isn't about Kubernetes, eBPF is so widely used for Kubernetes networking that it's a great illustration of using the platform to customize the networking stack.

In Kubernetes environments, applications are deployed in *pods*. Each pod is a group of one or more containers that share kernel namespaces and cgroups, isolating pods from each other and from the host machine they are running on.

In particular (for the purposes of this chapter), a pod typically has its own network namespace and its own IP address.[9] This means the kernel has a set of network stack structures for that namespace, separated from the host's and from other pods. As shown in Figure 8-5, the pod is connected to the host by a virtual Ethernet connection, and it is allocated its own IP address.

---

9 It's possible for pods to be run in the host's network namespace so that they share the IP address of the host, but this isn't usually done unless there's a good reason for an application running in the pod to require it.

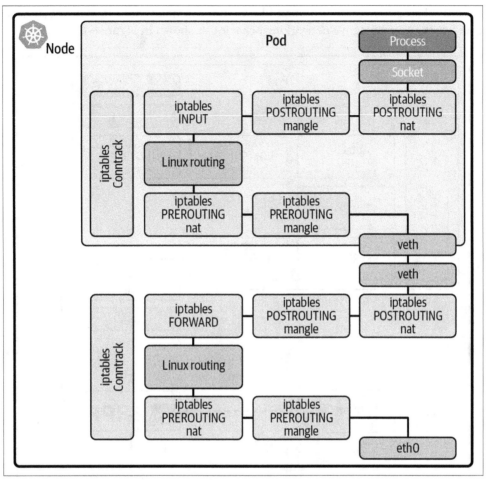

Figure 8-5. Network path in Kubernetes

You can see from Figure 8-5 that a packet coming from outside the machine destined for an application pod has to travel through the network stack on the host, across the virtual Ethernet connection, and into the pod's network namespace, and then it has to traverse the network stack again to reach the application.

Those two network stacks are running in the same kernel, so the packet is really running through the same processing twice. The more code a network packet has to pass through, the higher the latency, so if it's possible to shorten the network path, that will likely bring about performance improvements.

An eBPF-based networking solution like Cilium can hook into the network stack to override the kernel's native networking behavior, as shown in Figure 8-6.

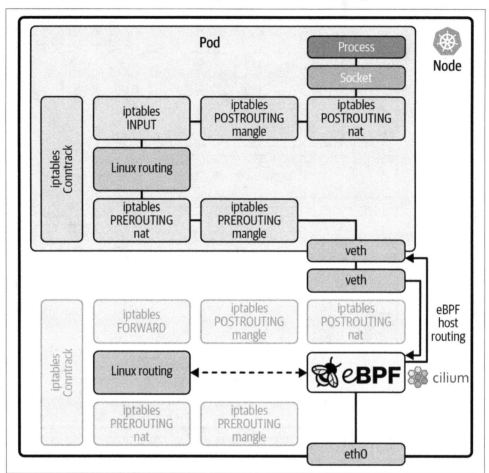

Figure 8-6. Bypassing iptables and conntrack processing with eBPF

In particular, eBPF enables replacing iptables and conntrack with a more efficient solution for managing network rules and connection tracking. Let's discuss why this results in a significant performance improvement in Kubernetes.

Avoiding iptables

Kubernetes has a component called kube-proxy that implements load balancing behavior, allowing multiple pods to fulfill requests to a service. This has been implemented using iptables rules.

Kubernetes offers users the choice of which networking solution to use through the use of the Container Network Interface (CNI). Some CNI plug-ins use iptables rules to implement L3/L4 network policy in Kubernetes; that is, the iptables rules indicate whether to drop a packet because it doesn't meet the network policy.

Although iptables was effective for traditional (precontainer) networking, it has some weaknesses when it's used in Kubernetes. In this environment, pods—and their IP addresses—come and go dynamically, and each time a pod is added or removed, the iptables rules have to be rewritten in their entirety, and this impacts performance at scale. (A talk (*https://oreil.ly/BO0-8*) by Haibin Xie and Quinton Hoole at KubeCon in 2017 described how making a single rule update to iptables rules for 20,000 services could take five hours.)

Updates to iptables aren't the only performance issues: looking up a rule requires a linear search through the table, which is an O(n) operation, growing linearly with the number of rules.

Cilium uses eBPF hash table maps to store network policy rules, connection tracking, and load balancer lookup tables, which can replace iptables for kube-proxy. Both looking up an entry in a hash table and inserting a new one are approximately O(1) operations, which means they scale much, much better.

You can read about the benchmarked performance improvements this achieves on the Cilium blog (*https://oreil.ly/9NV99*). In the same post you'll see that Calico, another CNI that has an eBPF option, also achieves better performance when you pick its eBPF implementation over iptables. eBPF offers the most performant mechanisms for scalable, dynamic Kubernetes deployments.

Coordinated Network Programs

A complex networking implementation like Cilium can't be written as a single eBPF program. As shown in Figure 8-7, it provides several different eBPF programs that are hooked into different parts of the kernel and its network stack.

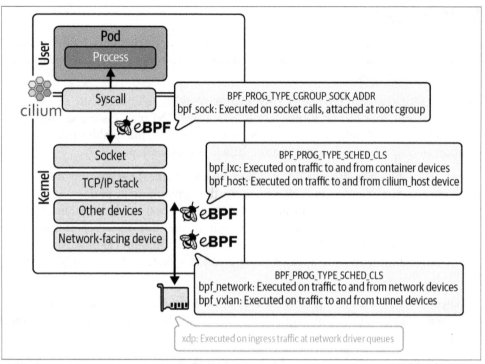

Figure 8-7. Cilium consists of multiple coordinated eBPF programs that hook into different points in the kernel

As a general principle, Cilium intercepts traffic as soon as it can in order to shorten the processing path for each packet. Messages flowing out from an application pod are intercepted at the socket layer, as close to the application as possible. Inbound packets from the external network are intercepted using XDP. But what about the additional attachment points?

Cilium supports different networking modes that suit different environments. A full description of this is beyond the scope of this book (you can find more information at Cilium.io), but I'll give a brief overview here so that you can see why there are so many different eBPF programs!

There is a simple, flat networking mode, in which Cilium allocates IP addresses for all the pods in a cluster from the same CIDR and directly routes traffic between them. There are also a couple of different tunneling modes, in which traffic intended for a pod on a different node gets encapsulated in a message addressed to that destination node's IP address and decapsulated on that destination node for the final hop into the pod. Different eBPF programs get invoked to handle traffic depending on whether a packet is destined for a local container, the local host, another host on this network, or a tunnel.

In Figure 8-7 you can see multiple TC programs that handle traffic to and from different devices. These devices represent the possible different real and virtual network interfaces where a packet might be flowing:

- The interface to a pod's network (one end of the virtual Ethernet connection between the pod and the host)
- The interface to a network tunnel
- The interface to a physical network device on the host
- The host's own network interface

> If you're interested in learning more about how packets flow through Cilium, Arthur Chiao wrote this detailed and interesting blog post: "Life of a Packet in Cilium: Discovering the Pod-to-Service Traffic Path and BPF Processing Logics" (*https://oreil.ly/toxsM*).

The different eBPF programs attached at these various points in the kernel communicate using eBFP maps and using the metadata that can be attached to network packets as they flow through the stack (which I mentioned when I discussed accessing network packets in the XDP example). These programs don't just route packets to their destination; they're also used to drop packets—just like you saw in earlier examples—based on network policies.

Network Policy Enforcement

You saw at the start of this chapter how eBPF programs can drop packets, and that means they simply won't reach their destination. This is the basis of network policy enforcement, and conceptually it's essentially the same whether we are thinking about "traditional" or cloud native firewalling. A policy determines whether a packet should be dropped or not, based on information about its source and/or destination.

In traditional environments, IP addresses are assigned to a particular server for a long period of time, but in Kubernetes, IP addresses come and go dynamically, and the address assigned today for a particular application pod might very well be reused for a completely different application tomorrow. This is why traditional firewalling isn't terribly effective in cloud native environments. It would be impractical to redefine firewall rules manually every time IP addresses change.

Instead, Kubernetes supports the concept of a NetworkPolicy resource, which defines firewalling rules based on the labels applied to particular pods rather than based on their IP address. Although the resource type is native to Kubernetes, it's not implemented by Kubernetes itself. Instead, this functionality is delegated to whatever CNI plug-in you're using. If you choose a CNI that doesn't support NetworkPolicy resources, any rules you might configure are simply ignored. On the flip side, CNIs are free to configure custom resources that allow for more sophisticated network policy configurations than the native Kubernetes definition allows. For example, Cilium supports features like DNS-based network policy rules, so you can define whether traffic is or isn't allowed not based on an IP address but based on the DNS name (e.g., "*example.com*"). You can also define policies for various Layer 7 protocols, for example, allowing or denying traffic for HTTP GET calls but not for POST calls to a particular URL.

 Isovalent's free hands-on lab "Getting Started with Cilium" (*https:// oreil.ly/afdeh*) walks you through defining network policies at Layers 3/4 and Layer 7. Another very useful resource is the Network Policy Editor at *networkpolicy.io*, which visually presents the effects of a network policy.

As I discussed earlier in this chapter, it's possible to use iptables rules to drop traffic, and that's an approach some CNIs have taken to implement Kubernetes NetworkPolicy rules. Cilium uses eBPF programs to drop traffic that doesn't match the set of rules currently in place. Having seen examples of dropping packets earlier in this chapter, I hope you have a rough mental model for how this would work.

Cilium uses Kubernetes identities to determine whether a given network policy rule applies. In the same way labels define which pods are part of a service in Kubernetes, labels also define Cilium's security identity for the pod. eBPF hash tables, indexed by these service identities, make for very efficient rule lookups.

Encrypted Connections

Many organizations have requirements to protect their deployments and their users' data by encrypting traffic between applications. This can be achieved by writing code in each application to ensure that it sets up secure connections, typically using mutual Traffic Layer Security (mTLS) underpinning an HTTP or gRPC connection. Setting up these connections requires first establishing the identities of the apps at either end of the connection (which is usually achieved by exchanging certificates) and then encrypting the data that flows between them.

In Kubernetes, it's possible to offload the requirement from the application, either to a service mesh layer or to the underlying network itself. A full discussion of service mesh is beyond the scope of this book, but you might be interested in a piece I wrote on the new stack: "How eBPF Streamlines the Service Mesh" (*https://oreil.ly/5ayvF*). Let's concentrate here on the network layer and how eBPF makes it possible to push the encryption requirement into the kernel.

The simplest option to ensure that traffic is encrypted within a Kubernetes cluster is to use *transparent encryption*. It's called "transparent" because it takes place entirely at the network layer and it's extremely lightweight from an operational point of view. The applications themselves don't need to be aware of the encryption at all, and they don't need to set up HTTPS connections; nor does this approach require any additional infrastructure components running under Kubernetes.

There are two in-kernel encryption protocols in common usage, IPsec and WireGuard[R], and they're both supported in Kubernetes networking by Cilium and Calico CNIs. It's beyond the scope of this book to discuss the differences between these two protocols, but the key point is that they set up a secure tunnel between two machines. The CNI can choose to connect the eBPF endpoint for a pod via this secure tunnel.

There is a nice write-up on the Cilium blog (*https://oreil.ly/xjpGP*) of how Cilium uses WireGuard[R] as well as IPsec to provide encrypted traffic between nodes. The post also gives a brief overview of the performance characteristics of both.

The secure tunnel is set up using the identities of the nodes at either end. These identities are managed by Kubernetes anyway, so the administrative burden for an operator is minimal. For many purposes this is sufficient as it ensures that all network traffic in a cluster is encrypted. Transparent encryption can also be used unmodified with NetworkPolicy that uses Kubernetes identities to manage whether traffic can flow between different endpoints in the cluster.

Some organizations operate a multitenant environment where there's a need for strong multitenant boundaries and where it's essential to use certificates to identify every application endpoint. Handling this within every application is a significant burden, so it's something that more recently has been offloaded to a service mesh layer, but this requires a whole extra set of components to be deployed, causing additional resource consumption, latency, and operational complexity.

eBPF is now enabling a new approach (*https://oreil.ly/DSnLZ*) that builds on transparent encryption but uses TLS for the initial certificate exchange and endpoint authentication so that the identities can represent individual applications rather than the nodes they are running on, as depicted in Figure 8-8.

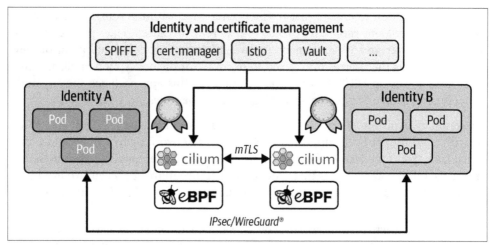

Figure 8-8. Transparent encryption between authenticated application identities

Once the authentication step has taken place, IPsec or WireGuard[(R)] within the kernel is used to encrypt the traffic that flows between those applications. This has a number of advantages. It allows third-party certificate and identity management tools like cert-manager or SPIFFE/SPIRE to handle the identity part, and the network takes care of encryption so that it's all entirely transparent to the application. Cilium supports NetworkPolicy definitions that specify endpoints by their SPIFFE ID rather than just by their Kubernetes labels. And perhaps most importantly, this approach can be used with any protocol that travels in IP packets. That's a big step up from mTLS, which works only for TCP-based connections.

There's not enough room in this book to dive deep into all the internals of Cilium, but I hope this section helped you understand how eBPF is a powerful platform for building complex networking functionality like a fully featured Kubernetes CNI.

Summary

In this chapter you saw eBPF programs attached at a variety of different points in the network stack. I showed examples of basic packet processing, and I hope these gave you an indication of how eBPF can create powerful networking features. You also saw some real-life examples of these networking features, including load balancing, firewalling, security mitigation, and Kubernetes networking.

Exercises and Further Reading

Here are some ways to learn more about the range of networking use cases for eBPF:

1. Modify the example XDP program `ping()` so that it generates different trace messages for ping responses and ping requests. The ICMP header immediately follows the IP header in the network packet (just like the IP header follows the Ethernet header). You'll likely want to use `struct icmphdr` from *linux/icmp.h* and look at whether the type field shows `ICMP_ECHO` or `ICMP_ECHOREPLY`.

2. If you want to dive further into XDP programming, I recommend the xdp-project's xdp-tutorial (*https://oreil.ly/UmJMF*).

3. Use sslsniff (*https://oreil.ly/Zuww7*) from the BCC project to view the contents of encrypted traffic.

4. Explore Cilium by using tutorials and labs linked to from the Cilium website (*https://cilium.io/get-started*).

5. Use the editor at *networkpolicy.io* to visualize the effect of network policies in a Kubernetes deployment.

eBPF for Security

You've seen how eBPF can be used to observe events across a system and report information about those events to user space tools. In this chapter you'll consider how to build on the concept of event detection to create eBPF-based security tools that can detect, or even prevent, malicious activity. I'll start by helping you understand what makes security different from other types of observability.

Example code for this chapter is in the GitHub repo (*http://github.com/lizrice/learning-ebpf*) in the *chapter9* directory.

Security Observability Requires Policy and Context

The difference between a security tool and an observability tool that reports on events is that a security tool needs to be able to distinguish between events that are expected under normal circumstances and events that suggest malicious activity might be taking place. For example, suppose you have an application that writes data to a local file as part of its normal processing. Let's say the app is expected to write to */home/<username>/<filename>*, so this activity isn't something you're interested in from a security perspective. However, you would want to be notified if the app writes to one of the many sensitive file locations in Linux. For example, it is unlikely that it needs to modify the password information stored in */etc/passwd*.

Policies have to take into account not just normal behavior when systems are fully functional, but also the expected error path behavior. For example, if a physical disk gets full, the application might start sending network messages to alert about this situation. These network messages shouldn't be seen as security events—even though they are unusual, they're not suspicious. Taking error paths into account can make it challenging to create effective policies, and we'll come back to that challenge later in this chapter.

Defining what is and isn't expected behavior is the job of a policy. A security tool compares activity to a policy and takes some action when the activity is outside the policy, making it suspicious. That action would typically involve generating a security event log, which would usually get sent to a Security Information Event Management (SIEM) platform. It might also result in an alert to a human who will be called on to investigate what happened.

The more contextual information that's available to the investigator, the more likely they will be able to find out the root cause of the event and determine whether it was an attack, which components were affected, how and when the attack took place, and who was responsible. As illustrated in Figure 9-1, being able to answer questions like this takes a tool from mere logging to deserving the nomenclature "security observability."

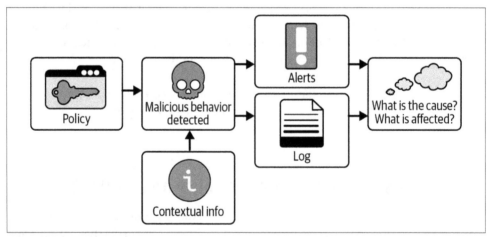

Figure 9-1. Contextual information is required alongside out-of-policy event detection for security observability

Let's explore some of the ways eBPF programs are being used to detect and enforce security events. As you know, eBPF programs can be attached to a variety of events, and one set of events that have been commonly used for security for many years are syscalls. We'll start our discussion with syscalls, but as you'll see, syscalls might not be the most effective way to implement security tooling with eBPF. We'll see some newer and more sophisticated approaches later in this chapter.

Using System Calls for Security Events

System calls (or syscalls) are the interface between user space applications and the kernel. If you can restrict the set of syscalls an app can make, that will limit what it is able to do. For example, if you stop an app from making syscalls in the open*() family, it won't be able to open files. If you have an application that you never expect to open files, you might want to create this limitation so that even if the app gets compromised, it won't be able to open files maliciously. If you've been using Docker or Kubernetes over the past few years, there is a very good chance you have already come across a security tool that uses BPF to limit syscalls: seccomp.

Seccomp

The name *seccomp* is a contraction of "SECure COMPuting." In its original, or "strict," form, seccomp is used to limit the set of syscalls a process can use to a very small subset: read(), write(), _exit(), and sigreturn(). The intention of this strict mode was to allow users to run untrusted code (perhaps a program downloaded from the internet) without any possibility of that code doing malicious things.

Strict mode is very restrictive, and many applications need to use a much larger set of syscalls—but that doesn't mean they need all 400 and more of them. It makes sense to allow a more flexible method for restricting the set that any given application can use. This is the reasoning behind the flavor of seccomp that most of us from the container world have encountered, which is more properly known as seccomp-bpf. Instead of having a fixed subset of syscalls that it permits, this mode of seccomp uses BPF code to filter the syscalls that are and aren't allowed.

In seccomp-bpf, a set of BPF instructions are loaded that act as a filter. Each time a syscall is called, the filter is triggered. The filter code has access to the arguments that are passed to the syscall so that it can make decisions based on both the syscall itself and the arguments that have been passed to it. The outcome is one of a set of possible actions that include:

- Allowing the syscall to go ahead
- Returning an error code to the user space application
- Killing the thread
- Notifying a user space application (seccomp-unotify) (as of kernel version 5.0)

 If you want to explore writing your own BPF filter code, Michael Kerrisk has some good examples at *https://oreil.ly/cJ6HL*.

Some of the arguments passed to syscalls are pointers, and the BPF code in seccomp-bpf is not able to dereference these pointers. This limits the flexibility of a seccomp profile, as it can only use value arguments in its decision-making process. Also, it has to be applied to the process when it starts—you can't modify the profile that is being applied to a given application process.

You may well have used seccomp-bpf without writing BPF code, as the code is often derived from a human-readable seccomp profile. Docker's default profile (*https:// oreil.ly/IT_Bf*) is a good example. This is a general-purpose profile intended to be usable with pretty much any normal, containerized application. That inevitably means it allows most syscalls and disallows only a few that are unlikely to be appropriate in any application, `reboot()` being a great example.

According to Aqua Security (*https://oreil.ly/1xWmn*), most containerized apps use somewhere in the range of 40 to 70 syscalls. For better security, it would be preferable to use a more constrained profile that is targeted at each specific application and only allows the syscalls it actually uses.

Generating Seccomp Profiles

If you ask the average app developer to tell you what syscalls one of their programs makes, you're likely to get a blank look. That's not intended to be insulting. It's just that most developers write in programming languages that give them higher-level abstractions far removed from the details of syscalls. For example, they might know what files their application opens, but it's less likely that they could tell you whether they are opened using `open()` or `openat()`. This makes it unlikely that you'll get a positive response if you ask the developer to handcraft an appropriate seccomp profile along with their application code.

Automation is the way forward: the idea is to use a tool to record the set of syscalls an application makes. In the early days, seccomp profiles were generally compiled using `strace` to gather the set of syscalls an application calls.[1] This isn't a wonderful solution in the cloud native age, as there's no easy way to point `strace` at a specific container or Kubernetes pod. It would also be more helpful to generate the profile not just as a list of syscalls, but in the JSON format that Kubernetes and OCI-compatible container runtimes can take as input. There are a couple of tools that do this, using eBPF to gather information about all the syscalls being called:

---

[1] See, for example, this post from Jess Frazelle, who developed the default seccomp profile for Docker: "How to Use the New Docker Seccomp Profiles" (*https://oreil.ly/EcpnM*).

- Inspektor Gadget (*https://www.inspektor-gadget.io*) includes a seccomp profiler that allows you to generate a custom seccomp profile for the containers in a Kubernetes pod.[2]
- Red Hat created a seccomp profiler in the form of an OCI runtime hook (*https://oreil.ly/nC8vM*).

With these profilers, you need to run the application for some arbitrary amount of time to generate a profile that includes the full list of the syscalls it might legitimately call. As discussed earlier in this chapter, this list needs to include error paths. If your application can't behave correctly under error conditions because the syscalls it needs to call are blocked, this might cause a bigger problem. And since seccomp profiles deal with a lower abstraction level than most developers are familiar with, it's hard to review them manually to see if they cover all the right cases.

Taking the OCI runtime hook as an example, an eBPF program is attached to the syscall_enter raw tracepoint (*https://oreil.ly/sbWSc*) and maintains an eBPF map that keeps track of which syscalls have been seen (*https://oreil.ly/czUM7*). The user space parts of this tool are written in Go and use the *iovisor/gobpf* library (*https://oreil.ly/sYCT3*). (I'll discuss this and other Golang libraries for eBPF in Chapter 10.)

The following are the lines of code (*https://oreil.ly/DOShA*) from the OCI runtime hook that load the eBPF program into the kernel and attach it to the tracepoint (a few lines have been omitted for brevity):

```
src := strings.Replace(source, "$PARENT_PID", strconv.Itoa(pid), -1)        ❶
m := bcc.NewModule(src, []string{})
defer m.Close()

...
enterTrace, err := m.LoadTracepoint("enter_trace")                          ❷
...
if err := m.AttachTracepoint("raw_syscalls:sys_enter", enterTrace); err != nil ❸
    {
    return fmt.Errorf("error attaching to tracepoint: %v", err)
}
```

❶ This line does something quite interesting: it replaces a variable named $PAR ENT_PID in the eBPF source code with a numeric process ID. This is a common pattern, and it indicates that this tool will load individual eBPF programs for each process being instrumented.

❷ Here, an eBPF program called enter_trace gets loaded into the kernel.

---

2 The documentation for Inspektor Gadget's seccomp profiler is quite dry, but this video overview from Jose Blanquicet (*https://oreil.ly/0bYaa*) is more accessible.

❸ The `enter_trace` program gets attached to the tracepoint `raw_sys calls:sys_enter`. This is the tracepoint at the point of entry to any syscall, which you've encountered in earlier examples. Whenever any user space code makes a syscall, this tracepoint will be hit.

These profilers use eBPF code attached to `sys_enter` to keep track of the set of syscalls that have been used, and they generate a seccomp profile to be used with seccomp, which does the actual job of enforcing the profile. The next class of eBPF tools we'll consider also attach to `sys_enter`, but they use syscalls to track the behavior of an application and compare it against security policies.

Syscall-Tracking Security Tools

The best-known tool that falls into this category of syscall-tracking security tools is the CNCF project Falco (*https://falco.org*), which provides security alerts. By default, Falco is installed as a kernel module, but there is also an eBPF version. Users can define rules (*https://oreil.ly/enufu*) to determine what events are security relevant, and Falco can generate alerts in a variety of formats when events happen that don't match the policies defined in these rules.

Both the kernel module driver and the eBPF-based driver attach to system calls. If you examine the Falco eBPF programs on GitHub (*https://oreil.ly/Q_cBD*) you'll see lines like the following that attach probes to raw syscall entry and exit points (plus a few other events, such as page faults):

```
BPF_PROBE("raw_syscalls/", sys_enter, sys_enter_args)

BPF_PROBE("raw_syscalls/", sys_exit, sys_exit_args)
```

Since eBPF programs can be loaded dynamically and can detect events triggered by preexisting processes, tools like Falco can apply policies to application workloads that are already running. Users can modify the set of rules being applied without having to modify the applications or their configuration. This is in contrast to seccomp profiles, which have to be applied to the application process when it is launched.

Unfortunately there is a problem with this approach of using syscall entry points for security tooling: there is a Time Of Check to Time Of Use (TOCTOU) issue.

When an eBPF program is triggered at the entry point to a system call, it can access the arguments that user space has passed to that system call. If those arguments are pointers, the kernel will need to copy the pointed-to data into its own data structures before acting on that data. As illustrated in Figure 9-2, there is a window of opportunity for an attacker to modify this data, after it has been inspected by the eBPF program but before the kernel copies it. Thus, the data being acted on might not be the same as what was captured by the eBPF program.[3]

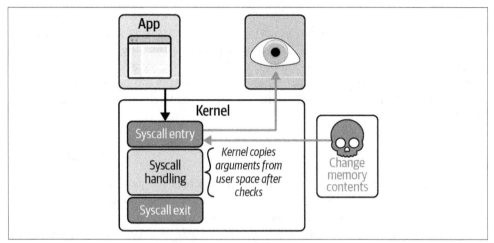

Figure 9-2. An attacker can change syscall arguments before they are accessed by the kernel

The same window would apply for seccomp-bpf, were it not for the fact that in seccomp-bpf the program is not allowed to dereference the user space pointer, so it's not possible to examine the data at all.

The TOCTOU issue does apply for seccomp_unotify, a recently added mode of seccomp where a violation can be reported to user space. The manpage for seccomp_unotify (*https://oreil.ly/cwpki*) explicitly notes that "It should thus be absolutely clear that the seccomp user-space notification mechanism *cannot* be used to implement a security policy!"

The syscall entry point might be very convenient for observability purposes, but for a serious security tool it's really not sufficient.

The Sysmon for Linux tool (*https://oreil.ly/pbtF3*) addresses the TOCTOU window by attaching to both the entry and exit points for syscalls. Once the call has completed, it looks at the kernel's data structures to get an accurate view. For example, if the syscall returns a file descriptor, the eBPF program attached to the exit can retrieve correct information about the object that the file descriptor represents by looking into the related process's file descriptor table. While this approach can result in an accurate

---

3 Exploiting this window was discussed in a DEFCON 29 talk titled "Phantom Attack: Evading System Call Monitoring (*https://oreil.ly/WguKq*)" by Rex Guo and Junyuan Zeng, and its impact on Falco was covered in more detail in the talk "LSM BPF Change Everything (*https://oreil.ly/17c-3*)" by Leo Di Donato and KP Singh.

record of security-related activity, it can't prevent an action from taking place, since the syscall has already completed by the time a check is made.

To be certain that it is inspecting the same information the kernel will act on, the eBPF program should be attached to an event that occurs after the parameters have been copied into kernel memory. Unfortunately, there is no single common place in the kernel to do this, as the data is handled differently in syscall-specific code. However, there is a well-defined interface where eBPF programs can be safely attached: the Linux Security Module (LSM) API. This requires a relatively new eBPF feature: BPF LSM.

BPF LSM

The LSM interface provides a set of hooks that each occur just before the kernel is about to act on a kernel data structure. The function called by a hook can make a decision about whether to allow the action to go ahead. This interface was originally provided to allow security tools to be implemented in the form of kernel modules (*https://oreil.ly/mF_OD*); BPF LSM (*https://oreil.ly/KzaMT*) extends this so that eBPF programs can be attached to the same hook points, as shown in Figure 9-3.

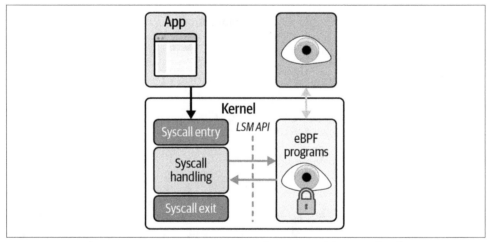

Figure 9-3. With LSM BPF, eBPF programs can be triggered by LSM hook events

There are hundreds of LSM hooks, and they're pretty nicely documented in the kernel source code (*https://oreil.ly/dO8jT*). To be clear, there isn't a one-to-one mapping between syscalls and LSM hooks, but if a syscall has the potential to do something interesting from a security perspective, processing that syscall will trigger one or more of the hooks.

Here's a trivial example of an eBPF program attached to an LSM hook. This example is called during the processing of a chmod command ("chmod" stands for "change modes" and is mostly used to change the access permissions on a file):

```
SEC("lsm/path_chmod")
int BPF_PROG(path_chmod, const struct path *path, umode_t mode)
{
    bpf_printk("Change mode of file name %s\n", path->dentry->d_iname);
    return 0;
}
```

This example simply traces out the name of the file and always returns 0, but you can imagine a real implementation that would make use of the arguments to decide whether to allow this change of mode. Returning a nonzero value would deny permission to make this change, so the kernel wouldn't go ahead with it. It's worth noting that making policy checks entirely within the kernel like this is highly performant.

The path argument to BPF_PROG() is the kernel data structure representing the file, and the mode argument is the desired new mode value. You can see the name of the file being accessed from the field path->dentry->d_iname.

LSM BPF was added in kernel version 5.7, which means that (at least at the time of this writing) it's not yet available on many supported Linux distributions, but I expect that over the next couple of years many vendors will develop security tooling that makes use of this interface. Before LSM BPF is made widely available, there is another possible approach, as used by the developers of Cilium Tetragon.

Cilium Tetragon

Tetragon (*https://oreil.ly/p-bdc*) is part of the Cilium project (also part of the CNCF). Rather than attaching to LSM API hooks, Tetragon's approach is to build a framework for attaching eBPF programs to arbitrary functions in the Linux kernel.

Tetragon is designed for use in a Kubernetes environment, and the project defines a custom Kubernetes resource type called a *TracingPolicy*. This is used to define a set of events to which eBPF programs should be attached, conditions that need to be checked by eBPF code, and actions to take if the conditions are met. The following is an extract from a sample TracingPolicy:

```
spec:
 kprobes:
 - call: "fd_install"
...
    matchArgs:
    - index: 1
      operator: "Prefix"
      values:
```

```
    - "/etc/"
  ...
```

This policy defines a set of kprobes to attach programs to, the first of which is the kernel function `fd_install`. This is an internal function in the kernel. Let's explore why you might choose to attach to a function like that.

Attaching to Internal Kernel Functions

The system call interface and the LSM interface are defined as stable interfaces in the Linux kernel; that is to say, they won't change in a backward-incompatible way. If you write code today that uses the functions in those interfaces, they will continue to work in future versions of the kernel. These interfaces represent just a tiny fraction of the 30 million lines of code that make up the Linux kernel. Parts of that codebase are de facto stable, even if they are not officially declared as such; they haven't changed for a long time and are unlikely to do so in the future.

It's perfectly reasonable to write eBPF programs that attach to kernel functions that aren't officially stable, with the expectation that they are likely to work for some considerable time to come. Also, given that it typically takes several years for a new kernel version to be widely deployed, it's a safe bet that there will be plenty of time to address any incompatibility issues that might arise.

The Tetragon contributors include a number of kernel developers who have used their knowledge of kernel internals to identify some good, safe places where eBPF programs can be attached for useful security purposes. There are several example TracingPolicy definitions (*https://oreil.ly/51yRN*) that make use of this knowledge. These examples monitor security events covering file operations, network activity, program executions, and changes to privileges—all the kinds of things a malicious actor would do as part of an attack.

Let's come back to that example policy definition that attaches to `fd_install`. The "fd" stands for "file descriptor," and the comment in the source code for this function (*https://oreil.ly/Tm6MN*) tells us this function "Install[s] a file pointer in the fd array." This happens when a file is opened, and it's called after the file's data structure has been populated in the kernel. It's a safe place to check the name of the file—and in the earlier TracingPolicy example, it's only of interest if the filename starts with "/etc/".

Just as in LSM BPF programs, Tetragon eBPF programs have access to contextual information to allow them to make security decisions entirely within the kernel. Rather than reporting all events of a given type to user space, security-relevant events can be filtered within the kernel so that only the out-of-policy events get reported to user space.

Preventative Security

Most eBPF-based security tools have used eBPF programs to detect malicious events, which notify a user space application that can then take action. As you can see in Figure 9-4, any action the user space app takes happens asynchronously, by which time it might be too late—perhaps data could have been exfiltrated, or the attacker could have persisted malicious code onto disk.

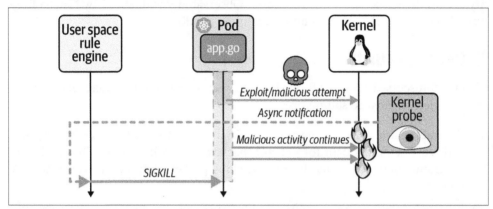

Figure 9-4. An asynchronous notification from kernel to user space allows some time for an attack to continue

In kernel versions 5.3 and up, there is a BPF helper function called `bpf_send_signal()`. Tetragon uses this function to implement preventative security. If a policy defines a Sigkill action, any matching events will cause Tetragon eBPF code to generate a SIGKILL signal that terminates the process that was attempting the out-of-policy action. As shown in Figure 9-5, this happens synchronously; that is, the activity the kernel was performing that the eBPF code determined to be out of policy is prevented from completing.

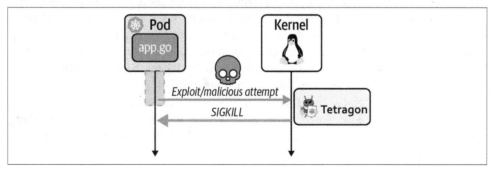

Figure 9-5. Tetragon kills malicious processes synchronously by sending a SIGKILL signal from the kernel

Sigkill policies need to be used with care, because an incorrectly configured policy could result in terminating applications unnecessarily, but it's an incredibly powerful use of eBPF for security purposes. You can start by running in an "audit" mode that generates security events but doesn't apply the SIGKILL enforcement, until you're confident that the policy won't break anything.

If you're interested in learning more about using Cilium Tetragon for detecting security events, there is a report titled "Security Observability with eBPF" by Natália Réka Ivánkó and Jed Salazar that digs into much more detail.

Network Security

Chapter 8 discussed how eBPF can be used very effectively to implement network security mechanisms. To summarize:

- Firewalling and DDoS protection are a natural fit for eBPF programs attached early in the ingress path for network packets. And with the possibility of XDP programs offloaded to hardware, malicious packets may never even reach the CPU!
- For implementing more sophisticated network policies, such as Kubernetes policies determining which services are allowed to communicate with one another, eBPF programs that attach to points in the network stack can drop packets if they are determined to be out of policy.

Network security tools are very often used in a preventative mode, dropping packets rather than just auditing malicious activity. This is because it's so easy for bad actors to mount network-related attacks; if you give a device a public IP address exposed to the internet, it won't be long before you start seeing suspicious traffic, so organizations are forced to use preventative measures.

In contrast, lots of organizations use intrusion detection tools in an audit mode, and they rely on forensics to determine whether a suspicious event was really malicious and what remedial action needs to be taken. If a given security tool is too blunt an instrument and is prone to detecting false-positives, it's not surprising that it needs to be run in audit mode rather than preventative mode. It's my belief that eBPF is enabling more sophisticated security tools with finer-grained, accurate controls. Just as we consider firewalls today to be sufficiently accurate to use in preventative mode, we'll see increased use of preventative tooling that acts on other, non-networking events. This could even include eBPF-based controls being packaged as part of an application product so that it can provide its own runtime security.

Summary

In this chapter you saw how eBPF's use in security has evolved from low-level checks on system calls to much more sophisticated use of eBPF programs for security policy checks, in-kernel event filtering, and runtime enforcement.

There's still much active development in the area of using eBPF for security purposes. I believe we will see tools in this area evolving and becoming widely adopted over the coming years.

eBPF Programming

In this book so far, you've learned a lot about eBPF and seen many examples of how it's used for a variety of applications. But what if you want to implement your own ideas based on eBPF? This chapter discusses your options when it comes to writing your own eBPF code.

As you know from reading this book, eBPF programming consists of two parts:

- Writing eBPF programs that run in the kernel
- Writing the user space code that manages and interacts with eBPF programs

Most of the libraries and languages I'll discuss in this chapter require you as a programmer to handle both parts, with an awareness of what is being handled where. But bpftrace, perhaps the simplest eBPF programming language, masks this distinction from the programmer.

Bpftrace

As described on the project's *README* page, "bpftrace is a high-level tracing language for Linux eBPF ... inspired by awk and C, and predecessor tracers such as DTrace and SystemTap."

The bpftrace (*https://oreil.ly/BZNZO*) command-line tool converts programs written in this high-level language into eBPF kernel code and provides some output formatting for the results within the terminal. As a user, you don't really need to think about the kernel–user space split.

You'll find several examples of useful one-liners in the project documentation, including a nice tutorial (*https://oreil.ly/Ah2QB*) that takes you from writing a simple "Hello

World" script up to writing more sophisticated scripts that can trace out data read from within kernel data structures.

 Get a feel for the range of capabilities that bpftrace provides from Brendan Gregg's bpftrace cheat sheet (*https://oreil.ly/VBwLm*). Or, for in-depth coverage of both bpftrace and BCC, see his book *BPF Performance Tools* (*https://oreil.ly/kjc95*).

As its name suggests, bpftrace can attach to tracing (also known as perf-related) events, including kprobes, uprobes, and tracepoints. For example, you can list the available tracepoints and kprobes on a machine with the -l option, like this:

```
$ bpftrace -l "*execve*"
tracepoint:syscalls:sys_enter_execve
tracepoint:syscalls:sys_exit_execve
...
kprobe:do_execve_file
kprobe:do_execve
kprobe:__ia32_sys_execve
kprobe:__x64_sys_execve
...
```

This example finds all the available attachment points that contain "execve." From this output you can see that it's possible to attach to a kprobe called do_execve. Here's a bpftrace one-line script that attaches to that event:

```
bpftrace -e 'kprobe:do_execve { @[comm] = count(); }'
Attaching 1 probe...
^C

@[node]: 6
@[sh]: 6
@[cpuUsage.sh]: 18
```

The { @[comm] = count(); } part is the script attached to that event. This example keeps track of the number of times the event was triggered by different executables.

Scripts for bpftrace can coordinate multiple eBPF programs attached to different events. For example, consider the *opensnoop.bt* script (*https://oreil.ly/3HWZ2*) that reports on files being opened. Here is an extract:

```
tracepoint:syscalls:sys_enter_open,
tracepoint:syscalls:sys_enter_openat
{
    @filename[tid] = args->filename;
}

tracepoint:syscalls:sys_exit_open,
tracepoint:syscalls:sys_exit_openat
/@filename[tid]/
```

```
{
    $ret = args->ret;
    $fd = $ret > 0 ? $ret : -1;
    $errno = $ret > 0 ? 0 : - $ret;

    printf("%-6d %-16s %4d %3d %s\n", pid, comm, $fd, $errno,
        str(@filename[tid]));
    delete(@filename[tid]);
}
```

This script defines two different eBPF programs, each attached to two different kernel tracepoints, at the entry to and exit from the open() and openat() syscalls.[1] Both of these syscalls are used to open files and take a filename as an input argument. The program triggered by either flavor of syscall entry caches that filename, storing it in a map where the key is the current thread ID. When the exit tracepoint is hit, the cached filename is retrieved from this map by the /@filename[tid]/ line in the script.

Running this script generates output like this:

```
./opensnoop.bt
Attaching 6 probes...
Tracing open syscalls... Hit Ctrl-C to end.
PID     COMM            FD ERR PATH
297388 node            30   0 /home/liz/.vscode-server/data/User/
                               workspaceStorage/73ace3ed015
297360 node            23   0 /proc/307224/cmdline
297360 node            23   0 /proc/305897/cmdline
297360 node            23   0 /proc/307224/cmdline
```

I've just told you there are four eBPF programs attached to tracepoints, so why does this output say there are six probes? The answer is that there are two "special probes" for the BEGIN and END clauses that the full version of this program includes to initialize and clean up the script (very similar to the awk language). I've omitted those clauses here for brevity, but you can find them in the source code in GitHub (*https://oreil.ly/X8wgW*).

If you're using bpftrace, you don't need to know about the underlying programs and maps, but for those of you who have read earlier chapters of this book, those concepts should be familiar to you by now. If you're interested to see the programs and maps that are loaded in the kernel while a bpftrace program is running, you can easily do this with bpftool (just as you saw in Chapter 3). Here's the output I got while running *opensnoop.bt*:

---

1 Being attached to syscall entry points means this script has the same Time Of Check To Time Of Use (TOC-TOU) vulnerability discussed in the previous chapter. That doesn't stop it from being a useful tool; it's just that you shouldn't rely on it as your only line of defense for security purposes.

```
$ bpftool prog list
...
494: tracepoint  name sys_enter_open  tag 6f08c3c150c4ce6e  gpl
        loaded_at 2022-11-18T12:44:05+0000  uid 0
        xlated 128B  jited 93B  memlock 4096B  map_ids 254
495: tracepoint  name sys_enter_opena  tag 26c093d1d907ce74  gpl
        loaded_at 2022-11-18T12:44:05+0000  uid 0
        xlated 128B  jited 93B  memlock 4096B  map_ids 254
496: tracepoint  name sys_exit_open  tag 0484b911472301f7  gpl
        loaded_at 2022-11-18T12:44:05+0000  uid 0
        xlated 936B  jited 565B  memlock 4096B  map_ids 254,255
497: tracepoint  name sys_exit_openat  tag 0484b911472301f7  gpl
        loaded_at 2022-11-18T12:44:05+0000  uid 0
        xlated 936B  jited 565B  memlock 4096B  map_ids 254,255

$ bpftool map list
254: hash  flags 0x0
        key 8B  value 8B  max_entries 4096  memlock 331776B
255: perf_event_array  name printf  flags 0x0
        key 4B  value 4B  max_entries 2  memlock 4096B
```

You can clearly see the four tracepoint programs, plus the hash map that's used for caching the filenames and the `perf_event_array` that is being used to pass output data from kernel to user space.

 The bpftrace utility is built on top of BCC, which you met elsewhere in this book and which I'll cover later in this chapter. bpftrace scripts get converted into BCC programs, which are then compiled at runtime using the LLVM/Clang toolchain.

If you want command-line tools for eBPF-based performance measurement, you may well find that your needs are met using bpftrace (*https://oreil.ly/u5FrJ*). But although bpftrace can be a powerful tool for using eBPF for tracing, it doesn't open up the full range of possibilities that eBPF enables.

To unlock the full potential of eBPF, you'll need to directly write eBPF programs yourself for the kernel and also handle the user space part. These two aspects can, and often are, written in entirely different languages. Let's start with the choices for eBPF code that runs in the kernel.

Language Choices for eBPF in the Kernel

eBPF programs can be written directly in eBPF bytecode,[2] but in practice, most are compiled to bytecode from either C or Rust. These languages have compilers that support eBPF bytecode as a target output.

 eBPF bytecode isn't a suitable target for all compiled languages. If the language involves a runtime component (like Go, or Java's virtual machine), it's likely to be incompatible with eBPF's verifier. For example, it's hard to imagine how memory garbage collection could work hand in hand with the verifier's checks on safe use of memory. Similarly, eBPF programs are required to be single threaded, so any concurrency features in a language couldn't be used.

Although not really eBPF, there is an interesting project called XDPLua (*https:// oreil.ly/7_3Fx*) that proposes writing XDP programs in Lua scripts that run directly within the kernel. However, the initial research in this project suggested that eBPF would likely be more performant, and as eBPF becomes more powerful with each kernel release (e.g., now being able to implement loops), it's not clear that there is much advantage other than the personal preference that some people might have to write code in Lua scripts.

I would hazard a guess that most people who choose to write eBPF kernel code in Rust would also opt for the same language for the user space code, since shared data structures wouldn't need to be rewritten. It's not obligatory, though—you can mix and match eBPF code with whatever user space language you choose.

Those who choose to write the kernel-side code in C also have the option to write user space code in C (you've seen plenty of examples of that in this book already). But C is a pretty low-level language that requires programmers to handle lots of details for themselves, notably, memory management. While some people are comfortable doing this, many people would prefer to write the user space code in another, higher-level language. Whatever your preferred language, you'd like a library that provides eBPF support so that you don't have to write directly to the system call interface you saw in Chapter 3. In the rest of this chapter we'll discuss some of the most popular options for eBPF libraries in a variety of languages.

---

2 For an example of this, check out Cloudflare's blog post "eBPF, Sockets, Hop Distance and manually writing eBPF assembly" (*https://oreil.ly/2GjuK*).

BCC Python/Lua/C++

Back in Chapter 2, the first "Hello World" example I gave you was a Python program written using the BCC library. This project includes plenty of useful performance measurement tools implemented using this same library (as well as newer implementations based on *libbpf* that I'll come to momentarily).

In addition to the documentation (*https://oreil.ly/Elggv*) that describes how to use the provided BCC tools to measure performance, BCC also includes a reference guide (*https://oreil.ly/WgeJA*) and a Python programming tutorial (*https://oreil.ly/hR3xr*) to help you develop your own eBPF tools in this framework.

Chapter 5 included a discussion of BCC's approach to portability, which is to compile the eBPF code at runtime to ensure that it's compatible with the target machine's kernel data structures. In BCC, you define the kernel-side eBPF program code as a string (or the contents of a file that BCC reads into a string). This string gets passed to Clang for compilation, but before that happens, BCC does some preprocessing on the string. This enables it to provide handy shortcuts for the programmer, some of which you've seen already in this book. For example, here are some relevant lines from the example code in *chapter2/hello_map.py*:

```
#!/usr/bin/python3                                     ❶
from bcc import BPF

program = """                                          ❷
BPF_RINGBUF_OUTPUT(output, 1);                         ❸
...
int hello(void *ctx) {
  ...
    output.ringbuf_output(&data, sizeof(data), 0);     ❹

    return 0;
}
"""

b = BPF(text=program)                                  ❺
...

b["output"].open_ring_buffer(print_event)              ❻
...
```

❶ This is a Python program, which will run in user space.

❷ The program string holds the eBPF program to be compiled and then loaded into the kernel.

❸   BPF_RINGBUF_OUTPUT is a BCC macro that defines a ring buffer called output. This is part of the program string, so it's natural to assume it's defining the buffer from the kernel's perspective. Hold that thought until we get to callout 6.

❹   This line looks like a ringbuf_output() method on an object called object. But wait a minute—methods on objects aren't even part of the C language! BCC is doing some heavy lifting here, expanding methods (*https://oreil.ly/vLVth*) like these into underlying BPF helper functions, bpf_ringbuf_output() in this case.

❺   This is where the program string gets rewritten into the BPF C code that Clang can compile. This line also loads the resultant program into the kernel.

❻   There is no other place in the code that defines the ring buffer called output, and yet it's accessible from the Python user space code here. BCC does double duty when it preprocesses the line in callout 3, as it defines the ring buffer for both the user space and kernel parts.

As this example shows, BCC essentially provides its own C-like language for BPF programming. It makes life easy for the programmer, handling things like shared structure definitions for both kernel and user space and providing convenient short-cuts to wrap around BPF helper functions. This means BCC is an accessible way to get into eBPF programming if you're new to the field, especially if you're already comfortable with Python.

 If you'd like to explore BCC programming, this tutorial aimed at Python programmers (*https://oreil.ly/0pHKY*) is a great way to walk through many more of the features and capabilities of BCC than there is space for in this book.

The documentation doesn't make it terribly clear, but as well as supporting Python as the language for the user space part of eBPF tools, BCC enables writing tools in Lua and C++. There are *lua* and *cpp* directories within the supplied examples (*https://oreil.ly/PP0cL*) that you can base your own code on, should you be keen to try this approach.

BCC may be convenient for the programmer, but because of the inefficiencies of distributing a compiler toolchain alongside your utility (discussed in more depth in Chapter 5), if you're looking to write production-quality tools that you intend to distribute, I recommend considering some of the other libraries discussed in this chapter.

C and Libbpf

You've seen lots of examples in this book of eBPF programs written in C, using the LLVM toolchain to compile into eBPF bytecode. You've also seen that extensions were added to support BTF and CO-RE. Many C programmers will also be familiar with the other major C compiler, GCC, and will be happy to hear that GCC from version 10 (*https://oreil.ly/XAzxP*) also supports compiling to eBPF as a target; however, there are still some gaps compared with the functionality provided in LLVM.

As you saw in Chapter 5, CO-RE and *libbpf* enabled an approach to portable eBPF programming that doesn't require shipping a compiler toolchain alongside every eBPF tool. The BCC project took advantage of this and, in addition to the original set of BCC performance tracing tools, it now has versions of these tools rewritten to take advantage of *libbpf*. The general consensus is that the versions of the BCC tools that have been rewritten based on *libbpf* are the better option to use, since they have a significantly lower memory footprint[3] and don't involve a start-up delay while the compilation step takes place.

If you're comfortable with programming in C, using *libbpf* can make a lot of sense. You've seen lots of examples of this already in this book.

 To write your own *libbpf* programs in C, the best place to start (now that you have read this book!) is *libbpf-bootstrap* (*https://oreil.ly/4mx81*). Read Andrii Nakryiko's blog post about it (*https://oreil.ly/-OW8v*) as a good introduction to the motivations behind this project.

There's also a library called *libxdp* (*https://oreil.ly/374mL*) that builds on *libbpf* to allow for easier development and management of XDP programs. This is part of xdp-tools, which also holds one of my favorite learning resources for eBPF programming: the XDP Tutorial (*https://oreil.ly/E6dvl*).[4]

But C is quite a challenging, low-level language. C programmers have to take responsibility for things like memory management and buffer handling, and it's very easy to end up writing code with security vulnerabilities, not to mention crashes due to mishandling pointers. The eBPF verifier helps out on the kernel side, but there is no equivalent protection for your user space code.

---

3 See, for example, Brendan Gregg's observation (*https://oreil.ly/fz_dQ*) that the *libbpf*-based version of open-snoop required around 9 MB compared with 80 MB for the Python-based version.

4 Watch me working through some of the XDP Tutorial examples in episode 13 of the eBPF and Cilium Office Hours" livestream (*https://oreil.ly/9SaKn*).

The good news is that there are libraries for other programming languages that interface to *libbpf*, or provide similar relocation functionality to allow for portable eBPF programs. Here are a few of the most popular ones.

Go

The Go language has been widely adopted for infrastructure and cloud native tooling, so it's natural that there should be options for writing eBPF code in it.

 This article by Michael Kashin (*https://oreil.ly/s9umt*) provides another perspective comparing different eBPF libraries for Go.

Gobpf

Possibly the first serious Golang implementation was the gobpf (*https://oreil.ly/pC0dF*) project that sits alongside BCC as part of Iovisor. However, it hasn't been actively maintained for a while, and as I write this, there's some discussion of deprecating it (*https://oreil.ly/MnE79*), so bear this in mind when making your library choice.

Ebpf-go

The eBPF Go library included as part of the Cilium project (*https://oreil.ly/BnGyl*) is widely used (I found around 10,000 references on GitHub, and the project has close to 4,000 stars). It provides convenient functions for managing and loading eBPF programs and maps, including CO-RE support, all implemented purely in Go.

With this library you have the option to compile your eBPF programs to bytecode and embed that bytecode into Go source code, using a supplied tool called bpf2go (*https://oreil.ly/-kDbH*). You need the LLVM/Clang compiler to do this generation as part of the build step. Once the Go code is compiled, you have a single Go binary that you can distribute that includes the eBPF bytecode and is portable to different kernels, without any dependencies other than the Linux kernel itself.

The *cilium/ebpf* library also supports loading and managing eBPF programs built as standalone ELF files (like the **.bpf.o* examples you have seen in this book).

At the time of this writing, the *cilium/ebpf* library supports the perf events for tracing, including the relatively recent fentry events, as well as an extensive set of network program types like XDP and cgroup socket attachments.

In this project's *examples* directory under *cilium/ebpf* (*https://oreil.ly/Vuf9d*), you'll see that the C code for in-kernel programs sits in the same directories as the corresponding user space code in Go:

- The C files start with `// +build ignore`, which tells the Go compiler to ignore them. At the time of this writing there is an update in progress (*https://oreil.ly/ymuyn*) to change to the newer `//go:build` style of build tag.

- The user space files include a line like the following, which tells the Go compiler to invoke the bpf2go tool on the C file(s):

```
//go:generate go run github.com/cilium/ebpf/cmd/bpf2go -cc $BPF_CLANG
                -cflags $BPF_CFLAGS bpf <C filename> -- -I../headers
```

Running `go:generate` on the package rebuilds the eBPF program and regenerates the skeleton in a single step.

Much like `bpftool gen skeleton`, which you saw in Chapter 5, bpf2go generates skeleton code for manipulating the eBPF objects, minimizing the user space code you need to write yourself (except it's generating Go code rather than C). The output files also include the *.o* object files containing the bytecode.

In fact, bpf2go generates two versions of the bytecode *.o* files, for big- and little-endian architectures. There are also two correspondingly generated *.go* files, and the correct versions for the target platform get used at compile time. As an example, the auto-generated files in the kprobe example from *cilium/ebpf* (*https://oreil.ly/CgwVd*) are:

- The *bpf_bpfeb.o* and *bpf_bpfel.o* ELF files containing eBPF bytecode
- The *bpf_bpfeb.go* and *bpf_bpfel.go* files, which define Go structures and functions that correspond to the maps, programs, and links defined in that bytecode

You can relate the objects defined in the auto-generated Go code to the C code from which it was generated. Here are the objects defined in the C code for that kprobe example:

```
struct bpf_map_def SEC("maps") kprobe_map = {
...
};

SEC("kprobe/sys_execve")
int kprobe_execve() {
...
}
```

The auto-generated Go code includes structures representing all the maps and programs (in this case, there is only one of each):

```
type bpfMaps struct {
    KprobeMap *ebpf.Map `ebpf:"kprobe_map"`
}

type bpfPrograms struct {
    KprobeExecve *ebpf.Program `ebpf:"kprobe_execve"`
}
```

The names "KprobeMap" and "KprobeExecve" are derived from the map and program names used in the C code. These objects are grouped into a bpfObjects structure representing everything that's being loaded into the kernel:

```
type bpfObjects struct {
    bpfPrograms
    bpfMaps
}
```

You can then use these object definitions and related auto-generated functions in
your user space Go code. To give you an idea of what this might involve, here's an
extract based on the main function from the same kprobe example (*https://oreil.ly/
YXAjH*) (omitting error handling for brevity):

```
objs := bpfObjects{}
loadBpfObjects(&objs, nil)                              ❶
defer objs.Close()

kp, _ := link.Kprobe("sys_execve",
                     objs.KprobeExecve, nil)            ❷
defer kp.Close()

ticker := time.NewTicker(1 * time.Second)              ❸
defer ticker.Stop()

for range ticker.C {
    var value uint64
    objs.KprobeMap.Lookup(mapKey, &value)              ❹
    log.Printf("%s called %d times\n", fn, value)
}
```

❶ Load all the BPF objects that were embedded in bytecode form, into the bpfOb
    jects I just showed you defined by the auto-generated code.

❷ Attach the program to the sys_execve kprobe.

❸ Set up a ticker so that the code can poll the map once per second.

❹ Read an item out of the map.

There are several other examples in the *cilium/ebpf* directory that you can use for reference and inspiration.

Libbpfgo

The *libbpfgo* project (*https://oreil.ly/gvbXr*) by Aqua Security implements a Go wrapper around *libbpf*'s C code, providing utilities for loading and attaching programs and using Go-native features like channels for receiving events. Because it's built on *libbpf*, it supports CO-RE.

Here's an extract from the example from *libbpfgo*'s *README*, which gives a good high-level view of what to expect from this library:

```
bpfModule := bpf.NewModuleFromFile(bpfObjectPath)        ❶
bpfModule.BPFLoadObject()                                ❷

mymap, _ := bpfModule.GetMap("mymap")                    ❸
mymap.Update(key, value)

rb, _ := bpfModule.InitRingBuffer("events", eventsChannel, buffSize)
rb.Start()
e := <-eventsChannel                                     ❹
```

❶ Read eBPF bytecode from an object file.

❷ Load that bytecode into the kernel.

❸ Manipulate an entry in an eBPF map.

❹ Go programmers will appreciate receiving data from a ring or perf buffer on a channel, which is a language feature designed to handle asynchronous events.

This library was created for Aqua's Tracee (*https://oreil.ly/A03zd*) security project, and it's also being used by other projects such as Parca (*https://oreil.ly/s8JP9*) from Polar Signals, which provides eBPF-based CPU profiling. The only concern about this project's approach is the CGo boundary between the *libbpf* C code and Go, which can cause performance and other issues.[5]

While Go has been the established language for lots of infrastructure coding for around a decade, there has more recently been a growing body of developers who prefer to use Rust.

Rust

Rust is increasingly being used for building infrastructure tools. It allows for the low-level access of C, but with the added benefit of memory safety. Indeed, Linus Torvalds

---

5 Dave Cheney's 2016 post "cgo is not Go (*https://oreil.ly/mxThs*)" remains a good overview of concerns related to the CGo boundary.

confirmed in 2022 (*https://oreil.ly/7fINA*) that the Linux kernel itself will start to incorporate Rust code, and the recent 6.1 release has some initial Rust support (*https://oreil.ly/HrXy2*).

As I discussed earlier in this chapter, Rust can be compiled to eBPF bytecode, meaning that (with the right library support) it's possible to write both the user space and kernel code for eBPF utilities in Rust.

There are a few options for Rust eBPF development: *libbpf-rs*, *Redbpf*, and Aya.

Libbpf-rs

Libbpf-rs (*https://oreil.ly/qBagk*) is part of the *libbpf* project, and provides a Rust wrapper around the *libbpf* C code so that you can write the user space parts of eBPF code in Rust. As you can see from the project's examples (*https://oreil.ly/6wpf8*), the eBPF programs themselves are written in C.

> There are further examples in Rust in the *libbpf-bootstrap* (*https://oreil.ly/ter6c*) project, designed to help you get off the ground if you want to try building your own code using this crate.

This crate is helpful for incorporating eBPF programs into a Rust-based project, but it doesn't fulfill the desire that many people have to write the kernel-side code in Rust as well. Let's look at some other projects that enable that.

Redbpf

Redbpf (*https://oreil.ly/AtJod*) is a set of Rust crates that interface with *libbpf*, developed as part of foniod (*https://oreil.ly/dwGNK*), an eBPF-based security monitoring agent.

Redbpf predates Rust's ability to compile to eBPF bytecode, so it uses a multistep compilation process (*https://oreil.ly/DuHxE*) that involves compiling from Rust to LLVM bitcode and then using the LLVM toolchain to generate eBPF bytecode in ELF format. *Redbpf* supports a range of program types including tracepoints, kprobes and uprobes, XDP, TC, and some socket events.

As the Rust compiler rustc gained the ability to generate eBPF bytecode directly, this was leveraged by a project called Aya. At the time of this writing, Aya is considered "emerging" according to the community site at ebpf.io (*https://oreil.ly/WynV6*), while *Redbpf* is listed as a major project, but my personal perspective is that momentum seems to be moving toward Aya.

Aya

Aya (*https://aya-rs.dev/book*) is built in Rust directly to the syscall level, so it doesn't depend on *libbpf* (or indeed on BCC or the LLVM toolchain). But it does support the BTF format, the same relocations that *libbpf* does (as described in Chapter 5), so it's providing the same CO-RE abilities to compile once and run on other kernels. At the time of this writing, it supports a wider range of eBPF program types than *Redbpf*, including tracing/perf-related events, XDP and TC, cgroups, and LSM attachments.

As I mentioned, the Rust compiler also supports compiling to eBPF bytecode (*https://oreil.ly/a5q7M*), so this language can be used for both kernel and user space eBPF programming.

 The ability to write both the kernel side and the user space side natively in Rust without the intermediate dependency on LLVM has attracted Rust programmers to this option. There's an interesting discussion on GitHub (*https://oreil.ly/nls4l*) about why the developers of the lockc project (*https://oreil.ly/_-L6z*) (an eBPF-based project that enhances the security of container workloads using LSM hooks) decided to port their project from *libbpf-rs* to Aya.

The project includes aya-tool (*https://oreil.ly/Kd0nf*), a utility for generating Rust structure definitions that match kernel data structures so that you don't have to write them yourself.

The Aya project strongly emphasizes developer experience and makes it easy for newcomers to get started. With that in mind, the "Aya book" (*https://aya-rs.dev/book*) is a very readable introduction with some good example code, annotated with helpful explanations.

To give you a brief idea of what eBPF code looks like in Rust, here's an extract from Aya's basic XDP example that permits all traffic:

```
#[xdp(name="myapp")]                                        ❶
pub fn myapp(ctx: XdpContext) -> u32 {
    match unsafe { try_myapp(ctx) } {                       ❷
        Ok(ret) => ret,
        Err(_) => xdp_action::XDP_ABORTED,
    }
}

unsafe fn try_myapp(ctx: XdpContext) -> Result<u32, u32> {  ❸
    info!(&ctx, "received a packet");
    Ok(xdp_action::XDP_PASS)
}
```

This line is what defines the section name, equivalent to SEC("xdp/myapp") in C.

❷ The eBPF program called myapp calls the function try_myapp to process a network packet received at XDP.

❸ The try_myapp function logs the fact that a packet was received and always returns the XDP_PASS value that tells the kernel to carry on processing the packet as usual.

Just as we've seen in C-based examples throughout this book, the eBPF program gets compiled to an ELF object file. The difference is that Aya uses the Rust compiler instead of Clang to create that file.

Aya also generates code for the user space activities of loading the eBPF program into the kernel and attaching it to an event. Here are a few key lines from the user space side of that same basic example:

```
let mut bpf = Bpf::load(include_bytes_aligned!(
    "../../target/bpfel-unknown-none/release/myapp"
))?;                                                              ❶

let program: &mut Xdp = bpf.program_mut("myapp").unwrap().try_into()?;  ❷

program.load()?;                                                 ❸
program.attach(&opt.iface, XdpFlags::default())                  ❹
```

❶ Read the eBPF bytecode from the ELF object file produced by the compiler.

❷ Find the program called myapp in that bytecode.

❸ Load it into the kernel.

❹ Attach it to the XDP event on a specified network interface.

If you're a Rust programmer, I highly recommend you explore the additional examples (*https://oreil.ly/bp_Hq*) in the "Aya book" in more detail. There's also a nice blog post from Kong (*https://oreil.ly/mUVIk*) that walks through writing an XDP load balancer using Aya.

 Aya maintainers Dave Tucker and Alessandro Decina joined me for episode 25 of the "eBPF and Cilium Office Hours" livestream (*https://oreil.ly/U7bRu*) where they demonstrated and gave an introduction to eBPF programming with Aya.

Rust-bcc

Rust-bcc (*https://oreil.ly/prP_K*) provides Rust bindings that mimic the BCC project's Python bindings, along with some Rust implementations of some of the BCC set of tracing tools (*https://oreil.ly/Dd2nO*).

Testing BPF Programs

There's a bpf() command, BPF_PROG_RUN (*https://oreil.ly/Y2xPC*), that allows for running an eBPF program from user space for test purposes.

BPF_PROG_RUN (currently) works only with a subset of BPF program types that are mostly networking related.

You can also get information about eBPF program performance with some built-in statistics information. Run the following command to enable it:

```
$ sysctl -w kernel.bpf_stats_enabled=1
```

This will show additional information in bpftool's output about programs, like this:

```
$ bpftool prog list
...
2179: raw_tracepoint  name raw_tp_exec  tag 7f6d182e48b7ed38  gpl
        run_time_ns 316876 run_cnt 4
        loaded_at 2023-01-09T11:07:31+0000  uid 0
        xlated 216B  jited 264B  memlock 4096B  map_ids 780,777
        btf_id 953
        pids hello(19173)
```

The additional statistics are shown in bold, and here they show that the program has run four times, taking about 300 microseconds in total.

> Learn more from Quentin Monnet's FOSDEM 2020 talk titled "Tools and mechanisms to debug BPF programs." (*https://oreil.ly/I5Jhd*)

Multiple eBPF Programs

An eBPF program is a function attached to an event in the kernel. Many applications need to track more than one event to achieve their goals. A simple example of this is opensnoop.[6] I covered the `bpftrace` version of this early in this chapter, and you saw that it attaches BPF programs to four different syscall tracepoints:

- `syscall_enter_open`
- `syscall_exit_open`
- `syscall_enter_openat`
- `syscall_exit_openat`

These are the entry and exit points to the kernel's handling of the `open()` and `openat()` system calls. These two system calls can be used for opening files, and the opensnoop tool tracks both of them.

But why does it need to track both entry and exit for these system calls? The entry points are used because that's when the system call arguments are available, and these include the filename and any flags being passed to the `open[at]` syscall. But at that stage it's too soon to know whether the file will be opened successfully or not. That explains why it's necessary to have eBPF programs attached to the exit points too.

If you look at the *libbpf-tools* version of opensnoop (*https://oreil.ly/IOty_*), you'll see there's just one user space program, and it loads all four eBPF programs into the kernel and attaches them to their events. The eBPF programs themselves are essentially independent, but they use eBPF maps to coordinate among themselves.

A complex application might even need to add and remove eBPF programs dynamically throughout a long period of time. There may not even be a fixed number of eBPF programs for any given application. For example, Cilium attaches eBPF programs to each virtual networking interface, and in a Kubernetes environment these interfaces come and go depending on how many pods are running.

Most of the libraries in this chapter handle this multiplicity of eBPF programs automatically. For example, *libbpf* and *ebpf-go* generate skeleton code that will load *all* the programs and maps from the bytecode in an object file or buffer in one function call. They also generate finer-granularity functions so that you can manipulate programs and maps individually.

Summary

The vast majority of people who use eBPF-based tooling won't need to write eBPF code themselves, but if you do find yourself wanting to implement something your-

---

6 As well as the `bpftrace` version of this tool, there are equivalents in BCC and in *libbpf-tools*. They all do very much the same thing, generating a line of trace whenever a process opens a file. There's a walkthrough of the eBPF code for BCC's version of opensnoop in my report "What Is eBPF?".

self, you have a lot of options. This is a changing field, so it's very possible that by the time you read this, new language libraries and frameworks might exist, or consensus may have gathered around some of the libraries I've highlighted in this chapter. You'll find an up-to-date list of the major language projects around eBPF on the Infrastructure page of ebpf.io's list of significant projects (*https://ebpf.io/infrastructure*).

For quickly collecting trace information, bpftrace can be a very valuable option.

For more flexibility and control, BCC is a fast way to build an eBPF tool if you're comfortable with Python, provided that you don't care about the compilation step that takes place at runtime.

If you're writing eBPF code to be widely distributed and portable across different kernel versions, you'll probably want to take advantage of CO-RE. The user space frameworks that support CO-RE at time of this writing are *libbpf* for C, *cilium/ebpf* and *libbpfgo* for Go, and Aya for Rust.

For further advice, I highly recommend joining the eBPF Slack (*http://ebpf.io/slack*) and discussing your questions there. You'll likely find the maintainers of many of these language libraries in that community.

Exercises

If you'd like to try one or more of the libraries discussed in this chapter, "Hello World" is always a good place to start:

1. Using one or more libraries of your choosing, write an example "Hello World" program that outputs a simple trace message.

2. Use llvm-objdump to compare the bytecode produced with the "Hello World" example from Chapter 3. You'll find lots of similarities!

3. As you saw in Chapter 4, you can use strace -e bpf to see when bpf() system calls are made. Try that on your "Hello World" program to see if it's behaving as you expect.

CHAPTER 11

The Future Evolution of eBPF

eBPF is not finished yet! Like most software, it's under continual development within the Linux kernel, and it's being added to the Windows operating system as well. In this chapter we'll look at some of the likely future paths for this technology.

Since it was introduced within the Linux kernel, BPF has evolved into its own subsystem with its own mailing list and maintainers.[1] As eBPF's popularity increased and interest broadened beyond the Linux kernel community, it made sense to create a neutral body that could coordinate among the different parties involved. That body is the eBPF Foundation.

The eBPF Foundation

The eBPF Foundation (*https://ebpf.io/foundation*) was set up in 2021 by Google, Isovalent, Meta (then known as Facebook), Microsoft, and Netflix, under the auspices of the Linux Foundation. The foundation acts as a neutral body that can hold funds and intellectual property, such that various commercial companies can collaborate with one another.

The intent was not to change anything about the way eBPF technology is developed by the Linux kernel community and contributors to the Linux BPF subsystem. The foundation's activities are directed by the BPF Steering Committee, which is entirely composed of the technical experts who build the technology, including the Linux kernel BPF maintainers and representatives from other core eBPF projects.

---

1 Shout-out to Alexei Starovoitov and Andrii Nakryiko from Meta, and Daniel Borkmann from Isovalent, who maintain the BPF subtree in the Linux kernel.

The eBPF Foundation focuses on eBPF as a technology platform and the ecosystem of tools that enable eBPF development. Projects that build on top of eBPF looking for neutral ownership may find a better home in other foundations. For example, Cilium, Pixie, and Falco are all part of the CNCF, which makes sense as they are all intended to be used in cloud native environments.

One of the key drivers of this collaboration beyond the existing Linux maintainers was the interest that Microsoft had in developing eBPF within the Windows operating system. This brings about a need to define a standard for eBPF,[2] such that programs written for one OS can be used on another. This work is being done under the auspices of the eBPF Foundation.

eBPF for Windows

Work is well underway at Microsoft to support eBPF for Windows (*https://oreil.ly/ArwkR*). As I write this in the closing months of 2022, there are already functional demos (*https://oreil.ly/H-0dv*) that show Cilium Layer 4 load balancing and eBPF-based connection tracking running on Windows.

I've said before that eBPF programming is kernel programming, and at first glance it might seem unintuitive that a program written to run in the Linux kernel and that has access to Linux kernel data structures would in any way be able to operate in an entirely different operating system. But in practice, particularly when it comes to networking, all operating systems will have quite a lot in common. A network packet has the same structure whether it was created on a Windows or Linux machine, and the layers of the network stack have to be handled the same way.

You'll also recall that eBPF programs consist of a set of bytecode instructions that are processed by a virtual machine (VM) implemented within the kernel. That VM can be implemented within Windows too!

Figure 11-1 shows the eBPF for Windows architectural overview, taken from the project's GitHub repo (*https://oreil.ly/Ii4j2*). As you can see from this diagram, eBPF for Windows reuses some open source components from the existing eBPF ecosystem, such as *libbpf*, and the support in Clang for producing eBPF bytecode. The Linux kernel is licensed under GPL, and Windows is proprietary, so the Windows project can't reuse any parts of the Linux kernel's implementation of the verifier.[3] Instead, it uses the PREVAIL verifier (*https://vbpf.github.io*) and the uBPF JIT

---

2 Dave Thaler presented on the state of this standardization work (*https://oreil.ly/4bo6Y*) at the Linux Plumbers Conference.

3 Well, it *could*, but doing so would require Microsoft to also release the Windows source code under the GPL license.

compiler (*https://oreil.ly/btrkJ*) (both of which are permissively licensed so that they can be used by a broader range of projects and organizations).

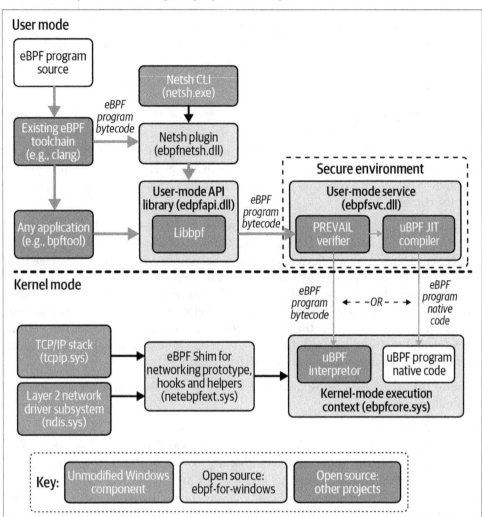

Figure 11-1. Architectural overview of eBPF for Windows, adapted from https://oreil.ly/ HxKsu

One interesting difference is that eBPF code is verified and JIT-compiled in a Windows Secure environment in user space rather than within the kernel (the uBPF interpreter shown in the kernel in Figure 11-1 is used only in debug builds and not production environments).

It would be unrealistic to expect that every single eBPF program written to run on Linux will work on Windows. But this isn't so different from the challenge of getting eBPF programs to run on different Linux kernel versions: even with CO-RE support, internal kernel data structures can be changed as well as added or removed between versions. It is the eBPF programmer's job to handle these possibilities gracefully.

Speaking of changes to the Linux kernel, what changes can we expect to see in eBPF in the coming years?

Linux eBPF Evolution

The capabilities of eBPF have evolved with practically every kernel release since 3.15. If you want to know what features are available in any given version, the BCC project maintains a useful list (*https://oreil.ly/4H5hU*). And I certainly expect more additions over the coming years.

The best way to predict what's coming is simply to listen to the people who are working on it. For example, at the 2022 Linux Plumbers Conference, eBPF maintainer Alexei Starovoitov gave a talk discussing how he expects to see the C language used by eBPF programs to evolve.[4] We've already seen eBPF evolve from supporting a few thousand instructions to practically unlimited complexity, with the addition of support for loops and an ever-increasing set of BPF helper functions. As additional capabilities are added into the C that's supported, and with the support of the verifier, eBPF C could evolve to allow all the flexibility of developing kernel modules, but with the safety and dynamic loading characteristics of eBPF.

Some of the other ideas being discussed and developed for new eBPF features and capabilities include:

Signed eBPF programs

Software supply chain security has been a hot topic for the past few years, and a key element is the ability to check that a program you're thinking of running comes from the expected source and has not been tampered with. One way to achieve this is, in general, to validate a cryptographic signature that accompanies a program. You might think this is something the kernel could do for eBPF programs, perhaps as part of the verification step, but unfortunately this is not straightforward! As you've seen in this book, user space loaders dynamically adjust programs with information about where maps are located, and for CO-RE purposes, which from a signing perspective is hard to distinguish from malicious modifications. This is a problem for which the eBPF community is keen to find a solution (*https://oreil.ly/ns03-*).

---

4 Alexei Starovoitov discusses the journey of BPF from restricted C language to extended and safe C in this video (*https://oreil.ly/xunKW*).

Long-lived kernel pointers

An eBPF program can retrieve a pointer to a kernel object using a helper function or a kfunc, but a pointer is valid only during that execution of the program. The pointer cannot be stored in a map for later retrieval. The idea of typed pointer support (*https://oreil.ly/fWVdo*) will allow for more flexibility in this area.

Memory allocation

It's not safe for eBPF programs to simply call memory allocation functions like `kmalloc()`, but there is a proposal that suggests (*https://oreil.ly/Yxxc5*) an eBPF-specific alternative.

When will you be able to take advantage of new eBPF features as they emerge? As an end user, the features you're able to take advantage of depend on the version of the kernel you're running in production, and as I discussed in Chapter 1, it can take several years for kernel releases to make it to stable distributions of Linux. As an individual you might opt for a bleeding-edge kernel, but the vast majority of organizations running server deployments use a stable, supported version. eBPF programmers have to take into account that if they write code that takes advantage of the newest features added to the kernel, the features are unlikely to be usable in most production environments for some years to come. Some organizations will have sufficiently urgent needs that it's worth rolling out newer kernel versions more quickly in order to early-adopt new eBPF features.

For example, in another forward-looking talk on building tomorrow's networking (*https://oreil.ly/IvPgd*), Daniel Borkmann discussed a feature called *Big TCP*. This was added to Linux in version 5.19 to enable network speeds of 100 GBit/s (and faster) by batching up network packets to be processed in the kernel. Most Linux distributions won't support a kernel this recent for a few years, but for specialist organizations dealing with large amounts of network traffic, it might well be worth upgrading sooner. Adding Big TCP support into eBPF and Cilium today means it's available for those massive-scale users, even if it's not something that can be enabled by most of us for a while.

Since eBPF allows kernel code to be adjusted dynamically, it's reasonable to expect it to be used to address problems "in the field." In Chapter 9 you read about using eBPF to mitigate kernel vulnerabilities; work is also underway to use eBPF to help support hardware devices such as human interface devices (*https://oreil.ly/JVYcY*) like mice, keyboards, and game controllers. This builds on existing support for decoding the protocols used by infrared controllers that I mentioned in Chapter 7.

eBPF Is a Platform, Not a Feature

Coming up to a decade ago, the hot new technology was containers, and it seemed as though everyone was talking about what they were and what advantages they would bring. We're at a similar stage with eBPF today, with lots of conference talks and blog posts—several of which I've referred to in this book—extolling the benefits of eBPF. Today, containers are part of daily life for many developers, whether they're running code locally using Docker or other container runtimes, or deploying code to Kubernetes environments. Will eBPF become part of everyone's regular toolkit too?

The answer, I believe, is no—or at least, not directly. Most users won't write eBPF programs directly or manipulate them manually with utilities like `bpftool`. But they'll interact regularly with tools built using eBPF, whether that's for performance measurement, debugging, networking, security, tracing, or a whole host of other capabilities yet to be implemented using eBPF. Users might not be aware that they're using eBPF, much as they might not know that when they use containers, they're using kernel features like namespaces and cgroups.

Today, projects and vendors with knowledge of eBPF highlight their use of it because it's so powerful and implies many advantages. As eBPF-based projects and products gain traction and market share, eBPF is becoming the de facto default technology platform for infrastructure tooling.

Knowledge of eBPF programming is—and will continue to be—a sought-after but relatively rare skill, just as kernel development today is much less common than developing, say, business applications or games. If you enjoy diving into the lower levels of systems and want to build essential infrastructure tooling, eBPF skills will serve you well. I hope this book has been of some assistance on your eBPF journey!

Further Reading

Throughout this book I have provided references to specific articles and documentation pages. Here is a list of some additional resources to help you on your eBPF journey:

- The eBPF community site *ebpf.io*
- The BPF and XDP reference in the Cilium documentation (*https://docs.cilium.io*)
- Linux kernel documentation on BPF (*https://oreil.ly/q8xh3*)
- Brendan Gregg's website (*https://www.brendangregg.com*) on using eBPF for performance and observability
- Andrii Nakryiko's website (*https://nakryiko.com*), particularly for more information on CO-RE and *libbpf*

- Lwn.net, a wonderful resource for updates to the Linux kernel, including the BPF subsystem

- Elixir.bootlin.com (*http://elixir.bootlin.com*), where you can browse the Linux source code

- eCHO (*https://oreil.ly/2AATZ*), a weekly livestream covering topics from across the eBPF and Cilium community (in which this author is a regular presenter)

Conclusion

Congratulations on reaching the end of this book!

I hope that reading *Learning eBPF* has given you insight into the power of eBPF. Perhaps it has inspired you to write eBPF code yourself or experiment with some of the tools I've discussed. If you've decided to do some eBPF programming, I hope the book has given you some confidence about how to get started. And if you have been completing the exercises as you worked through the book, bravo!

If you're excited about eBPF there are plenty of ways to get involved in the community. The best starting point is the website ebpf.io. This will point you to the latest news, projects, events, and happenings, and also to the eBPF Slack (*http://ebpf.io/slack*) channel where you're likely to find someone with the expertise to answer any questions you might have.

I welcome your feedback, comments, and any corrections to this text. You can provide your input through the GitHub repository that accompanies this book: *github.com/lizrice/learning-ebpf*. I'd also be happy to hear your comments directly. You can find me as @lizrice in many places across the internet.

Index

---

packet encryption/decryption, 157-160
transparent, 167
event
    attaching eBPF to kprobe events, 70
    attaching program to, 49-51
event buffer, 105
execve syscall function, 105

F
Facebook, Katran and, 3
Falco, 176
fentry programs, 130
fexit programs, 130
file descriptor, 63
firewalling
    defined, 144
    network policy enforcement and, 165
flow dissector, 138
frame pointer, 116
function calls, 29, 54-55
functions and function prototypes, BTF data
    for, 88

G
global variables, 51-53
Go, 193
gobpf, 193
GPL license, 116
Gregg, Brendan, 3

H
hash table map, 21-24
header files, C, 41
    application-specific headers, 93
    for CO-RE eBPF programs, 91-93
    generating a kernel header file, 89-90
    headers from libbpf, 92
    kernel headers, 92
helper functions, 126

I
infrared controllers, 139
inspecting loaded programs, 45-49
    BPF program tag, 47
    JIT-compiled machine code, 48
    translated bytecode, 47
instructions
    complexity limit, 4

for eBPF virtual machine, 38-40
verifier check for invalid, 122
verifier check for unreachable, 122
ioctl, 70-72
Iovisor project, xii
IP addresses, Kubernetes and, 165
ip link, 50, 68
ip route, 138
IPsec encryption protocol, 167
iptables, avoiding, 163

J
Jacobson, Van, 1
JIT compilation, 48
jump instruction, 29

K
Katran, 3
kernel
    adding new functionality to, 7-8
    basics, 5-7
    defined, 5
    evolution of features on, xii
    generating a kernel header file, 89-90
    inspecting loaded program in, 45-49
    loading eBPF program into, 45
    removing program from, 54
kernel header file, 89-90
kernel modules, 8
kfuncs, 127
kprobes, 128-130
    attaching eBPF program to kprobe event, 70
    attaching to syscall entry points, 129
    attaching to various kernel functions, 129
    origins, 3
kube-proxy, 163
Kubernetes
    avoiding iptables, 163
    cgroups and, 138
    CNI, 163, 165
    eBPF and Kubernetes networking, 160-168
    encrypted connections, 166-168
    policy enforcement, 165
    sidecar model, 12

L
libbpf
    accessing maps, 104

About the Author

Liz Rice is the chief open source officer with eBPF specialists at Isovalent, creators of the Cilium cloud native networking, security, and observability project. She sits on the CNCF Governing Board and on the Board of OpenUK. She was chair of the CNCF's Technical Oversight Committee in 2019–2022 and cochair of KubeCon + CloudNativeCon in 2018. She is also the author of *Container Security* published by O'Reilly.

She has a wealth of software development, team, and product management experience from working on network protocols and distributed systems and in digital technology sectors such as VOD, music, and VoIP. When not writing code, or talking about it, Liz loves riding bikes in places with better weather than her native London, competing in virtual races on Zwift, and making music under the pseudonym Insider Nine.

Colophon

The animal on the cover of *Learning eBPF* is an early bumblebee (*Bombus pratorum*), a bumblebee species found in most of Europe (especially the UK) and parts of Asia.

Bombus pratorum builds nests above ground in fields, parks, and sparse forest, even repurposing abandoned bird or rodent nests. The early bumblebee indeed emerges early in the year, typically from March to July, but in southern England, worker bees appear as early as February, making it quite common for two colony cycles to occur in a single year.

This species of bumblebee is quite smaller than others. While there are slight variations among queen, worker, and male drone types, the early bumblebee's appearance is generally black with a yellow collar, another yellow band on the abdominal segment, and a reddish or dull orange tail.

Early bumblebees form colonies with queen and worker bees but, unusually, queens use aggressive behavior rather than pheromones to establish dominance, using her mandibles to head-butt the strongest worker bees to maintain control of the colony. Worker bees forages for nectar and pollen of flowering plants such as white clover, thistle, sage, lavender; drones are created late in the hive cycle and leave the nest in search of new queens.

Many of the animals on O'Reilly covers are endangered; all of them are important to the world. The cover illustration is by Karen Montgomery, based on an antique line engraving from *The Animal Kingdom Illustrated*. The cover fonts are Gilroy Semibold and Guardian Sans. The text font is Adobe Minion Pro; the heading font is Adobe Myriad Condensed; and the code font is Dalton Maag's Ubuntu Mono.

Printed in the USA
CPSIA information can be obtained
at www.ICGtesting.com
JSHW061422060524
62622JS00009B/411

9 781098 135126